WOMEN'S IMPRISONMENT

WOMEN'S IMPRISONMENT

A study in social control

PAT CARLEN

Routledge & Kegan Paul
London, Boston, Melbourne and Henley

First published in 1983
by Routledge & Kegan Paul plc
39 Store Street, London WC1E 7DD,
9 Park Street, Boston, Mass. 02108, USA,
296 Beaconsfield Parade, Middle Park,
Melbourne, Australia, and
Broadway House, Newtown Road,
Henley-on-Thames, Oxon RG9 1EN
Set in Baskerville 11 pt by Columns, Reading
and printed in Great Britain by
T.J. Press (Padstow) Ltd, Padstow, Cornwall

Library of Congress Cataloging in Publication Data

Carlen, Pat.

Women's imprisonment.
Bibliography: p.
Includes index.
1. Women prisoners — Scotland — Case studies.
I. Title.
HV9649.S35C37 1983   365'.43'09411   82-21480

ISBN 0-7100-9441-8

Contents

Acknowledgments

This case study would not have been possible without the full cooperation of the Scottish Home and Health Department, the University of
Keele and the Governor, staff and prisoners of Her Majesty's Institution,
Cornton Vale. My greatest debt, however, is to the twenty prisoners,
who, though having problems enough of their own, were none the less
prepared to talk to me in the hope that this research might contribute
to a greater understanding of the problems of women similarly placed.

I was only able to talk with the prisoners and staff of Cornton Vale
as a result of receiving the full support and cooperation of the Governor,
Lady Martha Bruce. I am, therefore, extremely pleased to have this
opportunity to thank the Governor, the Deputy Governor, the prison
officers, the social workers, the Medical Officer and the Education
Officer of Her Majesty's Institution, Cornton Vale, for so generously
giving their time to talk to me about their jobs in the prison. Thanks
are also due to the Scottish Home and Health Department for funding
the project and to the Vice-Chancellor and Professor D. Thompson
of the University of Keele for allowing me a year's leave of absence
1980-1 to undertake the research.

Women's imprisonment in Scotland means many different things
to many different people and, for giving so much of their time to tell
me their own particular views on the topic, I am very grateful to the
following: the thirty Edinburgh and Glasgow police officers; the fifteen
Edinburgh and Glasgow sheriffs; the two Glasgow stipendiary magistrates; the eight Glasgow and Edinburgh court liaison officers; the
wardens of all the hostels and common lodging houses which I visited;
the General Secretary of the Scottish Prison Officers' Association; and
the staff of the Scottish Prison Service College. My thanks to all.

Many other institutions, organisations and individuals gave me
either information, advice or practical help and specifically I should
like to thank: the Governor and staff of Barlinnie Prison, Glasgow;
the Governor and prisoners of the Barlinnie Special Unit, Glasgow;
the Governor and staff of Saughton Prison, Edinburgh; SACRO (Edinburgh); SACRO (Glasgow); NACRO; the Edinburgh Council for the
Single Homeless; the Edinburgh and District Council on Alcoholism;

the Salvation Army; the Church of Scotland's Committee on Social Responsibility; the anonymous respondents to the questionnaires about the CQSW courses; and, also, Derek McClintock, George Moore, Bill Brittle, Chris Wood and George Sharkey. The specific form and substance of the arguments of this book are, of course, not directly attributable to any of the aforementioned officials, organisations, institutions or named individuals.

Whilst engaged in the investigatory part of the project in Scotland I received constant encouragement from Jacqueline and Sebastian Tombs and from Ruth and Kit Carson. Then, during the time I was writing the book at Keele, Mike Collison and Ronnie Frankenburg encouraged me by their continuing interest and support. Frank Burton of City University undertook the thankless task of reading the completed typescript and optimistically persevered with the even more thankless task of proffering criticism. I was, as always, extremely grateful for his advice. Throughout, I have received the greatest help from Jacqueline Tombs of the Social Research Branch at the Scottish Home and Health Department, and it is to her and to all members of the Social Research Branch that I owe an especial word of thanks.

Finally I must thank those who gave me secretarial and clerical assistance. Lisa Chamberlain in Edinburgh quickly transformed the long and often difficult tapes into coherent transcripts and Doreen Thompson at Keele typed the manuscript with equal speed. Jill and Daniel Carlen performed many editorial and clerical tasks and I am grateful to them for that — and for much else besides.

This book is, of course, dedicated to the twenty unnamed women prisoners whom I interviewed at Cornton Vale in the autumn of 1980.

Pat Carlen
(April 1982)

Introduction

The imprisonment of women in Scotland is not a problem. Few women go to prison and those who do find that Her Majesty's Institution at Cornton Vale is modern, clean and pleasant to the eye. Each prisoner has her own centrally-heated room with hot and cold water, there is provision for access to night-time sanitation and prisoners are neither brutalised by physical violence nor terrorised by psychiatric intervention. Cornton Vale is definitely not one of those overcrowded, brutalising institutions which provoke the cries of prison reformers, the recurring headlines about, and inquiries into, the 'prison crisis'. Rather, it might be seen by some reformers as being the prototype for the prison of the future.

This book, however, is not primarily about Cornton Vale, Scotland's one and only custodial complex for female offenders. Nor is it primarily about women — prisoners or otherwise. It is a book about the wider meanings of the moment of prison; a moment not to be confined within the interstices of Her Majesty's Institution; meanings not to be contained within the female subject of penology. As such, it is on the one hand, a book about the not-said, the irrelevant and irreverent of female subjectivity; on the other about an already-existent but always new penology.

The terrain is dominated (but not engulfed) by the prison and its female subjects. Criss-crossing and making the terrain what it is, however, are the lines of socio-biographies, histories and fantasies which ebb and flow, tighten and loosen in such a continuous transformative process that the meanings

1

of female imprisonment must be constantly open to question. So, it is also a book about men; and aunts; sheriffs and criminologists, families, social security offices, housing departments, transistor radios, husbands, and Miss Piggy; about alcoholism. . .madness. . .badness. . .sickness. About a type of dismissive society in general. About Melissa and nineteen other women in particular. Pre-eminently, but in the end not at all, it is about the twenty women who talked with me in the autumn of 1980 and whose moments of prison I have used as the occasion of an interrogation — an interrogation of the other, dispersed and always atrophied, moments which currently overdetermine, and consistently deny, the meanings of women's imprisonment in Scotland.

How is such a kaleidoscopic approach possible? Not by breaking the series of lenses which constitute the kaleidoscope itself. The aim of this book is more constructive. In the pages which follow I will try to trace out the ideological *non sequiturs*, the professional discourses and the domestic tragi-comedies which underpin the logics and imagery of the judicial and penal systems when they attempt to represent the delinquent or 'inadequate' woman. We will see how old ideologies coalesce to form new ones, how private griefs become public property, and how public servants act to reorganise and master private feelings and private relationships. The text will revolve around the talk of women prisoners, sheriffs, prison officers, JPs, policemen, social workers and others. Their talk poses, answers, reformulates and denies the questions of this book. The investigation was also designed with regard to several theoretical assumptions and within a politics.

1 *As regards method*: I worked on the theoretical assumption that empirical investigation and description of contemporary events is a desirable prerequisite to theoretical interrogation of political process and policy. Further, I worked on the assumption that what has usually been called the case-study method can, at its best, provoke questions which go beyond the particular case to a theoretical consideration of wider issues.
2 *As regards politics*: the wider issues which I had in mind whilst designing the practical investigation were twofold;

they concerned both the changing and various meanings of imprisonment within Great Britain and the invisible nature of the social control of women.

3 *Specifically of the case study I asked:*

(a) What is the meaning of Scotland's small population of female prisoners? Who are they? And why are they in prison?

(b) What is the moment of prison like in a modern, spacious and sanitary prison with a high staff-prisoner ratio?

(c) Is this the prototype for the prison of the future, and if so, what are the implications?

The case study

My interest in empirical research has once before directed me towards what many consider trivial, a non-problem. When I studied the magistrates' courts in the early 1970s (Carlen, 1976) several fellow sociologists thought the topic mundane and already well-researched, court officials and lawyers thought the subject trivial. Investigating the meanings of women's imprisonment in Scotland provoked similar reactions, the main one being that there are already plenty of prison studies. Actually, however, there are very few sociological studies of *women* and imprisonment in Great Britain. The major study of women's imprisonment is an historical account of the development of women's prisons in England, Wales and Scotland (Smith, 1962). The only other books giving insight into British women's experience of imprisonment are autobiographical accounts of ex-prisoners (eg. Buxton and Turner, 1962 and Henry, 1952) and an autobiographical account by an ex-prison governor (Size, 1957). The last thing I wanted to produce was a participant-observation study of a prison! My aim was to assess the 'moment' of prison: in other words, to theorize about the relationships between the biographies of women prisoners, the discourses which constitute them and the politics which render them the 'female' subject (albeit denied) of penology.

The fact that comparatively few Scottish women go to prison did not deter me. Quite the opposite. The fact that a large, technologically sophisticated complex is maintained to house in secure conditions the few Scottish women it is deemed necessary to incarcerate was itself intriguing. Who were these deviant few? What crimes had they committed? (Or was I already begging questions? Is the modern prison *necessarily* about crime and punishment at all?)

Finally, I was challenged by the negative profiles which these women (along with other petty offenders) were given. They could not be romanticised (I did not interview any female Jimmy Boyles!), their series of short-term sentences could not easily be turned into odysseys of psychological survival. None of the women were taking Open University degrees (only one indeed had stayed at school beyond the age of fifteen) and none of them had very liberal views on punishment. They were, however, in their sentence length and social background typical of the majority of prisoners in Great Britain. The fact however that *as women* they constitute only a minority group within the prison system has hitherto also made them invisible *as prisoners*.

Not only is there no study in existence of these 'invisible' Scottish women prisoners, there are very few studies concerned with British short-term prisoners in general (but see Davies (1974) and Prins (1980) for two excellent and comprehensive studies). They do not produce good stories like John McVicar (1974) and Wally Probyn (1977) and they pose some of the most intractable problems for penology whether that penology be called conservative, liberal, radical or whatever. They certainly pose problems for the researcher who wishes to talk with them! Within prison they are subdued, suspicious, tense; outside prison they tend to be either on the move (often straight back to prison via police cell and court) or watchful of the officialdom which has seldom boded well for them. These difficulties notwithstanding, I decided to interview twenty women prisoners at length, and also to interview the prison officers, prison social workers, sheriffs, JPs, policemen, court liaison officers and others who so repeatedly come into contact with them. As it turned out I had full cooperation from all groups approached and most of the practical investigative work was completed during the four months from the beginning of October 1980 to the end of January 1981.

First I interviewed the prisoners. I had told the Governor

that I would like to interview convicted prisoners over the age of twenty-one who either: (a) were currently serving a short term of imprisonment; or (b) had previously served a short custodial term after conviction; or (c) had previously been remanded in custody before trial; or (d) had previous convictions or (e) had previously been in trouble with the police. Although these criteria were wide, the women thereby excluded were the (mainly long-term) prisoners who had no previous convictions and who, prior to the offence for which they had been gaoled, had never been in any kind of criminal trouble.

The convicted women over the age of twenty-one are housed in two blocks called Sierra and Papa. Women arriving at the prison are initially housed in Sierra until they have been assessed as responsible enough to move to Papa, a block where women are generally expected to require less supervision. The women interviewed were all resident in Papa at the time of the interview. Initially only eighteen women fulfilled the criteria laid down for selection for interview. These eighteen were approached by letter, sixteen agreeing to the interview and two refusing. The remaining four women were approached as soon as they became resident in Papa and each agreed to be interviewed. Two tape-recorded focused interviews were conducted with each selected prisoner. (A list of the topics discussed is to be found in the Appendix B. Each interview was scheduled to last for an hour but some of the second interviews took less time.)

In this book the women are all referred to by fictitious names. Selected details of their biographies are as follows:

Ann Archer was in her late twenties and was serving her third prison sentence for theft for which offence she already had nineteen previous convictions. Youngest of seven children, Ann had lived mainly with her grandmother but for the last five years she had been associating with the man she hoped to marry. This man had also served prison sentences for theft. Ann had no children.

Bernice Bradley was in her early thirties and was serving an eighteen-month sentence for assault to severe injury. She served her first prison sentence in 1972 and thereafter had, according to her own account, been in prison 'nearly every other year since, mainly for housebreaking'. Her parents separated when she was five years old and her father served many prison sentences. At the age of eight Bernice was taken into care and then, at the age of thirteen, she was sent to what she called a 'training school'. At the age of sixteen Bernice married her first husband in order to 'get away from the Welfare'. They had two children (now in care) but soon Bernice left him to live with the man with whom she began her career in housebreaking. When she left him in 1972 she married her present husband. Since remarrying, Bernice has continued housebreaking, has become an alcoholic and has experienced many severe beatings.

Clare Carlton was in her late forties and was serving six years for culpable homicide (killing her second husband). Prior to this sentence she had served nine months for the attempted murder of her first husband. Clare told me that, although her first husband was an alcoholic, she herself had never suffered financial hardship. She stabbed her second husband and killed him after receiving many beatings and kickings from him. She had four grown-up children.

Daphne Daniels was in her late twenties, separated from her husband and was serving a two-year sentence for perjury. This was her first time in prison but, prior to this sentence, she had had convictions for disorderly behaviour, theft, reset, drugs offences and assault. Her husband was serving a life sentence. They had one child.

Eliza Eastwood was in her late fifties and her history, as she told it to me was extremely confused. Since 1963 she had been in and out of prison to serve short sentences for drink-related offences. When I visited her home town I found that she was known to all the police there and had been banned from more than one hostel or common-lodging house. Three days after her release in October 1980 she was back in Cornton Vale.

Freda Franklin was in her early thirties and had several close relations in gaol. At the time of interview she was serving a nine-month sentence for 'harbouring a fugitive from justice'. This was her first conviction although she had been remanded to prison on one previous occasion.

Georgina Green was in her mid-twenties, had a string of previous convictions for theft and was serving her third prison sentence. Prior to her last offence Georgina had left her husband and their three children and had set up home with someone else.

Hermione Hall was in her mid-thirties. She had well over twenty previous convictions and had served five prison sentences for offences of prostitution, theft and assault. Her husband had just completed a sentence for wife assault and her three children were in care.

Ingrid Ingham was in her mid-twenties, unmarried and had one child aged six. She was serving a twelve-month first prison sentence for serious assault. She had previous convictions for theft.

June Jones was in her mid-twenties and had served previous prison sentences for shoplifting. She was unmarried and had no children.

Kirsty King was in her mid-forties. She had been sent to an approved school at the age of twelve and had married at the age of twenty. Kirsty and her husband had had four children. They were divorced in 1973. Kirsty started drinking heavily in 1964 and, since then, according to her own estimate, had 'been in and out of prison over sixty times' for drink-related offences. When I visited her home town I found that she was well known to the social workers, police and hostels there.

Lisa Lobell was in her early twenties, had one child and was serving her fourth prison sentence in three years for offences ranging through prostitution, theft and assault. She also had many convictions for drink-related offences. A week after her release from prison in 1980 she was sentenced to imprisonment for breach of the peace.

Mandy MacDonald was a widow in her late fifties and currently serving a sixty-day sentence for breach of the peace. When I asked her how many prison sentences she had served Mandy said, 'I am never out of here.' She had one married daughter who lived abroad. For the past fifteen years Mandy had been in and out of prison for drink-related offences and had several times been in hospitals to seek treatment for her alcoholism.

Melissa Malcom was a single woman in her early thirties. She had been fostered at an early age and was moved from home to home until she was sent to an approved school at the age of fourteen. By the age of twenty she had had two children, had put them into care and had started drinking and 'skippering' (living rough). This pattern of life had continued, though Melissa had made regular attempts to 'dry-out' and gain a more settled way of life. She had served 'at least over thirty sentences' for offences ranging from breach of the peace to attempted murder. She herself had been raped and severely beaten up many times. In several cases her assailants had been charged and sentenced to long terms of imprisonment. Ten days after her release from Cornton Vale in October 1980 Melissa was back in prison for a drink-related offence.

Melody McDuff was a single woman in her early twenties and she had one child. She was serving her second custodial sentence for fraud and theft.

Netta Nelson was an unmarried woman in her early twenties. She had one child. Netta was serving a sixty-day sentence for shoplifting, having previously served twelve months for reset. The father of her child was also in prison.

Olive O'Brien was a married woman in her mid-forties. She had four teenage children and was serving ninety days for police assault. This was her tenth sentence of imprisonment for a drink-related offence. Olive said that she had no problems, though she did wonder if her heavy drinking was 'beginning to cause some trouble'.

Phyllis Prince was a single woman in her early twenties who was serving four years for child assault. This had been her first conviction but she had previously been in trouble with the police as a result of fighting at football matches.

Thelma Thompson was a married woman in her mid-thirties. She was serving a nine-month prison sentence for theft. Prior to that sentence she had served one term of imprisonment for forgery and another for attempted murder. She had three teenage children who did not normally live with her.

Vivienne Vincent was a divorced woman in her late forties. Her history as she told it to me was extremely confused but she had been in prison many times for drink-related offences and was well known to the police in her home town. She had four grown-up children.

When I had finished the interviews with the prisoners I interviewed a selection of prison staff: the Governor, the Deputy Governor, one of the three part-time doctors, the Education Officer, the three social workers and ten of the more senior prison officers. These interviews were not tape recorded. The interviews with the ten officers were semi-structured (a list of the questions asked is given in Appendix B) and the rest were unstructured. During the period that I was conducting these interviews I also did some observation, and informally talked with prisoners in Sierra and in Reception. On every occasion I had total cooperation from the staff and prisoners and there were many instances of officers going out of their way to discuss prison issues with me informally and to ensure that the research proceeded not only smoothly but pleasantly. During the rest of the investigative period I interviewed thirty police officers (ten in central Edinburgh, twenty in central Glasgow) on the topic of 'The arrest and prosecution of women offenders with particular reference to those committing drink-related offences'. I interviewed fifteen sheriffs (seven from Edinburgh and eight from Glasgow) and two of the three Glasgow stipendiary magistrates and I asked them about the sentencing of women offenders. Eight court liaison officers (four from Edinburgh and four from Glasgow) were asked about women offenders and the court system. I also made visits to, and talked with some of the personnel of, the following institutions and organisations: HMP Barlinnie, including the Special Unit; HMP Saughton, Edinburgh; the Scottish Prison Service College; SACRO (Edinburgh); SACRO (Glasgow); two common-lodging houses, one hostel for homeless women and one hostel for recovering alcoholic women; the Edinburgh and District Council for the Single Homeless; the Edinburgh Council on Alcoholism; the Scottish Prison Officers' Association (for an interview with the General Secretary) and a senior lecturer involved in the training of social workers at a Scottish College. Some Glasgow policemen kindly arranged a tour round central Glasgow during the day and a visit with them to some 'down and out spots' in the middle of the night. I observed the Glasgow sheriffs' courts in action and also managed some covert observation of practice at the alcoholism unit of the Royal Edinburgh Hospital when I escorted there, and attended the admission interview of, a SACRO referral. In order to observe police encounters with alcoholics I spent many hours in Edinburgh's Grassmarket and in Glasgow's George Square, Clyde Walkway and two main railway stations. Finally, in order that I might gain some insight into the prosecuting policies of the procurator fiscal staffs, the Social Research Branch of the Scottish Home and Health Department kindly made available to me the transcripts of twenty-five taped interviews with Ms Susan Moody conducted with procurator fiscal staffs in 1978 and 1979.

So, that is what I did. This book is what was made of it.

Part one
The denial of women's imprisonment

The felonies that took them there send shudders down the
   spine,
There are some who purloined property, and some drank
   too much wine,
And others, lost to decency who failed to pay a fine.

From 'The ballad of Holloway' by
Roger Woddis, first published in the
New Statesman (1972) and reprinted by
permission of the author and the
New Statesman

1 The meanings of women's imprisonment in Scotland

Scotland has only one female penal institution, Her Majesty's Institution, Cornton Vale, which is situated near Stirling. It provides for all female offenders over the age of sixteen. On one site it has remand, borstal, young offender and prison facilities. This book is mainly concerned with the convicted women prisoners over the age of twenty-one and it is based upon research funded by the Scottish Home and Health Department during 1980-1.

In 1978 23,280 females were proceeded against in the Scottish courts, a total of 821 of them eventually being received at Cornton Vale to serve sentence.[1] 657 of the 821 women received to serve sentence were aged twenty-one and over, and of Cornton Vale's average daily population of 169 females 73 of them were sentenced women over the age of twenty-one (see Appendix A). The average length of sentence imposed on women over the age of twenty-one was 74 days, though average length of sentence can be separated into whether the custodial sentence was imposed direct or whether it arose from failure to pay a fine. Approximately half of all Scottish women received under sentence are received as a result of failure to pay a fine and for fine-defaulters the average length of sentence was 35.9 days; for the directly sentenced women aged twenty-one and over received in 1978 the average length of sentence was 115 days. As will be seen from Table A (see Appendix A, p. 219), a third of all adult women received under sentence in 1978 had been convicted of breach of the peace; another third were guilty of crimes against property without violence.

13

In 1980[2] 692 females were received to serve sentence, 569 of them being aged twenty-one and over. The average daily population of Cornton Vale was 147, 65 of the 147 inmates being sentenced women aged twenty-one and over. Again, in 1980 half of these adult women prisoners had been received as a result of a failure to pay a fine, the average length of sentence for fine-defaulters being 36.4 days and for directly sentenced women aged twenty-one and over 116 days. Again also in 1980, and as can be seen from Table B (see Appendix A, p. 220), nearly a third of all adult women received under sentence had been convicted of breach of the peace, whilst another third had been convicted of crimes against property without violence.

When Cornton Vale opened as the new female institution in 1975 the press referred to it as a Spanish hacienda. Some residents of Stirling nowadays refer to it as a holiday camp. I have heard prisoners and local authority social workers call it a concentration camp. To me it seemed rather like an extremely quiet small-scale university campus. The blocks are spaced well apart from each other, linked by trim paths and interspersed with flower gardens. Inside, the common rooms are brightly furnished, very warm in winter and light and airy in summer.

The adult women who are convicted prisoners are housed in the two prison blocks, Papa and Sierra. Papa is the main prison block and Sierra is the observation and more secure block. Each block is organised into units of seven women each. Papa is organised into eight units and Sierra has four units. Each woman has her own centrally-heated cell and each unit has its own sitting-room, kitchen and bathing facilities. Units in Papa are designated 'open' or 'closed' according to the degree of freedom allowed to the women. The units in Sierra are all 'closed', but, because of the electronic locking of cells in Sierra, women there who are considered to be sufficiently trustworthy do have access to night-time sanitation. Thus the different degrees of freedom allowed to women depends both on the staff assessment of them and the design of the buildings in which they are housed.

Sierra Block has electronic locking of cells. This means that most women there have access to night-time sanitation. By pressing a button they can contact a central control point

and request that the cell door be opened. This is done elect-
ronically, the door being left open for seven-to-eight minutes.
It is reported by prison staff that this facility has not been
abused. Due to a financial restriction imposed during the
conversion and extension of the old Cornton Vale Borstal
into the new institution for women, Papa Block does not
have electronic locking. Women in three and a half of the
eight units have their own keys to their cells, however, and,
as a result, they too have access to toilet facilities at all
times. This leaves about twenty women who are usually
without access to toilet facilities during the night.

All women prisoners are initially housed in Sierra for
observation. Those who appear both to have settled down
to their sentence and to require minimum supervision are
then moved to Papa. Of the women who move to Papa the
more responsible are eventually allowed to have keys to
their rooms. This latter privilege is usually achieved only
after a woman has been in prison for at least six months.
It is, therefore, a privilege not available to the bulk of prisoners whose length of stay is much less than that.

But enough of facts and figures. As I have already said,
the elemental and usually denied meanings of women's
imprisonment in Scotland are to be found neither within
the walls of Cornton Vale nor within the official crime
statistics. Fragmented and transcribed, they are to be found
within discursive forms and practices which, conventionally,
are considered to be quite unrelated to penology — within,
for example, the conventions of the family and the kirk;
within traditional forms of public conviviality and ethics of
domesticity and masculinity; within some peculiar absences
in Scottish social work practice; within the ideological
practices of contemporary psychiatry; and within some over-
determined presences (e.g. alcohol, unemployment, poverty,)
within Scottish culture and society. Some of these elemental
meanings are singly analysed in the following chapters. In the
remainder of this chapter I will summarise those meanings,
showing, where possible, how they relate to the meanings of
women's imprisonment in general and to the meanings of
women's imprisonment in England and Wales in particular.
The focus of this chapter, therefore, is upon the *female* subject of Scottish penology. In the book's final chapter I will

place the study of Scottish women's (short-term)[3] imprisonment in its wider context and discuss its relevance to wider
issues within British penal politics.

The book's structure and argument

1 *The Scottish female offenders most likely to be imprisoned are those who have stepped outwith[4] domestic discipline.* The three chapters which comprise Part Two of the
book discuss the relationships between women, family and
imprisonment. Chapter 2 describes how some unsung elements of Scottish domestic life have traditionally disciplined
women in a multitude of non-penal ways. Chapter 3 suggests that when sheriffs and magistrates are faced with a
sentencing dilemma in the case of a female offender the
decision to imprison or not is made on their assessment of
the woman as mother. Chapter 4 describes how the general
organisational features of imprisonment increase women's
difficulties outside the prison at the same time as the prison
authorities are claiming that the prison's emphasis on domesticity can help rebuild family relationships. It is suggested
that, given that *most* of the women beginning short-term
sentences at Cornton Vale have either already had their
family lives impaired by imprisonment or have already rejected conventional family life altogether, the emphasis upon
domesticity is misplaced.

2 *Cornton Vale's disciplinary regime debilitates short-term
prisoners by contradictorily defining them as being both
within and without sociability, both within and without
femininity and both within and without adulthood.* Chapter
Five (Part Three, 'The Moment of Prison') indicates that
women's imprisonment in Scotland is imprisonment in the
general sense in that it has all the repressive organisational
features common to men's prisons; it also indicates that it
is a form of imprisonment specific to women in that two
modes for controlling many Scottish women outside prison,
i.e. family life and isolation from each other, are also incorporated into the prison regime to produce a very fine disciplinary web which denies the women both personality and
full adult status.

3 *The female petty offenders who are imprisoned in Scotland*

are those who are seen as being beyond care by the social services and beyond cure by the medical authorities. The three chapters of Part Four describe how certain women become the 'women that nobody wants'. Chapter 6 analyses contemporary Scottish social work practices and ideologies in relation to the supervision of offenders. Chapter 7 describes the world of the alcoholic and heavily drinking women offenders and the practices adopted by the various medical and non-medical agencies to distinguish between the 'curable' and the 'incurable'. Chapter 8 analyses those contemporary practices of psychiatry which result in female offenders with previous histories of mental illness being sent to prison on the grounds that they are *not* mentally ill, and, once there, being controlled by drugs on the grounds that they *are*.

4 *Women's imprisonment in Scotland is women's imprisonment denied.* The overall argument of the book is that the Scottish female prisoner is first debilitated by being defined as being both within and without sociability, femininity and adulthood; and then defined out of existence as being beyond care, cure and recognition. Throughout the empirical investigation I was faced with evidence of this denial. At my first meeting with the Governor of Cornton Vale she told me that although she was very interested in my research she had very few 'prisoners' for me to study. When I quoted the official prison statistics for Scotland in puzzlement at this statement she immediately clarified the issue by stating that she had not realised that I would be interested in interviewing fine-defaulters and drunks whom she did not count as real prisoners. In similar vein sheriffs denied that they *send* women to prison. Sometimes when they said that they never send women to prison they were referring to the fact that between 50-60 per cent of sentenced women at Cornton Vale at any time are likely to be there for failure to pay a fine. Sometimes they meant that Cornton Vale is not a real prison because it has none of the disgustingly insanitary and over-crowded conditions of many male closed prisons. Many prison officers also claimed that Cornton Vale is not like a 'real prison'. Some of the prison officers who made this point thought that it is not a real prison because the disciplinary regime is 'too soft'. Others thought that because so many of the prisoners have previous histories of mental illness the

institution is 'more like a mental hospital than a prison'. Yet others thought that because the majority of prisoners are in for so short a time 'you can't set up the training programmes that you'd have in a real prison.' Furthermore, some of the prison officers also claimed that the prisoners of Cornton Vale are not real women either. In fact several of the officers made the same point as Prison Officer No. 10 who said, 'Except for the embezzlers and one or two of the women serving long sentences the women coming here are not ordinary women. By and large, the normal ordinary woman who commits a crime doesn't get sent here.' Thus it is that Scottish women's imprisonment is denied and that so many officials within the judicial and penal systems were able to echo the sheriffs who said, 'I could talk for hours about *men* offenders but women are really no problem' (Sheriff No. 1); and 'Physically, we don't actually *see* them in the courts because *physically* we don't see them as a danger. Women don't constitute a social problem' (Sheriff No. 2).

Women's imprisonment in Scotland, England and Wales[5]

In general, the motto of those charged with the penal regulation of deviant women has been 'discipline, medicalise and feminise'! Women's imprisonment both in Great Britain and in the United States has traditionally been characterised by its invisibility, its domesticity and its infantilisation.

The invisibility of women within the American penal system has been widely commented upon. According to Jane Roberts Chapman, Lieber complained as early as 1833 that 'unhappily the small numbers of crimes committed in our country by women has caused a comparative neglect of female criminals' (Chapman, 1981:8-9). This neglect has continued for over one hundred years and by 1972 Hendrix was claiming that it has a sexist dimension. She claimed that, 'characteristically male officials in the criminal justice system regard the problem of female offenders as insignificant' (Chapman, 1981:4). In 1973 Helen Gibson summarised the more obvious reasons for the invisibility of women offenders and prisoners:

First, women represent only a small percentage of those arrested and an even smaller percentage of those incarcerated. Second, the crimes they commit are usually related to sex or property, and, instead of harming others, women criminals usually harm themselves. Finally, with the public and official awareness of a general increase in crime and serious prison disorders, the problems of women prisoners pale into insignificance. (Gibson in Crites, 1976:93)

In the main these reasons also hold as a part explanation for the invisibility of women prisoners in Scotland, England and Wales [6] though the recent rise in the numbers of women charged with violent crime has done much to sensitise the public to the 'problem' of female crime while pressure groups such as the National Council for Civil Liberties, the National Association for the Care and Rehabilitation of Offenders and the Howard League for Penal Reform have campaigned tirelessly to bring the plight of female prisoners to the attention of parliament and public (NACRO, 1978; Howard League 1978). [7] Officials, however, have not been alone in their neglect of women prisoners. The prison literature has also neglected them. In England and Wales, of course, the extreme secrecy of the Home Office in relation to prisons and prisoners has resulted in very little independent research access being granted either to male or to female institutions (Cohen and Taylor, 1978). That being recognised, however, the fact remains that more *is* known about the insides of British men's prisons than of women's, just as more is known about British male offenders in general.

Training for domesticity and motherhood has been a dominant feature of women's prison regimes both in Great Britain and in the United States. The so-called training programmes are nearly always linked to traditional (and totally unrealistic) conceptions of women's roles, idealisations in fact which working-class women have seldom had opportunity (and, maybe, not even inclination!) to realise. Training for domesticity, far from helping a woman develop as a person, can often increase her dependency upon the 'male'. As Price (1977) commented:

> In the women's institutions, usually small in size, the inmate is often more isolated than the male offender from the mainstream of normal community life. Because of the smaller size of the institution, work programmes are even more difficult to maintain. Women do the laundry, sewing and other 'female tasks' . . . Such programming does nothing to prepare a woman for employment, and in fact, increases her dependency . . . The inadequacy of current vocational training programs is one of the most serious problems in women's institutions which should be encouraging autonomy rather than dependency. (Price (1977) quoted in Widom, 1981)

The comparatively small numbers of women incarcerated in Scotland have also resulted in *all* of them being accommodated in one closed prison. Some prisoners therefore are imprisoned at great distances from their homes and, additionally, have no hope of ever moving to an open prison. There *is* no open prison for female prisoners in Scotland. Several of the women whom I interviewed were critical of this lack of a women's open prison and felt that in this respect (as in several others) they were disadvantaged when compared both with Scottish male prisoners and with English prisoners both male *and* female. Sheriff No. 2 thought that the very existence of Cornton Vale is anachronistic but contented himself with remarking that:

> 'there shouldn't be a Cornton Vale nowadays. Convention produces one. Perhaps, instead, there should be an open prison, for those who are unmanageable and for those who commit a grave offence.'

A senior lecturer in social work, however, was much more scathing about Cornton Vale's technologically sophisticated security system:

> 'Most of the people at Cornton Vale could be perfectly well accommodated in a proper hostel. A Colditz of that size and with all that technology isn't needed to contain the majority of the people there.'

Once women prisoners *are* accommodated in such a very closed institution, however, an oft-remarked phenomenon occurs; the comparatively few women prisoners who, because there are so few of them, are all accommodated in a single prison or custodial complex, are also often subjected to very secure and highly disciplined regimes organised to cope with the most difficult prisoner or the 'greatest security risk' who is (or ever has been or ever might be!) in residence. Helen Gibson has commented on this perhaps unexpected consequence of the minority status of women prisoners:

> While convention requires women's prisons to *look* like minimum security institutions economic reality decrees that they cannot *be* minimum security . . . a women's institution must accept every woman offender. . . . The result is an atmosphere that in spite of attractive facilities and peaceful surroundings is really very tense and oppressive. The inmate. . . is reduced to a state of childish dependency. . . . The reduction of women to a weak and dependent and helpless status is brought about by more subtle means than by the gun or the high wall. (Gibson, 1973 in Crites 1976:99)

These remarks well describe the present situation of Scottish women prisoners.

It is difficult to compare Cornton Vale with prisons in England because so little has been published about English women's prisons. Official reports and statistics do, however, give certain factual information. We know for instance that England has four closed and four open prisons for women (see Appendix A, Table D). We also know that whereas the numbers of Scottish women prisoners have remained fairly constant during the 1970s (with a slight drop in the last few years) the numbers of women and girls in custody in England have been steadily rising, reaching a peak figure of 1,646 on 15 March 1980 (Home Office, 1981a). In 1980, 1,900 adult females were received under sentence of immediate imprisonment and a further 716 were received in default of payment of a fine. It is suggested that had it not been for the industrial action of prison officers during the last three months of the year that the numbers of receptions would have been even higher. As it was, in 1980 the number of adult females received under sentence of immediate imprisonment was 65 per cent higher than in 1970 and 4 per cent higher than in 1979 (Home Office, 1981b:75). This is not, however, the place to discuss the meanings of women's imprisonment in England and Wales![8] What I will do instead is briefly indicate the similarities and dissimilarities between women's imprisonment in Scotland and women's imprisonment in England and Wales.

The most obvious difference between Scottish and English female imprisonment is that the greater numbers of English female prisoners result in a wider range of penal facilities. Female offenders in England and Wales can be sent to open prisons, and, at Askham Grange, Holloway and Styal prisons, there are mother and baby units.[9] Yet in England and Wales, as in Scotland, the majority of imprisoned women are petty offenders. This latter point was stressed by Dr M. Bull, Governor of Holloway, in her evidence to the *House of Commons Expenditure Committee* (House of Commons 1978-9):[10]

> The vast majority of offenders are committing minor offences and the majority of those are theft or handling stolen goods and I think it is something like 60 per cent of the people in prison here on that sort of charge. . . . On the whole, women are petty offenders. (Evans, 1980:60)

And of all adult women offenders in England and Wales in 1980 about 28 per cent of them were received into prison as fine-defaulters. Furthermore, the majority of the petty recidivist offenders are held in Holloway, London's closed local prison, and, at Holloway as at Cornton Vale, a high proportion of the prisoners have been diagnosed as having either 'personality disorders'[11] and/or alcohol and/or other drug-related problems. Magistrates in England and Wales are more likely to remand women in custody than men (Dell, 1970) and, according to Mawby (1977) the proportion of females remanded to prison and eventually sentenced to imprisonment is only half that of males. Indeed, in her evidence to the House of Commons Expenditure Committee Dr Bull expressed the view that remand in custody is 'simply a device to put women in prison for three weeks — perhaps just as a punitive way' (Heidensohn, 1981:127). The fact that in 1980 over 60 per cent of women sentenced directly to imprisonment in England and Wales received sentences of six months or less suggests that the majority of women in prison have been sent there for purely punitive purposes.[12]

About half the adult women imprisoned in England are accommodated in open prisons. Prisoners who exhibit strange behaviour together with the few prisoners deemed to be security risks and those with alcohol and other drug-related problems remain in the closed prisons. These closed prisons for women are notorious for the high degree of tension which they generate. In recent years, too, nearly all English closed prisons and some open prisons have had problems of severe overcrowding.[13] The only two Scottish prisoners whom I interviewed who had also served terms of imprisonment in Holloway both said that although the atmosphere there was tense the overcrowding meant that prisoners were not under such strict surveillance as they are at Cornton Vale and that at Holloway, therefore, prisoners could more easily subvert the prison regime.[14] They also pointed to the fact that, unlike their Scottish counterparts, English women prisoners are allowed to wear their own clothes. But women's imprisonment in England is as debilitating as it is in Scotland. English and Welsh prisoners are as cut-off from their families and friends as are Scottish prisoners, they are often accommodated in very bad and overcrowded conditions and it is as generally agreed in England and Wales as it is in Scotland that the overwhelming majority of female prisoners should not be in prison at all. Those that are there, according to the Home Office (1970) are 'depressingly normal' and it has long been recognised that though 'many of them look as mad as mad can be [they] are really reacting to prison life' (Gibbens, 1971). In fact, in 1970 an official Home Office publication stated that 'it may well be that as the end of the century draws nearer penological progress will result in ever fewer or no women at all being given prison sentences' (Home Office, 1970). Why is it, then, that twelve years later the numbers of women going to prison in England and Wales have increased by 65 per cent? The answers are complex and not to be found solely in analyses of either prison regimes or of prisoners. Certainly they are not all to be found in a study which specifically focuses upon the meanings of women's imprisonment in *Scotland*! However, insofar as *some* of the features of English and Welsh women's imprisonment are similar to those of Scottish women's imprisonment, it is to be hoped that the following analyses of the meanings of women's imprisonment in Scotland will also raise questions about, and contribute to, a greater understanding of the meanings of British women's imprisonment in general.

Part two

Women, domesticity and criminal justice

'God bliss Franscis' wrote Anna, Duchess of Buccleuch in 1720 or thereabouts, 'and give hime sones and no daughters.'
(Plant, 1952:2)

2 Family life

God hath revealed . . . that it is more than a monster in nature
that a woman shall reign and have empire above men. (John Knox,
1558)

In 1561 the wife of a baillie in Crail shouted to the congregation
to pull the minister owt the pulpit by the luggis. (T. C. Smout,
1969:78)

The meanings of women's imprisonment in Scotland are
manifold and complex. In this chapter I shall trace out the
ways in which the social position of Scottish working-class
women has turned upon a contradiction: how, on the one
hand, they have been given heavy responsibilities as bread-
winners and homemakers; how, on the other, they have
suffered a brutal industrial and familial repression at the
hands of bosses and husbands.

The glance at the historical position will be but a fleeting
one, as it is well-established that Scottish men have had their
family roles imbued both with the prudish authoritarianism
of Calvinism and the machismo traditionally associated with
a hard-labouring, hard-drinking and (with increasing industrialisation) an often demoralised and sometimes militant workforce (Hunter, 1979; Mechie, 1960; Mitchison, 1978; Young,
1979). The bulk of this chapter will be concerned with some
aspects of the contemporary position. Having indicated the
historical geneses of the contradictory elements in Scottish
domestic life, I shall examine the family experiences of the
women I interviewed in Cornton Vale. In indicating to what
extent the historical contradiction concerning Scottish

women's place in the family has persisted (both in practice and in discourse) to the end of the twentieth century, I shall also be arguing that it plays a major part in conditioning the meanings of *women's* imprisonment in Scotland today.

The kirk

Rosalind Mitchison in her book *Life in Scotland* (1978:33) has described how the 'Celtic emphasis on masculinity ... acquired divine sanction' after the Scottish Reformation in 1560. Scotland had always been a patriarchal society, and kinship had always been patrilineal, but it was Calvinistic misogyny which from the sixteenth century onwards strengthened the already existent masculine culture. A sentence in the 1560 *Confession of Faith* indicated that John Knox was not alone in his contention that women should be denied all authority: 'We flee the society with the Papistical Kirk in participation of their Sacraments; first, because their ministers are no ministers of Christ Jesus; yea, (which is more horrible) they suffer women whom the Holy Ghost will not suffer to teach in the congregation, to baptise' (Mitchison, 1978:33). Rosalind Mitchison comments:

> Hence came the tremendous masculine emphasis of Scottish social and ecclesiastical institutions in the seventeenth century, shown most revealingly in the way in which some parish registers record events of births and death. The form 'James Allan, a daughter' and 'James Allan, his wife's death' are common and the headship of the family might even be carried beyond the grave with 'James Allan, his relicts's death'. (*Ibid.*:34)

Mitchison argues that the kirk 'never accepted the idea that a different standard of probity was required of the two sexes' (*ibid.*:33) but certainly the long arm of church discipline fell more heavily on women than men, and not only because a woman's sexual misdemeanours often resulted in pregnancy. Both in ecclesiastical law and in common law married women were under the authority of their husbands. Further, however much the labouring classes in general ignored, or even resisted, the kirk's dictums on sex and other matters (Kellas and Fotheringham, 1976; Smout, 1976; and Young, 1979) the fact remains that when, in the years between 1560 and 1707, more than 3,000 people were judicially killed 'because their contemporaries thought they were witches ... the victims were mainly women, the wives of farmers, country and town craftsmen and cottars or poor old widows' (Smout, 1969:199-201). As Eveline Hunter (1979:3-4) comments: 'It is not inconceivable that many of the women burned in Scotland for their "witchcraft" were persecuted because of their knowledge of methods of ending unwanted pregnancies.'

Nor did the kirk do much for women in other spheres. The development of competing church schooling systems benefited boys more than girls. Mechie (1960), for example, notes that in 1748 after the Society for the Promotion of Christian Knowledge had established 134 schools in the Highlands, the combined rolls stood at 5,187 boys as against 2,618 girls. As for the Lowlands, once mill owners showed a marked preference for building up their workforce primarily from women and children there was little official pressure to send girls to school at all.

The kirk's blatant misogyny persisted well into the twentieth century. In 1959, the Glasgow Presbytery Special Committee, appointed to comment on a previous Assembly's Committee on 'The place of women in the church report,' observed that:

> every religion which has instituted priestesses, or otherwise afforded office to women, has become degenerate and corrupt. It is noteworthy that several of the discredited heresies of our faith (e.g. Gnosticism and Montanism) offered a greater place to women in their councils and are remembered today for the damage they did to the Christian cause. (Highett, 1960:113)

Here, inseminated into mid-twentieth-century discourse, is the kirk's historical justification for its oppressive disciplining of women. Women had to be disciplined into a chaste motherhood because in Calvinism (as in Roman Catholicism) they were depicted as the source of all depravity. Those entrusted with the disciplinary task were, of course, the husbands. This, according to Viscount Stair, compiler of the first chronicle of Scots' law in 1826, was a direct consequence of Genesis 111:16, 'where the Lord says to Eve, "the desire shall be towards thy husband and he shall rule over thee" ' (Hunter, 1979:6). Whatever epistemological status one accords to Genesis it may be reasonable to suggest that, despite his male omniscience, the Lord overlooked the fact that alcohol, hard labour and poor to non-existent housing were to wreak havoc with His agents' fitness for their task.

The home

The domestic life of Scottish working-class women has traditionally been haunted by the two spectres of slum housing and violent men. Yet the women who over the centuries have increasingly learned that alcohol can temporarily deaden the pain of their harsh working and living conditions have also traditionally shouldered the main domestic responsibilities, including the paying of bills and the holding of tenancies. Their domestic position has been one of responsibility without authority or privilege. T.C. Smout (1969) writes that 'at least in the South East, it had been customary as far back as the mid-seventeenth century for the rent of the labourer's one room hut to be paid for by the work of their wives.' This economic responsibility appears to have given the women little standing in the eyes of either the kirk or their husbands. A seventeenth-century traveller in Scotland commented:

> 'The peasant women wore linen skirts, with a plaid draped over their heads, pinned across the bosom and falling to their knees. They were not allowed by the Sessions to wear plaids over their heads in Church as this was conducive to sleep. *They went barefooted like the children yet the husbands have shoes*.' (Smout, 1969:152 my italics)

And, if it is well-documented that 'Highland women shared in the most laborious tasks of the peasant economy' (Richards, 1974) it is also to be noted that their lot was not improved by industrialisation. Indeed, James D. Young (1979:29) argues that 'Scottish industrialisation actually intensified the existing sexual and social enslavement of working women.' For, from the mid-eighteenth century, working-class women and girls provided the bulk of mill labour: 'The employers had ... doubly good reasons for seeking to build up their workforce primarily from women and children. They could do almost all the jobs (for less pay too) and since they were ... used to doing what they were told at home, they were more amenable to strict discipline at work' (Smout, 1969:407).

Mill work was not limited to women. Men also worked in the mills, and in the mines, and in a multitude of minor industries. Where their lives differed from their spouses was that they could, with impunity, regularly drown their sorrows in drink. Rosalind Mitchison argues that the Scottish cult of masculinity developed as a result of the uncertain and hard conditions of men's labour. The conditions under which women laboured were equally, if not more, arduous but no such licence to booze was given to them. Three inter-related social institutions — kirk, marriage and prostitution — ensured that the penalties for female inebriates would be heavy indeed:

> The pressures of industrial work can explain many of the features of the social ethos of the later nineteenth century, the detachment of men from the affairs of their families, the confining of recreation on which money was to be spent to the male sex, the assumption that opinions and conversations on matters to do with work, politics or sport are unsuitable in the female. . . . The respectable working man expected prudishness from his womenfolk because sexual promiscuity and prostitution were not only the inevitable life for women in [the] half-destitute world but also the quickest way into it. . . sexual prudishness, and a desire to limit and control the activities of women was one of the few areas where the more secure of the working-class agreed fully with the middle-class. (Mitchison, 1978:117)

It was not only industrial conditions which drove men to the pubs. The housing conditions of both rural and urban workmen resulted in many of them finding that only the heavy consumption of alcohol would ensure a few hours of conviviality followed by a few hours' sleep.

One of the most notorious features of working-class life in Scotland has been the low standard of its housing:

> In Glasgow in 1871 41 per cent of all families lived in single ends (one-roomed houses) and a further 37 per cent lived in two rooms. . . . By 1931 Scotland still had 35 per cent of its population living at a density of more than two people to a room — as compared with only 6.9 per cent of the population of England and Wales in similarly overcrowded conditions. (Dickson, 1980:246)

Bad housing was not solely an urban problem; housing was very poor in mining and rural areas too. What is amazing is that the nineteenth-century cholera and smallpox epidemics did not hasten sanitary reform in the cities. Many commentators explain this by pointing to the fact that the miasmic theory of disease had gained an ascendency over the contagion theory, but A. M. MacLaren agrues that here, as in all other areas of Scottish social life, the kirk had also played its part:

> Whilst the failure of any effective sanitary reform movement to develop in Scotland was related to the economics of public heath . . . it was also rooted in Calvinistic ideas concerning the 'unknowability' of God and the uselessness of any secular attempt to avert the workings of Divine Providence. (MacLaren, 1976:49)

However, whether one blames kirk or corporation for the nineteenth-century situation, Glasgow's housing problems have persisted throughout the twentieth century, whilst alcoholism is today recognised as one of Scotland's major social problems.

The actual domestic conditions of the Scottish labouring classes have not been such as to realise the ideal of family life and motherhood engendered first by the kirk and then by the welfare state (Beveridge, 1942). The miseries associated with excessive alcohol consumption and poor housing have been debated in Scotland for well over a century. Wife-beating has more recently been publicly recognised as a wide-spread, deep-rooted and, to some extent, approved custom (Dobash and Dobash, 1980). The evidence of it has been around for a long time. In 1831, for instance, 'James Logan . . . noted that a Scottish bride was expected to show reluctance and require a certain degree of violence which was neither thought unbecoming in the man nor a hardship to the woman' (Logan, 1831, quoted in Young, 1979) while Young himself claims that at the beginning of the twentieth century 'the extreme poverty and oppression of working people frequently culminated in death from starvation or wife-beating.' In the latter part of this chapter we will hear some working-class wives describing the violence which still characterises many marital relationships. While listening to them it may be as well to bear in mind some statistics relating to life in Glasgow in the 1970s. The first set concerns housing:

> A 1970 report showed that some 23 per cent of Glasgow's housing stock was unsatisfactory; 23 per cent of houses lacked hot water tap facilities, 32 per cent lacked a bath, 17 per cent lacked exclusive use of a water closet and 45 per cent had three rooms or less. . . . Another report indicated that of the 121 most socially deprived districts in Britain, Glasgow and surrounding areas accounted for 115. (Dickson, 1980)

The second set of figures concerns unemployment: 'Results of the collapse of heavy industry were catastrophic. Glasgow alone lost over 85,000 jobs in the fifteen years to 1977' (Dickson, 1980). Again, not conditions conducive to domestic harmony. But I shall not be suggesting that Scottish women go to prison *because* of poor domestic situations, nor that *because* there are so many elements in Scottish culture that contribute to the non-penal disciplining of women that Scottish women are downtrodden and lacking in spirit. Far from it. One history of Scottish working-class women is certainly one of oppression, but another is that of protest. It is to the history of female independence, dominance and protest in Scotland that I now turn.

Protest

Whatever doubts Scottish working-class men have entertained about their women's moral and spiritual strength — doubts which the kirk used to justify its rampant misogyny and husbands used to justify their insistence on female prudishness and isolation from the pleasures of public conviviality — they do not appear ever to have had the same doubts about women's physical strength. Rural life in seventeenth-century Scotland was no more idyllic for the majority of people than urban life was to be in the following centuries (see Smout, 1969). To get a living, Highland women had to engage in the same heavy work as their men. Child-care and other domestic work, however, was solely the province of the women. Perhaps it was because of their double investment of labour — in their homes *and* in the land — that women led the men into battle in the anti-clearance revolts of the 1820s.

> The pattern of anti-clearance revolt . . . is surprisingly
> consistent . . . the officer delivering the summons was
> set upon and humiliated. The second confrontation
> would involve a much larger body of constables whose
> approach was never secret. They would be met at some
> point by a body of women . . . at the rear would be the
> men. (Richards, 1974)

This fighting spirit was carried into the mills. Eveline Hunter (1979) writes that 'as trade unions became legal, [women], like men, formed themselves into societies and they also withdrew their labour in support of demands (for example . . . Glasgow spinners and weavers in 1833).' But the majority of trade unionists never wholeheartedly supported women's struggles. Scottish working women (like their contemporaries in the rest of Great Britain) usually had the privilege of either partly or wholly supporting their families financially whilst at the same time being castigated for neglecting them emotionally, physically, and spiritually. Even the left-wing socialists of Clydeside initially kept women out of politics. It is, therefore, not surprising that in the years between 1897 and 1978 only ten women ever made it on to the STUC General Council

(Hunter, 1979). Yet Scottish working-class women have continuously struggled on the domestic front. They've had to.

In 1915 women led the rent strikes and continued to do so through to the 1920s (Young, 1979). After the 1939-45 war the implementation of the *Beveridge Report* resulted in women being seen as pivotal agents in the distribution of welfare (cf. Wilson, 1977a). Family allowances were paid to women; women were expected to attend Health Centres with their children, to look after under-fives and the elderly at home, to be at home to the Health Visitor when she called, to negotiate with education, housing and other 'welfare' authorities and, in Scotland more frequently than in other parts of Britain, to take on the tenancy of council accommodation. Elizabeth Wilson (1977b) has made the same point about British women in general:

> The division of labour within the community usually
> means that it is women who go to the rent-office, women
> who attempt to grapple with schools, women who are
> interviewed by the social worker. A large element in
> social work consists of attempts to get them to do their
> job 'better'.

It is in this context that E. Richards's (1974) description of women's resistance to the Highland Clearances has a metaphorical relevance at the end of the twentieth century. Richards wrote that, 'in many incidents when the people were in actual confrontation with the representatives of authority, the women were found at the head, often taking the worst injuries.' As metaphor, this well describes the position of many Scottish women today as their men (sometimes unemployed, ill, or in prison; more often exercising what they see as their traditional male prerogative) leave them to cope alone as the unrecognised agents (though always recognised objects) of the professional distributors of state welfare. Most women manage — somehow. Others fail — spectacularly. These latter are the women who — of all female lawbreakers in Scotland — end up at Cornton Vale ... again and again and again.

In the remainder of this chapter I shall depict some of the

unsung dimensions of family life in contemporary Scotland. Mainly this will be done by using the words of women imprisoned at Cornton Vale. When I talked with them I did not particularly ask Melissa and the others about the family, except to record the conventional details relating to marital status, etc. Yet, as they talked about their lives outside the prison, about their views of themselves, the women's talk was always inseminated with notions of themselves as family members — or not. This situating of self both within and without a notion of familiness was all the more striking as most of them lived outwith the family and marriage in the conventional sense, and a small minority had never known one or both parents either. Still the talk centred on the family; on the family life which they thought other people had and which they themselves hoped to have one day; on the family life which they had rejected; on the family life which, somehow, had eluded them; on the family life which had left them physically bruised and emotionally battered; on the family life which, in a minority of cases, had engendered in them (too late?) a burgeoning awareness of the rights and wrongs of women.

What the women prisoners had to say about certain dimensions of family life in Scotland was not peculiar to them. To a large extent their views were shared by sheriffs, policemen, prison officers and social workers. For when they talked with me about women and imprisonment in Scotland, judicial and prison personnel again and again made sense of, and underlined, what they were saying by referring to the position of women in general in Scotland. As they, and the prisoners, talked about Scottish domesticity, intimacy and family life the following facts and themes emerged.

Family variations

Although most of the women I spoke to held a notion of the nuclear family as the normal unit of domesticity, their own experience of family life appears to have departed sharply from the ideal. (This ideal was never made explicit; how could it have been? The women's discourse constantly denied it. Fragments from the interviews, however, suggest that it was the romanticised and conventional one: a man and wife bound by ties of affection living together with their off-spring in the marital home.) The following facts give some indication both of the circumstances of the prisoners' domestic lives at the time of interview and of their varied family histories.

During their terms of imprisonment only two of the women were receiving effective support from their families of origin, though the father of one of them was serving a fourteen-year prison sentence himself. Five of the other women had been separated from their parents at an early age, four of them being taken into care and, before the age of ten, experiencing several different 'homes'. Two of these women had then gone straight from a foster home to an approved school at the age of fourteen. Of the remaining twelve women, only one claimed to have had a very unhappy childhood though most of the others found either that they had drifted away from their families when they married or that their families had turned against them when they got into trouble. Ironically, the only two women who were still very close to their families of origin whilst they were inside were two women whose families were, according to the authorities, 'well-steeped in crime' and who were, therefore, from the official viewpoint, seen as a bad influence!

Although most of the women I interviewed had initially paid lip-service to fairly conventional views on family and marriage their own attempts to found families, to realise their own (at least earlier) domestic ideals, had not been wholly successful for a variety of reasons. The state of marital play at the time of the interviews was as indicated in Table 1. Five of the older women had grown-up children who had left home and two of the unmarried women had no children. The remaining thirteen women had between them twenty-eight children under the age of sixteen. Only eleven of these children normally lived at home with their mothers. Seventeen of the children were in care and did not normally live with their mothers even when the latter were not in prison. Four of the seven single women had one child each who lived with them when they were not in prison and a fifth had two children in care. The eleven children who usually lived at home with their mothers were being cared for in the following ways while their mothers were in prison: the four teenage children of one woman were being looked after by a neighbour; the mothers of three of the women were between them caring for four children; the sisters of two of the women were looking after one child each and one of the unmarried mothers was having the baby cared for by his father with whom she normally cohabited.

Table 1 Domestic arrangements

	No.	No fixed Abode
Married and still living with husband in marital home	1	
Married, not living with anyone else, but husband in prison	2	
Twice married but second husband in prison	1	1
Twice married but woman in prison for culpable homicide of second husband	1	
Married, separated from husband and cohabiting with male	1	1
Married, separated from husband and not cohabiting	3	1
Divorced and living alone	2	1
Divorced and cohabiting	1	1
Widow living alone	1	1
Single and not cohabiting	4	1
Single but cohabiting	2	
Single, cohabiting but man in prison	1	
	20	7

It was often difficult to establish where the woman lived. Seven actually had no fixed abode at the time they commenced their term of imprisonment and a further six had no

home to go to when they were liberated. Of the remaining
seven, one lived with her widowed mother, one lived with
her sister and five had their own rented houses. But many of
the living arrangements were temporary, the women often
moving not only from house to house but from town to
town as they sought better lives than those which they were
currently enduring, lives too frequently bedevilled by family
violence, alcohol problems and a nagging sense of increasing
isolation and futility.

Family violence

In our . . . analysis of 3,020 cases of violence occurring
in two Scottish cities in 1974 . . . we found that assaults
against wives was the second most common violent offence.
The largest category was violence between unrelated males
(39%), second to that was assault of wives (26%). Of the
3,020 violent offences 1,044 involved family members . . . .
A closer scrutiny of violence among family members
revealed that 76% was husbands assaulting their wives and
1% was wives assaulting their husbands. (Dobash and
Dobash, 1980)

'It's all linked up with the masculine image — the hard
man.' (Director, Edinburgh and District Council on Alcoholism)

I did not ask the women specifically about violence in the
family but, just as much of their talk centred around the
'family', particularly the 'man', so it was also studded with
references to, and accounts of violent attacks which they had
suffered both at the hands of family members and at the
hands of males in general. The following list indicates the
range and seriousness of physical attacks which thirteen of
the women had suffered:

Bernice Bradley had suffered severe beatings at the hands of
her second husband. A social work report contained the
comment: 'Her face shows a million battle scars which
she attributed to her husband.'

Clare Carlton had suffered beatings and kickings from both husbands. Subsequently she had attempted to murder the first and had succeeded in killing the second.

Daphne Daniels had been beaten up several times by different men. She had once had a swastika carved on her forehead.

Georgina Green left her husband because of the frequent beatings and kickings which she suffered and went to live with a man from whom she subsequently experienced the same degree of violence.

Hermione Hall had suffered a series of beatings and kickings and her husband had completed a term of imprisonment for wife assault.

Ingrid Ingham referred to the 'several black eyes' she had received from her husband.

Lisa Lobell had lost an eye at the hands of her cohabitee, the father of her baby.

Mandy MacDonald claimed to have been hit by her uncle and by the police.

Melissa Malcom had been beaten up many times and had been raped on two occasions, on the first occasion by one man, on the second by two men. The latter were subsequently brought to trial and sentenced to twelve years' imprisonment. Melissa knew that they had threatened to 'throw acid in her face' upon their liberation from gaol.

Netta Nelson referred to the 'black eyes' which she had frequently received from her cohabitee, the father of her child.

Olive O'Brien had filed a complaint against a policeman for hitting her in the mouth and breaking a tooth.

Phyllis Prince had been hit on several occasions by her cohabitee.

Thelma Thompson had in adolescence been beaten by her mother with an electric cable.

The reluctance of the judiciary, the police, social workers and the community in general to take seriously the injuries of battered wives has been well-documented both in England (Pizzey, 1974) and in Scotland (Dobash and Dobash, 1980). Dobash and Dobash (1980:7) give a succinct account of the reasons why:

In this century numerous ideas about the nature of the family and the marital relationship also left women to struggle alone against oppression. Beliefs in the sanctity of the family were closely associated with belief in personal privacy and the rejection of intervention in family affairs. . . . The cult of domesticity and belief in family harmony and bliss made the idea of outside intervention in domestic affairs seem a needless violation of the sanctity and privacy of the home.

This is a general explanation. In Scotland the cult of domesticity was not just a result of the growth of an individualism and a family privacy both of which were concomitant with the development of capitalism (Zaretsky, 1976), it also had its roots in the Calvinist legacy of misogyny and the close-knit masculine camaraderie associated with the hard physical labours of the mining, shipbuilding and other heavy industries. Most of the Cornton Vale women were insistent that this cult of aggressive and assertive masculinity had persisted longer and in a more homogeneous form in Scotland than in England. In this they were supported by prison officers, sheriffs and policemen. It is not surprising that Clare Carlton, imprisoned previously for the attempted murder of her first husband and currently serving six years for the culpable homicide of her second husband, had ruminated at length about the continuing domestic violence of Scottish men.

'In Scotland, men still have all this aggressiveness. "I'm the man!" No, "I'm the *master*!" Not the man, the *master*, and I think that this is why they get into their head that if a woman steps out of line it's a punishment to keep her in line. If the boys in the family see the father giving the mother a punishing they say "that's the way to act", so when they get married they just act exactly the same way as their fathers.'

A prison officer, a sheriff and a policeman made the same point:

'Many of the women have battering husbands. They're much behind Englishmen.' (Prison Officer No. 11, female)

'Women here put up with a lot of violence from their
men. Men still beat women a lot in Scotland. The women
may leave them but it's still the women who suffer most.'
(Sheriff No. 2, male)

'Many of the women are punch drunk. They've been
beaten all their lives and I think it's getting worse. There's
a lot of male chauvinism in Scotland.' (Policeman No. 8)

It was frequently stressed by prison officers, policemen
and sheriffs that a corollary to the tradition of male violence
towards women was that the women put up with it. The
women I interviewed in Cornton Vale, however, were to
some extent, the ones who had *not* put up with it. Many
women had left their husbands because of either their violence, their drinking, their gambling or all three, and we shall
see, at the end of this chapter, how several women had, in
their increasing isolation from the world outside the home,
developed also a positive sense of independence from the
ideological constraints of the 'man, marriage and family'
syndrome. Clare Carlton and Melissa Malcom had, in different ways, protested from the beginning, although they
now recognised that it had cost them dearly. They justified
their own extreme acts of violence on the grounds that legitimate and effective protest was not open to women. Two
reasons were given for this unequal state of affairs: first,
that women were not so well-practised in culturally accept-
able physical violence as men; second, that within marriage
a majority of working-class women were in a relationship
characterised by total economic dependency upon their
husbands. Melissa Malcom's life-style had particularly ex-
posed her to male violence and the effects of this had been
recognised in a psychiatric report after Melissa had been
charged with attempted murder of a man who had been
'aggravating' her. Having stated that Melissa had no paranoid
traits, hallucinations and delusions, the report continued:

The repeated sexual assaults to which she was subjected
have left their deep mark on her and I am prepared to
accept that sexual advances to her could be totally unacceptable in the light of her previous past experiences. If

these advances were made more forcibly, one can understand that in the light of the past history she could lose control of herself and that her responsibility could be substantially diminished for her actions.

Melissa had, none the less, received three years imprisonment for attempted murder. Her own explanation was terse and to the point:

'I was getting sick of it, you know. I didn't want the same thing to happen that had happened before. You can take so much violence towards your own person, then you will retaliate. I know. I was raped when I was twenty and I was raped a few years ago by a lot of men. I was left at death's door four times and I wasn't taking anymore. I'm fed-up with getting battered and when you do get fed-up with it you will retaliate. You don't care what you've got in your hand and you don't care about the consequences afterwards.'

Clare Carlton also decided to take no more:

'I've been lying in a pool of blood and him kicking hell out of me and the police have just said, "Oh a husband and wife fight" and walk out. What are you supposed to do, just take it and take it until you're kicked senseless? You just can't take it all the time.'

But verbal rebellion is no match against physical force and economic dependence; as Clare says:

'They come and bring all their drinking cronies home and you've got to get up out your bed and entertain all his drunken friends. But I wasn't that kind, you see. I got out my bed all right, to throw them out! And nine times out of ten I got a punching for it, but I still got rid of them. No way was I going to have that in the house. But then again, you get wee lassies that are feared of their men, they wouldn't stand up to them. Especially if there's kids, they've no-where to go. I was in that position. I had to take him back because you can't get help. It's better to stay with a man and have grub on the table for to feed the kids and a roof over your head.'

And when the crunch comes, when women can stand no more, they have to use a weapon and something more effective than the traditional and much parodied rolling-pin:

'It's funny, the idea of a woman retaliating. I mean, like the old cartoons that you see, the women with a frying-pan or a rolling-pin. You've got to use a weapon. It's only a weapon that's going to stop a man, because if you just hit him with something like a rolling-pin you're going to get an awful kicking.' (Clare Carlton)

Most women who are the victims of their husbands' violence do not effectively 'stop' them. They put up with them. And in any case, the non-penal and informal disciplining of women does not usually take the form of extreme physical violence. The Cornton Vale women who had entered into either formal or informal relationships with men had soon found that they were controlled and increasingly isolated in a multitude of non-violent ways, ways which initially they had found difficult to define, blaming themselves for their sense of unease, frustration, isolation and powerlessness. For many of them, too, alcohol had begun to play a large part in their lives.

Drinking, marriage and the cult of masculinity

Thirteen of the women interviewed admitted to a 'drinking problem' of some kind and even more mentioned that they had been drinking at the time of the offence which had landed them in prison. Indeed, such a high proportion of women were in prison for drink-related offences that a later chapter of this book is wholly devoted to a discussion of female alcoholic offenders in Scotland. Here, however, I want to limit the discussion to the relationship between Scottish male drinking habits and the cult of masculinity. The aim will be to highlight the effects which the two combined have on the marital relationship.

Although at the time of the interviews there were several women claiming that they would not be living with a man when they were released from prison, only one of the women interviewed had *never* attempted to set up home with a man. Not one of the others had been wholly satisfied with their domestic experiences. Indeed to imply that they merely experienced the usual dissatisfactions and irritations with their partners would be an understatement. Ten had experienced violence at the hands of their men; eight had had husbands or cohabitees who had been, or were currently, in prison; seven claimed that their men had severe drink problems; and eleven claimed that they alone had been responsible for running the home, paying the bills, dealing with the authorities and bringing up the children. Several had more specific complaints: Lisa Lobell had been forced into prostitution by her cohabitee, Hermione Hall by her husband; Thelma Thompson's husband was a heavy gambler; Bernice Bradley's cohabitee had initiated her into housebreaking; Hermione Hall's husband regularly left her while he went on drinking sprees to London; and Freda Franklin had been the family breadwinner since her husband had given up work on the day they had wed. In fact the women who had entertained the romantic notion that marriage would give them protection, full-adult status and companionship had found instead that it gave them the triple burdens of increased responsibility, increased dependency and a deadening sense of increasing isolation from the world outside the home. What, however, came as a nasty surprise to young newly married women indoctrinated with the ideology of the ideal nuclear family situation was already well-known to many others. Sheriffs, social workers and prison officers were quite explicit as they depicted the contradictions which obtained historically, and which *still* persist within the family roles of Scottish women. An Assistant Governor at Cornton Vale explained:

'In theory, and the men believe this, the wife is subject to the man and he's in charge of everything. In practice, it's the mother who runs the house, pays the bills, etc. and the men don't want to know.'

Others were prepared to make the same point and to make it specific to Scotland:

> 'We now have here a great population of single parents, and even many women who are married have all the responsibility.' (Sheriff No. 1)

> 'Women often get into trouble because they have the whole burden of housekeeping on them.' (Sheriff No. 4)

> 'A large number of women in Scotland are the mainstay of the family in a way that the father isn't.' (Sheriff No. 14)

> 'In Scotland, the domestic situation is different from England. Here women run the homes and men don't concern themselves with the finances.' (Court Liaison Officer No. 3)

By the time the women reached Cornton Vale they had learned these lessons and many were rebelling (or had rebelled) against the harshness of their pedagogy. Their enlightenment had usually begun early in their married lives (cf. Dobash and Dobash, 1980). Netta Nelson, for instance, had given up a good job as a bookbinder to live with the father of her child. She had thought that with the coming of the baby they would have 'a normal life', but she soon found that *she* was tied to the house while *his* life-style remained unchanged:

> 'Well, to tell the truth he didn't have as much time with Flora as I would have liked him to. He still jumped about with his pals. When we had Flora I thought he should spend more time with her. But as far as he was concerned I was the mother and my place was in the home. I'd given up work and I would have liked more income and I missed the company. He wasn't a man for staying in every night and everyday. He was out quite a lot you know, so it was just me and her in the house.'

Netta's husband didn't work but he would not stay at home and look after the child so that she could work. The fact that their husbands didn't work had irritated several more of the women. Some, like Kirsty King, had left their husbands for that reason:

> 'Well, I left him. He wouldn't settle down. He was always used to money in his pocket and we were only getting £29 a week to keep the lot of us. I couldn't afford to give him £10 in his pocket so he started drinking and gambling and I left him. Then when I went on the drink in 1962 I went on it heavy myself.'

This, according to several other people I spoke to, was a common sequence of events. Community Liaison Officer No. 3 in Glasgow remarked: 'Some women have been very anti-drink, then they get desperate and take to drink themselves.' Two of the senior prison officers spoke at length about the relationships between drink, marital violence and female crime as they had seen them over the years:

> 'Because their marriage has broken down they choose friends "lower down" and at the same time they're struggling financially with children. Then they drink alone in pubs and meet a partner who is drinking and involved in crime.' (Prison Officer No. 3)

> 'Many of the women have battering husbands, husbands who have left them. Those who have men often have men who can't face up to their problems; the woman is left with them. Then maybe the children get taken away, they turn to drink and their health goes down. At the same time they get caught up with social security, because if their husband has left them they're likely to take up with someone else, still claim . . . and there's trouble again!' (Prison Officer No. 4)

Before they get to this stage, however, many women struggle with the loneliness of the marital home. Married men, unlike married women, can seek company and relaxation in the pubs. Netta, although only in her early twenties, had soon learned this:

'I think it's a man's world. I think men would even take prison better than women do. See, men are not with their families as much, men are usually out drinking with their pals.'

Thelma Thompson also felt that women were disadvantaged in the marital relationship:

'If I'd have been a man I could have put my jacket on and went down to the pub and had a pint and stood there and had a chat with some of my friends and forgot about it.'
Pat Carlen: 'What about if you *had* gone to the pub?'
Thelma: 'He'd have gone crazy. See? It's all right for them to do it, but not for you.'

Particularly vexing to Thelma and the other women was the way in which men went to the pubs to avoid any discussion of problems relating to the marriage, family or home.

'We could never discuss problems. He just wouldn't discuss them. The minute I started speaking about them it was "Hush! I don't wish to discuss it any further. Anymore of it and that'll be it." You know, he'd put his jacket on and go for a drive in the car, or he'd go for a pint and come back and the matter had to be closed.'

Other women made the point that not only did men go to the pubs to avoid confronting domestic problems, they also could use the *threat* of going to the pub to discipline their women into silence. Clare Carlton gave a long disquisition on Scottish men's drinking habits. I am reproducing it in full as it summarises points made by other women and by prison officers and social workers.

'It's the same in any pub in Scotland. If you get a woman walking into a bar — in Scotland it's just not done. Well, maybe the younger ones are doing it more, but years ago you never saw a woman in a bar. There are still a lot of bars where women are just not allowed in the public bar — it's men only. The women's got to go into the lounge. It's a wee room where women can sit on their own and get a drink. Scotsmen think that drinking is just for men. They don't have a social drink, just try to get down as much in as short a time as possible. And, if a wifie goes in, it's "You should be in the lounge beside the women." It's the same if you suggest a children's room. "Oh, that's not right taking bairns into a pub" — but they'll leave them outside or at home playing with matches or something. As I say, men think that drinking is just for them alone. Even when they go out on a Saturday night with their wives or their girlfriends, they're away to the bars talking to their pals and the lassies are left sitting talking to women in the same position as themselves. And they come over now and then, "You alright, Hen? Like another drink, Hen?" and they're away again. I went with him one night and I stood at the bar with him and you should have seen the looks I was getting. He was saying "Away you go and sit down." I says, "I'm not sitting down on my own. I'd rather stand here and talk to you." "Oh it's men's talk." I said, "I don't care," and he got more and more embarrassed and he says, "Come on, we'll go home, I'll get a carryout." He came home rather than have me stand at the bar with him.'

According to all accounts Clare Carlton's husband had tradition on his side. A prison social worker told me that 'There's a long history in Scotland of women not going into pubs', and an Assistant Governor of a male prison emphasised that Scottish drinking habits are different from those south of the border: 'Scottish pubs', he said, 'are places for men, drinking places, not like the south.'

In concluding this section on Scottish drinking habits, marriage and the cult of masculinity it is of course only fair to remember that thirteen of the women I interviewed had their own drinking problems. As we shall see in Chapter 7, however, most of these women were lone drinkers, not locked into the masculine drinking-culture of the pubs. Furthermore, they had all begun their heavy drinking after they had been married or cohabiting for some time. Their drinking habits were more often those born of isolation than of excess conviviality. Within marriage (actual or common-law) they had *at least initially* suffered more from their men's regular and taken-for-granted drinking habits than from any latent drinking propensities of their own. The male warden of a Glasgow hostel for homeless women could sum up the general situation in a few words: 'There *are* many women in Scotland suffering from alcohol problems; but even more are suffering from the alcohol problems of their husbands.'

Isolation

'When you get married in Scotland you're expected to give up all your friends, but he keeps his. He goes out, you stay home. Many of the women in the prison are there because they can't get away from a man, *literally* can't get away, not when they've got children.' (Prison Officer No. 11)

'A woman can still go to work when they're first married — but a woman's not expected to keep her friends!' (Clare)

Eleven of the women claimed that they had no friends outside prison. Three of them were women of no fixed abode, either moving from common-lodging house to common-lodging house or intermittently skippering (living rough). (The particular problems of this latter group are discussed in Chapter 7.) The majority of women who experienced loneliness and isolation, however, were those who were either married or cohabiting with a male, though it has to be noted that many of the women had felt very much alone in the world since childhood.

The childhood experiences of many of the lonely women had not been happy. Lisa, for instance, had, at the age of fifteen, been taken away from the foster parents with whom she had lived since the age of four:

'I felt awfully rejected when I was fifteen cos I had lived with these foster parents since I was four. But I got in trouble and they took me away to a strange place in Glasgow. Since then everything went to hell.'

Some of the women who had lived at home with their parents had felt unwanted. Others, like Phyllis Prince, Melody McDuff, and Clare Carlton found that their relatives had not wanted to know them once they were in trouble. Mandy MacDonald, Bernice Bradley and Vivienne Vincent all claimed that at some time or other their own kin had turned them over to the police; as Vivienne commented, 'There's kin for you!' Yet the majority of the women who felt isolated were not so much concerned with estrangement from parents, brothers and sisters — though three claimed that such estrangement had occurred because of friction between their families and their husbands. Rather; they were concerned with their sudden isolation from the outside world once they were married and had children (cf. Gavron, 1968). As the women searched around for reasons for this state of affairs, the recurring themes (apart from the ubiquitous references to boozing and beatings) were inter-related. They concerned: female dependency and sexual politics; the contradictions ensuing from the fact that whilst for the homebound working-class wife the home is the site of her labour, for her husband it is the refuge from his; and the contemporary emphasis on emotional self-sufficiency as the ideological hall-mark of the successful nuclear family.

Far from being put off family domesticity by their childhood experiences, the women who had had the most unhappy childhoods had sought to establish permanent relationships with men at a comparatively early age. I asked Bernice Bradley why she had married at sixteen:

> *Pat Carlen*: 'Did you just assume that every normal woman got married?'
> *Bernice*: 'Aye, I did. . . . No, I don't think I even thought of that, it was just a thing that was going to get me away from the Welfare.'

Lisa Lobell, involved in prostitution, and with a severe drinking problem, had desperately wanted a baby to alleviate her loneliness. Now, with a six-month-old child, she found that she had new fears:

'I've got a terrible fear in life and that's if someone tried
to take my wee boy from me. It's probably because I've
no-one else there and he's the only one I care about.'

No woman mentioned the pursuit of sexual pleasure as a
reason for setting up home with a man. This silence may
have been due either to a reluctance to talk about sex with
a stranger or to an assumption that such a reason would
be taken-for-granted. Against that, however, four women
spontaneously stated either that they 'could do without
it', or that they could 'take it or leave it', while others
specifically mentioned a regular income, a father for the
children or a home and independence as being the consideration uppermost in their minds when they had married.
At the same time, not one (even of those who had engaged
in prostitution) approved of any kind of promiscuity, and
several of them pointed out that at the time of their marriage and even at the births of their children they had been
totally ignorant of the facts of life. This was especially true
of those who had been brought up in institutions. Melissa
said that she had been 'just ignorant' and Bernice elaborated
on the same theme:

'When I was pregnant with that baby I wasn't sure where
that baby was going to come from, and that's the gospel
truth. . . . I think that people that are brought up in
homes like that, they should educate them more on
the facts of life, but they don't, they shelter them.'

But being in some kind of proprietary relationship with a
man *was* important to the women's self-esteem. Though
they often complained of their husbands' extreme jealousy,
they all reiterated that (at least at one stage of the relationship) they themselves could have forgiven anything
other than sexual infidelity; 'Beatings, black eyes, anything
. . . so long as he didn't go with another woman' (Ingrid).
For in their isolation, both from their families of origin
and from other women, many of the women (even leaving
aside their economic dependency) could not easily envisage
life without a man. Again and again when I asked badly
beaten and visibly scarred women why they were going back

to the men who had disfigured them, I received the slightly surprised reply, 'Because he's my man. I've got no one else.' As they talked on, however, some of the women realised that it was their husband's behaviour which had brought about this state of affairs, a state of affairs with which, some thought, their husbands were not dissatisfied.

> *Pat Carlen*: 'Have you many friends outside?'
> *Lisa*: 'No true friends I would say. There's not an awful
>   lot of people I trust. I've trusted my husband on a
>   few occasions and he's let me down. But he doesn't
>   like anyone else to help me. He likes to see me stranded
>   so that I can crawl back to him like an idiot.'

Hermione, Vivienne and Netta all gave their husband's jealousy as a reason for not working themselves: 'He's awfully jealous', said Hermione, 'that's why he doesn't like me working.' But it was not only other men who were seen as rivals. The woman's place was seen not only as being in the home, but in her *own* home *alone* and in no one else's.

Clare Carlton explained:

> 'I used to get rid of anyone who was in the house before
> he came in from work (even though *my* name was in the
> rent book) because I knew he could just be quite blunt
> and say, "Come on, out you go." And most Scotsmen are
> the same. When they come in from their work they don't
> want anyone in the house but their own family.'

Netta and Clare thought that there were also other reasons why the housewives did not mix. Netta said that she never invited other women into her home because she 'felt inferior, you know really. My house was clean and all that, but it was really plain, nothing fancy.' Clare had the same view:

> *Pat Carlen*: 'In the area you lived, did the women mix?'
> *Clare*: 'No, they didn't mix. I think they daren't because
>   they were trying to be one better than their neighbours.'

So the women had borne their individual burdens of loneliness — alone. And the 'house' had begun to loom in their lives as the major symbol of their bondage. Olive O'Brien, approaching middle-age, with her four children in their teens and her husband away on an oil-rig, told me how she *had* to go out for a drink — to get away from the 'house':

> 'My husband doesn't think I should get fed-up because I don't have any money problems. But he thinks I should stay in the house. I can't stay in the house. I hate the house.'

Likewise Kirsty, who, when I asked her what she thought had gone wrong with her life, replied, 'I would blame myself ... but I don't take the blame for everything 'cos I have to go back in my life and see me sitting alone in the house for years.' Olive, Kirsty and Thelma had sought consolation and company in the bottle and gradually, in exchange for boredom, had taken all the risks associated with heavy drinking. Thelma described a stark cause and effect:

> 'I was bored. I was really and truly bored. I felt I was a slave to the house. I was going out and down the street and into the pub and getting into the wrong company. And I started drinking heavily.'

Clare Carlton, on the other hand, had not taken to drink; instead, on two occasions she had lifted a knife. Consequently she had had plenty of time to reflect on her two disastrous marriages.

> *Pat Carlen*: 'Can you see that anything would have made the pattern of the last ten years different?'
> *Clare*: 'I think if there was someone you could talk to it makes an awful difference. When you sit for days on end, weeks on end, sitting worrying, worrying, and worrying, there's going to be something that bursts. Some turn to drink. I never drank. I went to the Bingo if I felt lonely. There was days I just used to sit and watch television, kids' programmes; or have the wireless on, just for a voice in the house.'

None of the women who had experienced isolation had felt that they could take their problems to other people, mainly because all the people they knew had problems similar to their own. Also married couples and couples living together were expected to keep their troubles to themselves:

> 'They've got their own problems and I've got mine.'
> (Melissa)

> 'Yes, I've a few friends, but I felt you cannot take your matrimonial problems to them. You cannot go and burden your family with them because they've got their own lives to lead as well. I've ended up taking an overdose of tablets rather than discuss it with someone, you know.' (Thelma)

> 'My mother believed that if you make your bed you lie on it. It's your problem, not hers.' (Clare)

In isolation the women prisoners had experienced (albeit in extreme form) some of the unsung elements of Scottish domesticity. But I do not want to give the impression that they were merely downtrodden, weak or broken. Their very situation, of course, accurately defined most of them as losers but, at the same time, there were still many fighters amongst them. Although most of them expected to lose and lose again, they had learned some lessons about family life. In spelling out those lessons to me many of the women pursued a new theme — a desire for independence, from the 'man' and the family — at least as they had known them.

Independence

Lisa, Thelma and Hermione blamed their husbands directly for their law-breaking activities (though many more felt that their domestic situation in general was indirectly to blame for their being in prison). Certainly their descriptions of family life give the lie to the ideal. Hermione, for instance, gave a graphic description of her contemptuous and careless entry into prostitution:

'He used to call me names and everything, you know, and he used to say, "Do you know how to sell it? You'd get good money for it, you know." And it was just one day he was going on and I walked out the house and I went down to Glasgow Green. I was sitting there with a drink and a man approached me and I ended up with him for £10, and again that night for £40. I went home and says "Well, you always says it to me."'

Lisa felt contempt for the man who knew (and didn't care) that she was prostituting in order to feed him and his child:

'I often wonder . . . if he'd been coming in with a steady income at the end of the week whether I'd be in here. I mean I was going out prostituting again for my wean and I need a drink before I prostitute, you know. There's the alcohol gives me confidence to do that. I mean, I wouldn't do it sober.'

Thelma Thompson described a situation which several of the sheriffs had described — although she had not found that they had been particularly sympathetic to her:

'Twice I've been in trouble because of his gambling. Each time we've been split up it was because of his gambling. It was only because he promised that he would work and I'd get my fair share of the housekeeping that I went back to him and I ended up stealing, and selling the stuff to get money for to pay my electric bill, to pay my light, my rent, to save getting myself evicted. Where do I land? Nine months imprisonment. When I appealed they wouldn't let my husband go up and speak and say it was his fault that I was in prison. So what chance do you have? I mean, I had to find some way of keeping my roof over my head, but the law won't listen to that. They're not interested.'

Thelma's experience and her response to it had been typical. By the time they had been in prison several times, however, some of the women were wondering if they would not be better off if they attempted to become altogether independent of male-related domesticity. Even those who were not prepared to give up an existent relationship vowed that it either had already, or would in the future, become different. When I asked Hermione why she had put up with her husband stealing her money and beating her she replied wearily but with vehemence:

'I just stuck it. I used to be frightened of him but I'm not now. He starts anything now I'd hit him with anything . . . and I've seen him running from me you know.'

I asked both Lisa and Netta if they thought that they could live without a man and both said that they could, although Lisa was scared of being lonely. Netta was more certain. Her man had beaten her and kept her short of money and like others in the same situation she definitely thought that she would be better off without him.

'I think that if a father's like the way he was, the child's better off with just one parent than having two. I've had a few black eyes and I've learned a lot. I wouldn't let it happen again. The next one would have to be a lot different.'

As far as married women's isolation was concerned Clare was once more reflective, using her own experience to make a general point concerning the way in which women are, from an early age, schooled for housewifely isolation from each other.

'When I was first married I never bothered about having friends. My man, my house and my kids were all that I wanted. Which, I know, now that I'm older, is wrong. But that was the way I was brought up, that my family and my home were to come first, no friends or neighbours or anything, and I think its wrong. Cos, as I say, if I'd had somebody to talk to, even a friend, it would have helped an awful lot. Maybe I wouldn't have been in here.'

Yet, however coolly the women analysed their situation, they did not believe they could free themselves of their dependency upon men. They felt trapped, not by their own desire, but by their economic and social situation. (Each time they went to prison, of course, both their social situations and their economic situations became worse, as we shall see in the following chapters.) Several of them could well conceive of life without a man, if only they could support themselves economically. I asked Lisa if she could live without a man and she replied, 'Aye, I think so. I would get depressed but the wee wean would make me stronger.' Bernice Bradley sketched out a scenario that would have no man in it at all:

> 'Well — I know this is going to sound stupid — I would actually like to have another baby and I think — it sounds mixed-up and daft — I wouldn't like there to be a father there at all. I'd just like to be on my own bringing that kid up and, if possible, through nursery schools and that, I'd like to go out and get a job on top of that as well. The way I see it, the majority of women are much better off without a man, tied to them in marriage. I would never get remarried again. It doesn't matter how I felt. Often, when I think back I wish I'd just led my own life, independently, and not clung to relationships the way I did.'

Bernice, however, was desperately realistic:

> *Pat Carlen*: 'So you won't go back to him?'
> *Bernice*: 'Oh, I don't know . . . I'm going to end up going back to him, just because it's an immediate roof over my head.'

In isolation from other women it is difficult, maybe impossible, to break the ideological and economic bonds which keep women in their traditional place.

Earlier, I wrote that Thelma's experience was typical. The women's law breaking *had* often, initially at least, been a response to a domestic situation, elements of which are by all accounts, shared with many other Scottish women, women who do not break the law, who suffer in silence. So why, then, had the Cornton Vale women offended? Often, in the first instance, to conventionalise a domestic situation which they had experienced as departing sharply from the ideal. But that is not why they were in prison, and this book is primarily about imprisonment, not about lawbreaking. The women's actual imprisonment was usually decided by factors other than their initial lawbreaking — though as we shall see in the next chapter, their domestic situations had certainly influenced the sentencing decisions of the sheriffs and magistrates. Other factors which help decide whether or not Scottish women go to prison are discussed in Chapters 6, 7 and 8. Before we consider these other factors, however, I shall, in Part Three, describe the moment of prison itself. We shall then see how ideologies relating to women's place in the family inseminate both the sentencing process and the prison experience. We shall also see that women's imprisonment is a very specific form of social control especially tailored for the disciplining of women. For the majority of these imprisoned women have not merely broken the law. As women, mothers and wives they have, also, somehow stepped out of place.

3 Women, family and the courts

'No-one likes to believe that the hand that rocks the cradle may be a shaky one.' (Curlee, 1968)

Scotland has the distinction of imprisoning an infinitesimal proportion of its female population, and then (with a few notable exceptions) mainly imprisoning women who commit the least serious crimes. Half of the sentenced women at Cornton Vale at any time have been received because of failure to pay a fine but a high proportion of women sentenced directly to imprisonment have also committed comparatively minor crimes.

Whether a woman goes to prison or not is dependent upon many factors. The sentence or the remand, though obviously the necessary and immediate causes, are not the only causes. In later chapters I shall discuss some other factors which condition the meanings of women's imprisonment in Scotland. First, however, I will examine the reasoning behind a sheriff's or a magistrate's decision to send a woman to prison (or not).

The sheriffs' tale

Most of the fifteen sheriffs interviewed made the point that they hate sending anyone — man or woman — to prison. All fifteen of them, however, claimed that they particularly hated sending a woman there. The two Glasgow stipendiary magistrates expressed views similar to those of the sheriffs, though one of them — before whom several of the women I interviewed had appeared at one time or another — emphatically expressed the view that only a certain type of woman finishes up in court, let alone in prison.

> 'If we have a woman in court and she is still with her husband we are amazed. Most who are in court don't take marriage seriously. They may be legally married but shacking up with someone else. Divorce is easy nowadays. Shotgun marriages are common and the children are the last ones thought of.' (Glasgow Stipendiary Magistrate)

As we shall see later, this stipendiary magistrate took a fairly hard line about alcoholic women also and a sheriff claimed that the JP courts in general would be equally hard — a major reason, he suggested, why a higher proportion of women than would have been expected (on the basis of the trivial nature of their crimes) are sent to prison by district courts.

> 'The structure of the Magistrates' Bench in Scotland is working class. Therefore they are less sympathetic to alcoholics and women who have no family.'

However, although this same point was made by three other sheriffs and a court liaison officer, the sheriffs' own reasoning in the cases of women offenders was not, upon further investigation, found to be as straightforwardly chivalrous towards *all* women as it had at first been made to appear. In fact their reasoning was both complex and, in many cases, contradictory.

One sheriff was unequivocally against sending women to prison:

> 'There shouldn't be a Cornton Vale nowadays. Convention produces one. There could perhaps be an open prison for women who commit very grave crimes. Most women are hardworking and they commit crime because they are short of money. Bringing them before the court is an embarrassment for them and an embarrassment for me. They are clearly a case for social workers [cf. Wilson, 1977a and Donzelot, 1980] but the fiscals insist on prose-

cuting them. Women earn money for the housekeeping and men drink it.' (Sheriff No. 2)

This same sheriff admitted sending women to prison, none the less:

'What can you do with them? If you don't send them to prison they cannot be fined. How can they be fined? They haven't the same money as men. At a certain stage you are engaged in a war of attrition with a woman. She tries to wear you out and you try to wear her out. At the end of the line is prison. Not sending them to prison just gives them a tolerance of courts.'

The contradiction does not arise because the sheriff was hypocritical; on the contrary, he was very aware of the contradiction between his words and deeds. It arises from the sheriff's recognition of the dissymmetry between the logic of a sentencing tariff which has prison as the ultimate sanction, and economic conditions which ensure that for the many people who are unable to pay the financial penalty prison is the *only* possible sanction.[1]

There was only one type of crime, i.e. the crime of violence, where the fifteen sheriffs unanimously agreed that they would be inclined to treat a woman in the same way as a man — and even then, on second thoughts, most of them added that they would want to look at the crime, the woman's circumstances and all the factors surrounding both, very carefully indeed. The other crimes frequently committed by women and which the sheriffs thought posed them with the greatest sentencing dilemmas were those of fraud and embezzlement, crimes most usually committed by women in the course of their employment; and persistent or professional shoplifting. The problem with the fraud and embezzlement cases was that the offenders were usually first-time offenders and often middle-class or upper working-class women who were on the one hand not a threat to the public and, on the other, respectable wives and good mothers running 'decent' homes. As with the crimes of violence, however, the sheriffs felt that they would be flying in the face of public opinion if they didn't impose prison sentences. One sheriff summed up the dilemma which several other sheriffs had described:

'I am disturbed about the female cashier who puts her hand in the till. It may be the first time she has offended and if she goes to prison she may never offend again ... but how do you know that she wouldn't if you didn't imprison her? And what does the general public think when a woman takes £2,000 and gets away with it, as they see it?' (Sheriff No. 4)

'I served my first Community Service Order on a woman who had committed an enormous fraud. When I made inquiries I found that the boy was doing well at school — she had sent him privately — and that it would have been terrible to have had his mother in gaol for a year. So I imposed a Community Service Order and it was a major success!' (Sheriff No. 1)

Here we have the crux of the matter: *when the sheriffs I interviewed are faced with a sentencing dilemma in a case where the offender is female, they mainly decide their sentence on the basis of their assessment of the woman as mother.*

When the sheriffs and the stipendiary magistrates were initially asked what special factors (if any) they would take into account when deciding whether or not to sentence a woman to a term of imprisonment, twelve of the sheriffs and both of the stipendiary magistrates said that their major concern would be to find out about the women's domestic circumstances. As we know from other sources, sheriffs are generally much more likely to ask for a Social Inquiry Report on a woman than on a man (e.g. Chambers, 1979) and eleven of the fifteen sheriffs interviewed, and both of the stipendiary magistrates, said that they would be much more likely to ask for a Social Inquiry Report in the case of a woman. They gave the following reasons:

(a) because women involved in serious crimes are often first offenders in whose cases there is a statutory requirement to obtain Social Inquiry Reports before terms of imprisonment can be imposed (*First Offender (Scotland) Act 1960*);

(b) because 'women are more likely to be mad than bad'

(Sheriffs Nos 1 and 3);

(c) because they want to find out to what extent the woman can be exonerated because of family or general social circumstances beyond her control;

(d) because they want to find out if a woman can pay a fine, and if not, why not;

(e) finally (and mentioned by all eleven sheriffs and the two stipendiaries who particularly favoured obtaining Social Inquiry Reports on women offenders) because they want to assess the degree of hardship which the children will suffer if the mother goes to prison.

The first reason given requires little discussion, and in any case the major focus of this study is on the female recidivist petty offenders who eventually become the short-term recidivist prisoners. The idea that women are more likely to be 'mad than bad' is a ubiquitous theme in criminology (cf. Crites, 1976; Smart, 1976) and certainly has had effects in that when women offend they are much more likely to be seen as being in need of care and protection or psychiatric help rather than as deserving more overt penal sanctions. Rose Giallombardo (1966) amongst others, states that:

> Whereas male criminals are usually feared as dangerous men, in the eyes of society the disgraced or dishonoured woman has always been considered pathetic. . . . Women who commit criminal offences tend to be regarded as erring and misguided creatures who need protection and help.

Certainly some of the sheriffs thought that deviant women in general tend to be disturbed, though some only referred to menopause-related disturbance. One sheriff thought that women were at the back of much male crime! This, the old Adam and Eve theory of crime, was put very forcefully by Sheriff No. 2:

> 'There is a vast amount of subliminal disturbance caused by women, which doesn't appear to be related to them; but many young men commit crime to show off to women who have egged them on.'

This was a minority view. When many of the sheriffs said vague things like: 'I tend to think with women committing crime that it's usually a symptom of something else,' (Sheriff No. 6), further discussion usually revealed that the 'something else' referred to was more related to social than psychological factors.

All of the sheriffs were very aware of the difficult family lives endured by many of the women appearing before them. Sheriff No. 7 stressed the fundamental problem:

'Some women come from areas where there is no community, high-rise flats and high crime. Or rather, there may be a community but not one that helps them. These areas have high unemployment for men and absolutely no work for women. Obviously there's little money to spend if you have a family. You'd have to be a saint not to offend in those circumstances. Many of them would have to move away completely to avoid crime.'

Other sheriffs were more specific. Three said that they were always interested to find out if a woman was totally responsible for the financial running of the home (a common feature of the domestic lives of many Scottish women). Three others mentioned that they were usually sympathetic to women if upon inquiry they discovered that they had heavily-drinking or wife-beating husbands. A more instrumental reason for pursuing these types of inquiry was related to the assessment of the woman's ability to pay a fine appropriate to the offence. The word 'embarrassment' was used more than once to describe sheriffs' feelings when a woman appears in court as accused. Their embarrassment is not entirely related to chivalry (although some claimed that that played a part). Women in court are 'embarrassing' simply because, as objects of a penal system weighted towards financial penalties for all but the gravest of offences and the most incorrigible of offenders, they are not financially competent. This, of course, is true of many male offenders (both employed and unemployed) and should be an 'embarrassment' to anyone engaged in the pursuit of 'justice'. But it is even more true of those women who are known only to have access to money by grace and favour of husbands who might well refuse to give it to them for payment of a fine. Sheriffs appear to be so 'embarrassed' by the situation of these women that they displace responsibility for imprisoning them on to public opinion:

> 'You never know how much money is available for a fine. Unless the woman is receiving regular money from her husband she will find it very difficult to pay a fine.' (Sheriff No. 4)

> 'Women normally can't pay a fine . . . and if the offence is serious enough for a large fine then they have to go to prison if they can't pay it. If people cannot pay a fine then they have to be admonished. In those cases where the public would not think it appropriate for a person to be admonished they have to go to prison.' (Sheriff No. 6)

> 'With women who cannot pay a fine I have to impose a very small alternative prison sentence.' (Sheriff No. 10)

Sheriffs, however, are not prepared to satisfy public opinion at the expense of the women's children. A further sifting occurs.

> 'Other things being equal, the appropriate sentence should indicate the appropriate measure of social disfavour. Then you add on and take off marks for particular social circumstances — a few marks on for having children, a few marks off if you haven't any! (Sheriff No. 3)

A high proportion of the women who eventually are selected to appease the public's punitive obsession are those who in the eyes of the sheriffs have failed as mothers.

Of the twelve sheriffs who said that they would want to find out what would happen to her children if a woman went to gaol, three stated that they would want to find out not only if the woman was a mother but if she was a *good* mother; five more sheriffs and one of the stipendiaries said that if the woman's children were already in care then they would be more likely to send her to prison than if her children had been living at home with her. Additionally, three sheriffs mentioned that family, husband and children act as good disciplinary controls on a woman and that if she is living at home within a conventional family consisting of husband and children then the female offender will be less likely to reoffend in the future (cf. Dahl and Snare, 1978).

'Women who live more ordered lives don't commit crime because with a husband and children to look after they don't have the time.' (Sheriff No. 1)

'If she has a husband he may just tell her to stop it.' (Sheriff No. 2)

'Not many women with steady husbands or cohabitees commit crime. They're kept occupied.' (Sheriff No. 6)

Some of the sheriffs are obviously relieved when they find that a woman's children are in care: it solves the sentencing problem:

'If she's a good mother, we don't want to take her away. If she's not a good mother, it doesn't really matter.' (Sheriff No. 13)

'If upon inquiry you discover that a woman has no children then it clears the way to send her to prison. If she has children but they are in care then I take the view that she is footloose and fancy-free and I treat her as a single woman.' (Glasgow Stipendiary Magistrate)

Another sheriff went further; he justified imprisonment by entertaining the idea that the woman's domestic difficulties might be partly remedied as a result of imprisonment:

'One often finds out, when inquiries are made, that the women have left their husbands and that their children are already in care. In those cases it may seem a very good idea to send them to prison for three months — to sort themselves out and to see what the Governor's and her staff's skills can impart to them.' (Sheriff No. 5)

In fact, once a sheriff has decided to send a woman to prison
he forgets some of his other stereotypes of working-class
women — as victims of beating and drinking husbands, as
responsible and financially overburdened women running
homes in the absence of feckless husbands — and now,
only concentrates on the very bad woman/wife/mother
before him:

> 'Most of us do not like to think that a woman is bad but
> when they do go wrong they are usually very bad indeed.'
> (Sheriff No. 1)

> 'When women *do* turn to crime they are often extremely
> clever about it, and very tough too.' (Sheriff No. 12)

> 'One tends to find that when a woman goes off the rails
> she tends to get into a terrible state.' (Sheriff No. 5)

The process of imprisonment becomes indicative *in itself* of
the woman prisoner's complete badness:

> 'A woman who goes to prison is usually very bad indeed;
> one who's had all the chances.' (Sheriff No. 8)

> 'Women who get sent to prison have earned it. By the time
> they get there, they're pretty bad.' (Glasgow Stipendiary
> Magistrate)

Finally, having transformed the offending woman into the
bad woman/mother/wife, the sheriffs strangely justify their
imprisonment of her by claiming that Cornton Vale is not
really like a prison at all!

> 'I have no qualms about sending a woman to Cornton Vale
> since I visited it.' (Sheriff No. 8)

> 'In one way I am less reluctant to send a woman to prison
> because it's not so bad as a men's prison.' (Sheriff No. 5)

Only four of the fifteen sheriffs had visited Cornton Vale and
these four had been very impressed with what they had seen.

They, plus five more who had never been to Cornton Vale, talked in glowing terms of what the prison could do for a woman. As they talked, female imprisonment was quite openly transformed into paternal discipline. Instead of being like a prison Cornton Vale was more like a mental hospital ... a maternity home ... a refuge ... an alcohol recovery unit ... a drugs recovery unit ... a domestic science college.

'I sent a young girl there last week. She had been sleeping rough and no hostel would take her any more. She wouldn't cooperate with the hospital. Her crime was comparatively trivial. She was shouting and swearing and there was a doubt whether she had committed any crime at all. But no one else could cope with her any longer, and this was one way of dealing with it.' (Sheriff No. 6)

'It's better for women to go to Cornton Vale if they are pregnant, living wild or drinking heavily. At least they will get medical care there and be properly looked after.' (Sheriff No. 4)

'In Cornton Vale a woman can be taught hygiene.' (Sheriff No. 2)

'Cornton Vale does try to do something. If a woman is not a good housewife at least they will try to teach her some basic skills.' (Sheriff No. 14)

Cornton Vale prison is of course a prison and does not pretend to be anything else. But the sheriffs were not only wrong about Cornton Vale, they were also operating with some other assumptions which need further examination.

What seemed most extraordinary about the sentencing views expressed by the sheriffs was that they could isolate their knowledge of the very hard domestic lives led by some Scottish working-class women from their beliefs that women who had children in care were, by definition, bad mothers. Moreover, they also appeared to consider it to be perfectly proper that they should take into account a woman's performance as a mother when deciding whether or not to sentence her to a term of imprisonment.

Of the women interviewed in Cornton Vale whose children were in care, two had in fact had their children first taken into care when they had gone to prison for the first time (both women had served their first term of imprisonment for breach of the peace). Three women had put their children into care when they had left 'battering' husbands. The children of another had been put into care when their mother had left a husband who was drinking and gambling away the housekeeping money. These particular facts illustrate two important general points: first, that the initial prison sentence can have not only *disastrous* effects but also *snowballing* effects as one consequence of the first imprisonment (i.e. the children going into care) becomes a partial justification for the subsequent custodial sentences; second, that the sheriffs' sympathy for the wife of the drunkard or the bully does not extend to the women who have rebelled against such masculine privilege and family discipline by leaving their husbands and putting their children into care. Already some of the meanings of women's imprisonment in Scotland become clear!

In the main, Scottish women go to prison for trivial crimes. A woman prisoner is more likely to be a *persistent* offender than a *dangerous* offender. A woman who is still running a household and looking after her children is more likely to be a candidate for a non-custodial penalty than is her sister who, in rebelling against marital tyranny, has also stepped outwith domesticity and motherhood. The latter goes to Cornton Vale — again and again and again.

4 Women, family and imprisonment

Society may as well start with poverty because it is identifiable, preventable and it is society's business. The other more personal, emotional problems will anyway be better dealt with by women if they are not exhausted, impoverished, worried about the rent, hungry and disheartened! (Morris, 1965)

The official tale

'We can do so much to rebuild family relationships.' (Governor, Cornton Vale, 1980)

The main, and in most cases only, type of work traditionally provided for Scottish women prisoners has been domestic work, though at least by 1957 'it was at last acknowledged that women prisoners should be returned to society trained as efficient "housewives" rather than as efficient "house-maids"' (Smith, 1962:299). Even 'educational' classes were (and still are) devoted to this aim.

For the women prisoners at Greenock the educational programme was designed to help them to be more competent in looking after their homes upon liberation. Training was given in planning a family budget and in simple letter-writing. The class in cooking was very popular; the women made out their own recipe books and worked out the cost of ingredients. Instruction in home nursing and mothercraft was given under a trained nurse. (Scottish Home and Health Department, *Report on Prisons in Scotland*, *1957*:16)

By 1966 the situation was largely unchanged and we find that 'the cookhouse and laundry continued to employ women serving longer sentences and these areas [were] considered of first-rate importance in the domestic training of such prisoners' (*RPS, 1966*:19).

Although mention was made also of the following recreational facilities for male prisoners — football, basketball, quoits, billiards, darts, cards, tennis — at the women's prison at Greenock recreation consisted of making handicraft articles such as soft toys, fine knitting, sewing and crochet work (*Ibid*:21).

The 1968 Report stated that typing and shorthand classes had been added to those in cooking, child-care and home-nursing. By then, also, women were employed on the manufacture of women's clothing. But the ulterior (domestic and maternal) motive had not been forgotten:

> 'In this field the benefit of the training given by the dressmaking instructress was seen clearly in the improved standard of workmanship and — perhaps more important — in the delight of the women in discovering their ability not only to make clothes for personal use but also to make dresses for their children.' (*RPS, 1968*)

In 1975 the new female institution at Cornton Vale was opened. Since then, the main work on offer to women has been in machining (fabrics), gardening and general domestic work. A few women have received general office training and typing tuition and the occasional long-termer has been allowed to study for a university degree. The main training emphases are still upon the acquisition of domestic skills and health education. In the *Report on Prisons in Scotland, 1977* we read that 'at Cornton Vale Institution health education formed an integral part of a course on family and the home' (p. 12). Given the high proportion of imprisoned women with drinking problems it is not surprising that there is an emphasis upon health education. What *is* surprising is that there is still such an emphasis upon family and the home.

The main training emphasis is upon home and family. The organisation of the blocks is based upon the 'family concept' of small groups of seven women to each unit. The idea that women prisoners need to be in small units has been prevalent in prison circles abroad for many years (cf. Giallombardo, 1966). It is not being suggested that women prisoners would be better off in the overcrowded and brutal conditions of many male prisons in Britain. Nor is exception being taken to anyone being taught to cook. There are many 'survival' skills (like cooking, mending a fuse) which are not taught to some people (usually on grounds of either class, IQ level or gender) and which could usefully be taught to *anyone* finding difficulty in coping with some of the practical aspects of living. But women at Cornton Vale are not being taught *general* survival skills — skills which would enable them to live successfully without a man. They are being taught skills which will the better enable them to fill their ideal place in the ideal family. Before, therefore, one joins in the general acclaim that Cornton Vale receives from British visitors — used only to the disgusting physical conditions prevalent in a high proportion of Britain's male prisons — one might consider the following propositions:

(1) that it is ironic (and maybe even a waste of time in terms of the relevance it can have to the women's lives) that training for family life should be offered to women who have already rejected the type of 'family life' which is likely to be available to them in the present cultural and economic conditions of Scotland;

(2) that it is hypocritical that there should be a proclaimed concern about the preservation or restoration of family life in an institution which undermines family relationships even when they are good and almost certainly destroys them when they are already bad;

(3) that (in the context of other, specified organisational features) the division of the blocks into small 'family' units results in women prisoners being rigidly disciplined in a way that further increases their isolation and dependency.

The women's tale

> 'They used to give me probation, deferred sentence, or something like that. But now that my family's all grown-up they say, "Three months imprisonment."' (Kirsty King)

> Inmates live in small units . . . . One woman in each unit is given the role of 'homemaker'. She acts as 'mother', supplies meals for the unit and is responsible for keeping the place tidy while other members of the unit are at work. Many inmates whose home circumstances have been very poor go back with higher standards and as a result look after their families better. (From *Women in the Scottish Prison Service*, 1980, Scottish Information Office)

As approximately one-fifth of all receptions to Cornton Vale in any one year are classified as being of 'no fixed abode' the above optimistic sentiments apply, presumably, only to the remaining four-fifths of prisoners undergoing Cornton Vale's training (unless of course it can also be presumed that the others go back and make improvements in the domestic arrangements of their common-lodging houses and derelict 'skips'). Yet, *most* of the women beginning short-term sentences at Cornton Vale have either already had their family lives impaired by previous terms of imprisonment or have already rejected conventional family life altogether. Of the twenty women I interviewed seven were of 'no fixed abode' when they began their terms of imprisonment and six more did not know where they would go when they were liberated. The non-relevance of training for domesticity in these circumstances should be obvious. I have nothing against cooking, sewing, and housework. I agree entirely with the Prison Education Officer who said, 'It does not hurt a woman to know about sewing, cooking and health education.' But neither does it hurt a man to know about these things and no-one has as yet suggested that they should be taught to the male prisoners of Barlinnie. Indeed, at men's prisons in Scotland courses are held in such subjects as general construction, painting, decorating, etc. Even though these courses mainly benefit the long-term prisoners (as do the business studies courses at Cornton Vale) at least there is an assumption that it is desirable for men to earn their living upon their liberation. No such assumption is made about women. The training at Cornton Vale is predicated upon the assumption that a woman's place is in the home — or, in the case of these women, in an institution. In this latter connection there was truth, as well as bitterness, in Mandy MacDonald's assertion:

'It's people like me keeps this place going. At least the Governor knows that I'll get the work done while I'm here.'

And the Education Officer repeated one woman's comments on the non-relevance of the domestic training given:

'One woman came up to me and said "Are you the person in charge of these courses? That woman has been teaching us how to work out how much carpet we would need to cover a floor. I've never had a house, let alone a bloody carpet."'

Just as women who 'cannot take' domesticity are discriminated against in the courts so also, according to one prison officer, are they disadvantaged once they arrive at Cornton Vale:

'The problem with the idea of making these units as much like home as possible is that many of the women can't take it. So they have to be put in the secure unit.' (Prison Officer No. 12)

But what is there to take? Is it really a genuinely rehabilitative experience which the women cannot take? After all, most of them recognise that they have fairly deep-rooted social problems to face when they are liberated. The majority of them told me that they could do with some help of one kind or another. Yet all of them said that they hated Cornton Vale, that the Cornton Vale experience was totally inappropriate to their needs. It was not merely that the women were undergoing a training which assumed that most of them had homes (when they didn't) and children (when according to the sheriffs one of the strategic reasons for the women being in prison at all was that their children were already in care), it was because they knew that they were being disciplined into a regime which by its very nature atrophies *any* outside relationships (familial or otherwise) and which also, by its very nature, diminishes a person's independence and self-respect.

Though some of what follows is specific to women's imprisonment in Scotland, much of it is applicable to prisons and imprisonment throughout Great Britain. Indeed, much of what I will be describing in the rest of this chapter has been described time and time again. It has to be said again, here, simply because so many Scottish sheriffs, policemen, social workers and members of the general public hold to a false notion that women's imprisonment in Scotland is not really imprisonment at all. *Women's imprisonment in Scotland is imprisonment in the general sense that it has all the repressive organisational features common to men's prisons; at the same time, it is a form of imprisonment specific to women in that it has repressive features not to be found in men's prisons.* To these general and specific features I now turn. The major argument of the remainder of this chapter is that the general organisational features of imprisonment especially increase women's difficulties outside prison at the same time as the prison authorities are claiming that the prison's domestic training can help rebuild family relationships.

Women, imprisonment and family

Incarceration in a prison is a circumstance likely to have negative effects on anyone's domestic life. For the women who end up at Cornton Vale the effects can be disastrous. Most of them already have severe domestic problems even before they are imprisoned, but seven of the women I interviewed did normally live at home with their children and six of them admitted to missing their children terribly. Loss of maternal responsibilities was not the only cause of worry and anguish. There were other causes. Protection of property was one. Without exception the women came from areas and domestic circumstances wherein property and possessions

are best not left untended. Seven of the women interviewed
had at one time or another lost a tenancy as a result of
imprisonment, and seven had either had their houses vandalised or had had property stolen from them whilst they had
been in Cornton Vale. Damaged personal relationships
provided cause for further anxiety. Three women were worried that their cohabitees would leave them whilst they were
in prison and one woman had been notified that her husband
was filing for a divorce. Two more women had received
notification that their cohabitees were applying for custody
of their children and a third was worried that her mother-in-
law would attempt to gain custody of her daughter. It is not
surprising that Ann Archer asked me: 'If people couldn't
cope before they came in, how will they be able to do so
when they go out again?'

The women described their one greatest cause of tension
as being the sheer frustration at their inability to cope with
any problems whilst they were at Cornton Vale. Bernice
described the general feeling, 'In here, if there's problems
your hands are tied. You know you cannot do anything.'
Other women described more specific problems:

> 'There's a woman in my unit, her husband's trying to
> take her baby off her and there's not a lot she can do
> about it. She's got time to contest it but what can she
> do in here? Her hands are tied.' (Thelma Thompson)

> 'When I came in I had the child benefit book in my pro-
> perty and I thought they should have told me to send
> that out, but they never. Then I thought, "maybe I should
> ask the social" but then I thought "I shall be out by the
> time I've been through all that rigmarole." But I thought
> the social worker should have told me.' (Netta Nelson)

Women, like Netta and Melody for instance, who were having
their children looked after by relatives were often worried on
the one hand that their relatives were having to bear an
additional financial burden and, on the other, concerned
that if either they or the relatives sought help that the
children would be put into an institution. This situation,
where women prisoners are ignorant of how to proceed

with the management of their outside affairs, is not helped by the fact that if they wish to see a social worker they have to make the request through an officer, and often in front of other prisoners:

> 'See, when you request for a social worker they ask you what it's for and something you think is urgent might not be something they think is urgent. So therefore they say "Och, wait" and maybe by the time you see her it's too late.' (Netta Nelson)

The prisoners said that in these circumstances they would rather just keep quiet.

The prisoners' main contact with their relatives and friends is via visits and letters. The number of visits allowed to prisoners varies according to the length of their sentences. Visits for short-term prisoners do not happen very frequently. For women serving three months the allowance of visits is usually two visits of twenty minutes each. Women serving longer periods are allowed a one-hour visit once a fortnight. Not all short-term prisoners take their allowance of visits for several reasons. A few women, of course, have no one to visit them. The relatives of others cannot afford to travel to Cornton Vale. An official in the prison service recognised that 'there are special problems of visiting at Cornton Vale because it is the only prison for women in Scotland.' The reluctance of relatives to travel down from say, Wick, in the north of Scotland to Stirling in central Scotland, is not diminished by the fact that regardless of the time and money they have spent in getting to Cornton Vale they are still only allowed twenty minutes with the short-term prisoners. 'What's the point', exclaimed Olive O'Brien, 'Of coming from Dundee, wasting all that money on train fares, for twenty minutes? It doesn't make sense.'

Melody McDuff's mother only had to travel from Glasgow but with Melody's child to arrange for as well she found that visiting her imprisoned daughter took a whole day. When I went to visit Mrs McDuff she told me, 'It's a whole day when I go to visit Melody. I have to take Alasdair to my other daughter first, then the train to Stirling, then another bus, then a walk.' When I myself travelled through from

Edinburgh to Cornton Vale to visit Melissa (imprisoned yet again, ten days after being released from Cornton Vale!) I found that though the round trip took five hours, the actual time spent with Melissa accounted for only twenty minutes of that time.

Another factor inhibiting visits is the fact that both before and after the visit prisoners have to strip and submit to being searched.

'I've had one visit, all the time I've been in here and that was my friend and her husband. It's a waste of time. They come all the way from Glasgow for twenty minutes, plus you're as long sitting in Reception as you are at your visit. Then you get took back down to Reception and put into one of the dog boxes and you get searched. Some of them search you right thoroughly — know what I mean? Others just strip you down to your underwear.' (Hermione Hall)

'I keep the two visits to two weeks before I get out and get the two of them together because you only get twenty minutes otherwise. The officers are there and you've got to sit with your hands up here so that they can see what you're doing. And then they take you down and strip you. I know lassies that'll not take a visit for that reason.' (June Jones)

'You get searched after your visit which I think is terrible, it's degrading. Half the times I won't even have a visit because of the idea of getting stripped. Sometimes it's pretty thorough and sometimes it's just stripping you down to your bra and pants and that's as far as they go. But some of them just go beyond that and the lassies object to it.' (Melissa Malcom)

When all obstacles have been surmounted and a visit does take place it is likely to increase the prisoner's pain and tension. When I went to visit Melissa two officers stood about three yards away (no more!) and the tables accommodating other prisoners and their visitors were even closer to each other and to us. I sympathised with Mrs McDuff who had commented: 'You can't talk about anything on a visit with the screws standing so close all the time.' For women who are missing their children the strains of a visit are intense. Freda Franklin describes a typical dilemma of mothers in prison. She describes how she was torn between her desire to see her children and her desire to shield them from the pain of seeing her in prison:

'When I first came in I just didn't want to see the weans because I knew how hard it would be for them to go away and for me to see them go away. Then I got desperate. I'd never seen them for the first couple of visits, then I just had to see them, I felt as though I had to. And when they came up, my eldest daughter — she's awfully, awfully close to me — it was a shame for the wean, so it was. At the end of the visit I says "You'll have to go now" and she just gives me a kiss and just bolted out the door. 'Cos I'd always said "If you greet, I'll never ask you to come up again because you're only upsetting me as well." She's been up several times now but still she's the same, just gives me a kiss and bolts right out the door before her tears start. It's really heartbreaking.'

Mrs McDuff, however, had given up taking Alasdair to see Melody because it upset him so much:

'Alasdair greets at night. I only took him to see Melody once. When we came away he was greeting so much that I didn't take him again. She said last week, "I see you've not brought Alasdair" and I said, "No, it's me that's got to struggle with him, Melody."'

Melody herself was ambivalent about this at first, but then she decided that her mother was right.

'I said to my mum, "I don't know whether I want him to come and visit me or not." I desperately want to see him — but to bring him to this place — no way. It's a place I want to forget and I don't want him to say later on "I was there, Mum. I remember coming to see you in prison." '

A prison officer commented that 'visits are mixed blessings' and another said, 'I have seen family visits where everyone is in floods of tears' (Prison Officer No. 1).

Censorship of letters means that letter writing is also inhibited as a means of maintaining contact with relations and friends. Letter writing did not come easy to the women I interviewed. When they had written a letter they did not take kindly to being told to write it again.

> 'Half the times I've written letters and ripped them up. Censoring your letters is terrible. You're not allowed to write what you want so I just rip them up.' (Melissa Malcom)

> 'I got called down to the office and I was to rewrite this letter. So I re-wrote it and I wrote the same thing because I couldn't see what harm I was doing, and I had to re-write it again. I says, "No, I'm not re-writing it." I tore it up, plus the 10 pence stamp, which means a lot to me, a 10 pence stamp — I tore it up rather than write it again.' (Freda Franklin)

Waiting for letters can also cause tension, particularly when there is no way of finding out why the long awaited letter does not come.

> 'This place makes you awfully, awfully bitter. I've not had a letter from my ma for four months and I don't know why.' (Phyllis Prince)

Several women expressed irritation that telephone calls are not allowed. Whilst I was at Cornton Vale Melody had spent an agonised weekend wondering why her mother had not arrived for a visit as expected:

> 'If we could just have a telephone call, even if we had to save it up for an emergency. Then if your letters don't come or your visit doesn't turn up you could phone and see what's wrong. Even if it was just to phone my mum to say "Is everything OK?" and she just said "Yes, fine" and put the phone down I'd be over the moon for the rest of the week.' (Melody McDuff)

'If only you could get to phone your house. I could get
to phone my man up — but you're not allowed, and the
social worker's not allowed to do that for you.' (Olive
O'Brien)

Prisoners did not believe that letters were censored purely
for security purposes. Several women said that officers had
referred in casual conversation to something that had been
written to them in a letter. I myself was present when a
young officer in Sierra entertained four other officers by
reading aloud a letter sent to a prisoner. The officer caused
a great deal of mirth by pronouncing the ill-spelt words
phonetically! During the same week I read a note in Thelma
Thompson's file which was indicative of one of the functions
of censorship:

Only having Thelma's side to the story regarding her
husband's behaviour I asked the staff who censor letters
and take visits if they could clarify just what the situation
is.

That such clarification is sought and obtained was confirmed
by a senior prison officer, though this same officer was
against censorship altogether.

'We learn a lot about prisoners through censoring mail.
They know that everything is screened and we make them
deceitful. Because they have no uninhibited contacts with
the outside, visits can be very emotional.' (Prison Officer
No. 3)

In such a context, where the women are both without power
to act and without privacy in which to communicate, they
learn to cope with their problems by affecting not to think
about them at all. But the problems do not go away. The
problems are outside, the women are inside. Imprisonment
becomes unreal — an existence both within and without a
life. The women found it difficult to describe:

'In this place you're in a sort of limbo. Nothing outside is
real. I just imagine — and this *is* imagination — that I'm

coming out of space. I feel I've been in one planet and I'm going to another planet. 'Cos outside the world's different from in here.' (Ann Archer)

'In here — oh, how can I explain it? It's like an existence. Nothing seems real. It's when you go home that the worries start.' (Ingrid Ingham)

'This is out of limits, this place. You're standing outside your existence. A lot of lassies going out of here are going out with blank minds. Your problems are not sorted out in here. They're all piled up for you waiting at the gate when you go out, so they are.' (Melissa Malcom)

So much for the sheriffs' views on the rehabilitative powers of Cornton Vale! Of course, they are right to assume that women in ill-health will be well looked after in the prison, that pregnant women will be properly cared for. But prisons are not run as surrogate nursing homes or kindergartens. Babies are *not* welcome in the prison. Both the Governor and her staff think that prison is a quite inappropriate place for babies.

Domestic problems, far from being alleviated, tend to get worse while a woman is in Cornton Vale. After they had been released, I went to visit Kirsty in Edinburgh and Ingrid in Glasgow. They are two very different people. Kirsty is notorious in Edinburgh for her heavy drinking. Although she has a flat she often stays in hostels or elsewhere when she has a drink in her. Ingrid, by contrast, has a lovely and beautifully kept council flat and a charming six-year-old son. Their experiences upon being liberated were typical of many other prisoners in circumstances similar to theirs.

Pat Carlen: 'What happened last time you went out of prison?'

Kirsty: 'At first I got drunk. You always do. I mean it's something that I can't understand. You say to yourself "I'm not going to take a drink, I'll go to the pictures or something", but you're so glad to get away from here. You're so glad to get away from the atmosphere, the shouting and bawling and cleaning and all the rest of

it, that you say, "Och, I've just got to take that wee drink
down." Then I went out stealing again, shoplifting.'

The above conversation took place in prison, the day before
Kirsty was liberated. I went to see her three weeks later and
we had coffee in an Edinburgh cafe. Things had not been
going too well:

'Och, Miss Carlen, I was so upset when I got home last
Thursday. The council hadn't shut up my place. They'd
wanted £16 to do it and where would I get £16 from?
Anyhow, when I got back two men had been in and
vandalised it. I've just been up to see the social worker and
he's coming down this afternoon. I got rid of those two
men but I couldn't stay there it was in such a state. I could
have cried. I went to the Sally Ann but I got into trouble
last night for doing some washing. This young lieutenant
came up to me and said I was breaking the rules. So I said,
you know what I said Miss Carlen? "Up you!" and they
want me out by Monday!'

When I saw Ingrid two weeks after her liberation she too
was very depressed. She had thought that the social workers
in Cornton Vale had sorted out her rent for her, but she had
received a demand for rent arrears as soon as she had arrived
home. Whilst she had been in prison her common-law husband had stayed in the flat, run up some bills and then had
left, taking with him one or two essential household goods
(e.g. the electric kettle).

Pat Carlen: 'And how was Jamie?'
Ingrid: 'He won't leave me for a moment. He's terrified
    I'm going away again, he's very unsettled.'
Pat Carlen: 'And your husband?'
Ingrid: 'That's finished. He came up to me mam's and told
    her he'd been with another woman. That was the worst
    thing he could do, to do that when I was in there.'
Pat Carlen: 'How did you feel when you got out?'
Ingrid: 'Very disappointed. After all that time, all I came
    out to was worries. I never did think that I should get
    away with what I did but I never thought it would be

so bad when I came out either. It goes on and on and no-one to help you. I've lost my man, and my job and now I can't even give Jamie what he needs.'

The unofficial tale

Most of the prison officers were completely frank about their own assessment of the negative effects which imprisonment must have on a woman's family and domestic life. One, commenting on the total inappropriateness of holding out family and marriage as being the major goal to which every woman should aspire, said sadly of the Borstal girls: 'When they're under twenty-one they all hope to get married and have children. Then, when they do, their children are taken into care' (Prison Officer No. 9). Others made the point that when an imprisoned woman did have children at home then 'family discipline' and the yoke of maternal responsibility inseminated and strengthened the organisational discipline of the prison, thereby containing the imprisoned mother in a psychological vacuum of being — both without and within the family.

'The woman is expected to be at home to look after the children. Therefore when she comes in here she can feel more guilty.' (Prison Officer No. 8)

'Women with children are often less trouble. They don't want to lose remission.' (Prison Officer No. 12)

Freda Franklin and Clare Carlton agreed with these remarks:

'I've never been on report here because I've got two kids to think about. I think of the remission I'd get taken off me. On my sentence I need only do six months. That six I want done as quick as possible and get out to the weans.' (Freda Franklin)

'If women have kids outside they'll take any amount of stick off anybody.' (Clare Carlton)

Thus the woman's place in the family is constitutive of, and conditions, the meanings of her imprisonment from the sentencing stage onwards. Many Scottish working-class women, like their contemporaries elsewhere in Great Britain, have not had the opportunity to negotiate a public realm of existence. When they offend against the criminal law, therefore, the private realm of family life conditions public knowledge about the 'bad' woman, the female subject of penology. Whether the woman is actually within or outwith the family is immaterial. What, ironically *is* material is that whether the woman has family or not, there is no judgmental space where she, the crime and the punishment can be constituted as being family-immune. Yet, the 'very bad' women who, according to the sheriffs, have been sent to prison as 'a last resort' are, upon their arrival at Cornton Vale translated back into social beings outwith society, 'puir creeturs', victims of drink, violence and unemployment whose family life is described by prison officers as being 'generally chaotic' and 'beyond belief'. Once the women are seen again as being harmless, pathetic creatures the justifications for their imprisonment undergo a further transformation. Scottish women are imprisoned for their own, rather than the public, good. Prison becomes home and prison officers become next-of-kin.

> 'Most of them are isolated outside. All the friends they've got are staff.' (Prison Officer No. 9)

> 'After they've been in here, many of them find it difficult to live outside. We become their next-of-kin.' (Prison Officer No. 3)

Thus are both the private and the public realms of family life and the discourses which constitute it incorporated into the state's regulatory processes and agencies. This fusion of the private and public realms of family discipline with the penological regulation of deviant women has, in fact, received nominal recognition. Cornton Vale's main prison block is, appropriately, called Papa!

Part three
The moment of prison

5 Papa's discipline: disciplinary modes in the Scottish women's prison

'We do not need to carry batons; we rely on talk.' (Comment by a female prison officer when I remarked on the fact that female officers, unlike their male colleagues, do not carry batons.)

A constant theme in feminist writings from Wollstonecraft to de Beauvoir and beyond concerns the debilitating contradictions which have been inherent in the social constructions of both femininity and female subjectivity. Much of contemporary feminist struggle is concerned with confronting and theorizing the contradictions which have atrophied women's abilities to make sense of themselves in a world publicly defined by men. Even today, after feminist writings and sustained campaigns have resulted in some significant legislative and ideological victories, the contradictory conditions within which individual women struggle for autonomy can still cause anguish and pain. For though women may nowadays be more aware of the ideological sources of these contradictory definitions – definitions both of legitimate womanhood and the conditions which engender such a state – they are, none the less, still constituted within them.

At the same time, of course, the very existence of the diffuse but ideologically powerful women's movement has enabled many women to confront successfully (and thereby change) the conditions of their own existences. The progressive effects of the women's movement have, however, been partial. There remain many women whose oppression is still made possible by a stubborn matrix of ideological and economic conditions. The women whose family life I described in

Chapter Two are a case in point. Brought up both in ignorance of, and yet dependent upon, male-related authority and domesticity, these women were, at an early age, quickly isolated in domestic conditions and family relationships over which they felt they had no control. It has been argued that it is this feeling of futility and powerlessness which has resulted in the mystery illnesses and often life-long depressions to which middle-class women have been perennially subject and which were particularly prevalent at the turn of the century (Ehrenreich and English, 1979). Depressed (or oppressed) working-class women, however, have not had the option of comfortable invalidity at home. For them the alternatives have been stark — either to put up with their lot or to reject it altogether. Rejection of family and domesticity has often led to the bottle or to the mental hospital. Even when it has led to neither, many women who have rejected maternal responsibilities have found themselves further isolated — as women out of place. As we saw in Chapter 3, if they then get into criminal trouble, their lack of maternal responsibilities, the fact that they are outwith domestic discipline, may go against them in the courts. If they go to prison they will yet again become victims of contradictory and debilitating definitions of womanhood.

In this chapter, therefore, I shall show how contradictory definitions both of legitimate womanhood and the conditions engendering it are dominant both in the penal discourses and the extra-discursive practices of the women's prison. I shall show how, together, they weave a fine web of penal control around women prisoners. Within the fractured and discontinuous elements of these discourses and institutional practices imprisoned women are again and again deconstructed and reconstructed to the point of debilitation. The features of the disciplinary regime which are specific to women's imprisonment elevate, fracture and realign opposed ideological elements of the prisoners' subjective experience until they have been constructed as women both irrevocably within and irretrievably without adult female subjectivity. Women prisoners are contradictorily defined as being: both within and without sociability; both within and without femininity; and, concomitantly with the two previous conditions, both within and without adulthood.

Imprisoned – within and without sociability

The short-term prisoners in Cornton Vale's Papa Block, the main focus of this part of the study, feel that they are the most restricted prisoners within the prison. Many of them expressed a sense of injustice that this should be so. By and large their crimes have been less serious than those of the long-term prisoners; they have been moved to Papa Block because, through their behaviour whilst under observation, they have demonstrated that they can conduct themselves reasonably with less supervision than the women whose behaviour has caused them to be kept in Sierra, the secure block. Many of Papa's short-term prisoners have been in Cornton Vale so frequently that they are well-known to the staff and are trusted by them. So why the severity of their treatment? It is because they are the ones for whom the disciplinary organisation of the prison – and all general prisons – is devised. The prisoners doing Open University degrees, receiving specialist training, living in specially devised units are the exceptions, not the rule, within the prison system. None the less, it is likely that the women in Papa Block at Cornton Vale receive an even stricter and more coercive surveillance than do their counterparts in men's prisons.

According to the Governor of Cornton Vale the short-term prisoners in Sierra have to be allowed more latitude because they are the most difficult prisoners to contain. The longer term prisoners in Papa's open units are allowed 'association' (i.e. the freedom to sit in each other's rooms in the evenings and to watch television from 6.30 pm to 8.00 pm) as a privilege. The majority of prisoners, however, are serving much less than six months; they are locked into their rooms from 6.30 pm during the week and, unless they have a twenty-minute visit on a Saturday afternoon, from 1.30 pm until the next morning on Saturdays and Sundays. Several prisoners remarked on the fact that Cornton Vale's much publicised gardens are 'only for show', that the women prisoners are not allowed to exercise in them and are only occasionally allowed to sit outside in the fresh air. Lack of relaxing exercise (as opposed to hard physical labour working in the gardens or humping dustbins) was often complained about — and in this context, as in several others relating to recreational facilities, the women thought that they were much worse off than male prisoners, even the short-term male prisoners. Certainly at Saughton prison men are able to associate on two nights a week and during Saturday and Sunday afternoons after only two months' imprisonment. At such times male prisoners are allowed to play darts, cards, table-tennis, dominoes, etc. None of these activities were available to the women prisoners at Cornton Vale even to those allowed association. Thus, at the most elementary and physical level the women felt that they were more restricted than the general fact of their imprisonment warranted.

'I'd do anything to pass the time, so when I came in I asked if they had a netball team and they said "Oh no, nothing like that."' (Freda Franklin)

'Likes of Sierra and Romeo have exercise, but we don't get nothing. If we were allowed out even for a game of football every now and then it would help — at least it would help me, because it would get rid of my excess energy.' (Phyllis Prince)

Not all the women felt so energetic but many of them wanted to do more than just sit and watch television:

'In the open units they have a record player — but we're not allowed one. In men's prisons they have table tennis; I've not even seen a pack of cards over here.' (Hermione Hall)

'Men's prisons are different from women's; they have cards and pool and table-tennis.' (Kirsty King)

Though to this last Olive O'Brien added darkly, 'They wouldn't tolerate this carry-on in a men's prison.'

The majority of women prisoners at Cornton Vale are not in 'association' at all. When they are not at work, cleaning the unit or eating their meals they are locked alone in their rooms. Apart from listening to their transistors they have little to do but churn over their problems. Reading does not come easy to most of the women at any time. In a prison cell many of them find it even more difficult. Some find it impossible:

> 'You try to concentrate on a book but your thoughts go back to home. People who say they really concentrate on a book in here must be really good, they must be used to it. 'Cos it's very difficult. I read a fair amount outside, here I can't. I pick up a book, I read a bit and then my mind wanders — to home, my children, my father — are they all right? And then I start to worry.' (Thelma Thompson)

Talk can relieve tension but the short-term prisoners at Cornton Vale get little time to talk to each other. Georgina Green was expressing a general opinion when she commented: 'I think we're locked up far too much. We don't get any time to sit and talk to other prisoners.' As a result of this enforced seclusion, when the prisoners do meet at mealtimes the talk can be frenetic and not have a cathartic effect at all. Ingrid Ingham described what often happens and why:

> 'When I was in the closed unit it was hard, because you're always locked up. All day Saturday and Sunday you're locked up. You feel as if the walls are closing in on you. Then, when you all get out for tea or supper you're all squawking at the same time; talk, talk, talking because you've been locked up all that time. I don't think I ever really got a clear conversation with anybody because it was all stupid things we talked about; for the sake of talking when we got out.' (Ingrid Ingham)

Thelma Thompson who had previously been in Holloway claimed that this isolation is peculiar to Cornton Vale:

> 'In the English prison you have more free time to communicate more with the other inmates. So there, instead of bickering about small, silly things when you do get to meet them, you're getting to understand them. Taking away your freedom is a true word in every sense in Scotland.'

The purpose of the 'family' concept of organisation at Cornton Vale is, according to the Governor, that women 'should have their self-respect restored to them within a disciplined setting'. The women tell a different tale, a tale of isolation from each other and of self-estrangement.

The women who outside the prison are denied the legitimate pleasures of public conviviality and communality are yet again denied any real communicative experience once they get to prison. The division of the women into family units of seven allows for a rigid surveillance and control. Women from one unit are not allowed to communicate with women from another unit. Within each unit conversations between members are constantly monitored by officers, the permitted modes of conversations and the legitimacy of the topics discussed arbitrarily changing according to the dictates of the officers on duty. Further, the women are required to be sociable without being allowed to engage in the types of exchanges considered to be constitutive of sociability outside the prison. This constant emphasis on social behaviour outwith the normal channels of sociability makes the women tense in their relationships with each other and distrustful of their own ability to develop or maintain any sense of individual autonomy or self-direction. The major disciplinary effect of Cornton Vale's 'family unit' system is that the women prisoners are, both literally and symbolically, both physically and mentally, spaced-out.

Several women complained of the strict surveillance by officers over their movements within the blocks and of their confinement to the same small groups: 'If you go from one unit to another unit without asking permission you can get put on report for it.' (Thelma Thompson)

'The lassies in the open units aren't really supposed to speak to the lassies in the closed units. For what reason I've no idea. I got into trouble for it one day, so I did. I went down to Unit 5 to take the milk jug and I put my head in to say "Hello" to the lassies and I got called into the office and told that if I didn't want my privileges taken off me not to speak to prisoners in other units.' (Freda Franklin)

Many prisoners just get fed-up with being with the same small group. After all, several of them, like Melissa Malcom, had decided to live outwith domesticity because, as they described themselves, they were 'loners'. Melissa in fact often went days without speaking to anyone other than to those officers who addressed her directly. Others said that they experienced a certain amount of strain from being forced into close company with people with whom they had nothing in common other than the fact of their incarceration. Phyllis Prince said, 'I'm not one for crowds, so this place just beats me,' whilst Ann Archer felt disdain for the company she was being forced to keep:

> 'There's a lot of people in here — no harm to them — I just don't like them. But I've got to put up with them. If you're in the same unit with somebody you don't like, (say, you hate her) and she doesn't like you, you've just got to put up with each other and it causes a lot of tension. Tension builds up here.'

However, even when women do get on with each other within the units, even when they wish to communicate with, and help, each other, there are many bars to sociability. The women in the closed units are not allowed to go into each other's rooms. The women in the open units are inhibited by the possibility that the intercom button in their rooms may be on, the officers thereby being able to listen-in on their conversations. Bernice Bradley described what could happen:

> 'They've got these intercom things on the wall, and sometimes you can be sitting there and they can be listening to every word you're saying. While I was in the open unit we were all sitting talking one day and the officer just came belting out over this intercom thing. It was a good job it was an officer that was all right, but she'd heard every word we'd said.'

In the closed units officers are always present when the women are talking:

'You can't have a joke without them asking what you're laughing about.' (June Jones)

'You can't have a laugh and joke without them telling you to shut-up. Yet you cannot talk privately without them sticking their noses in.' (Phyllis Prince)

Freda Franklin (along with others like Bernice Bradley and Phyllis Prince who had both at one time been in open units and found the artificiality of the enforced sociability too much of a strain) pointed out to me that I should not fall into the error of assuming that women in the open units had greater access to privacy than those in the closed:

> 'Having a key means that you can open your own door. But the officers still come into your room when they want to, even if your key's on the other side of the door. It doesn't keep them out.'

A more frequent complaint was that the officers even monitored mealtime talk and behaviour:

> 'When you get your food in the sitting room an officer is there. She comes in and sits there. I don't call that freedom. I mean they're right outside in any case but they come in and sit just next to you. Why don't they leave you alone to your meals? The only time you feel you've got freedom is when they lock the doors when you're in your room.' (Vivienne Vincent)

Thus one ironical result of the women's recognition that they are being forced into a coercively monitored sociability is that they are driven into even greater isolation, a debilitating isolation outwith both sociability and privacy. Yet several women thought that they *should* communicate more with other people, that keeping themselves to themselves was not a good thing (indeed it had been a part of the ethic of respectable female domesticity which they had earlier rejected), that lack of communication with others had been one of their problems in the past. Melissa admitted that she was often bad-tempered and 'hated' other people just because 'alone I have bad thoughts' while Thelma Thompson, continually told-off by officers for talking too much, knew quite well why she did it:

> 'As I say, I talk a lot. Sometimes I'm rambling on and on and it's of no interest to anyone else, it's just relieving my tension. I *can* sit and have a reasonable discussion with anyone if they're willing to but before the discussion's closed you're back in your room. By the time you get back you've forgotten what you were discussing in the first place. So therefore you don't carry it on, you go on to something else and everything's one big mumbo-jumbo. You've no time to get anything off your chest. I *am* inclined to talk a lot, it's just my way of relieving my nerves. Some of them say "Do you never get tired of speaking?" And it used to worry me, but why should it, if talking is helping me and saving me from cracking up?' (Thelma Thompson)

Some women are *so* overburdened by their own problems that their inclination is to avoid engaging in the exchanges which would entail hearing about other people's troubles. The prison officers encourage this attitude of non-involvement in the affairs of other prisoners:

> 'A lot of the women think "Oh, I've got enough on my plate myself without bothering about anybody else" and in here it is sometimes better to be like that because if something does blow-up you're pulled into it. Then you're told that you shouldn't be talking to other people or that you shouldn't be finding out about each other, that it's an officer's job.' (Clare Carlton)

Not only are the women discouraged from discussing their own affairs they are, in fact, actually forbidden to engage in many of the expected civilities of normal social life. June Jones was very indignant that she had had her lighter taken from her and that she had also been put on report for giving someone a light, 'I mean, if everyone's sitting round and somebody says "Give us a light,", you're not going to say, "No, you're not getting one."' She (amongst others) was also indignant that having been forced to live with a homeless woman in a 'family' unit she was then not allowed to give that same woman information that could help her upon liberation:

> 'There's a woman in our unit who's got nowhere to go when she gets out. So I gave her my address and I got locked up for that. The officer just took the address off me and tore it up.' (June Jones)

Sharing of privileges and skills is also forbidden:

> 'If you get books sent in you must keep them to yourself and when you've finished those books they go right into your property. One lassie got five books sent in and she asked if she could put them in the library so the other lassies could go and get them. But no way.' (Freda Franklin)

> 'I've got City and Guilds. One of the girls who's going out says to me that she could get a job as a waitress, a living-in position, so that she wouldn't have to worry about where she's going to stay. But she says "I'm not a good waitress." I says "Well, come on, get the knives and forks out and I'll show you" and I was saying "Put this, this side and that, that side" and I got into serious trouble. The officer says to me "*You* can't tell people what to do on the outside." They don't like you to know anything. They'd rather think you're all dumb and stupid.' (Melody McDuff)

Olive O'Brien summed up the general feeling of contempt for a disciplinary system which though purporting to engender a sense of social responsibility in those subject to it at the same time attempts to extinguish all signs of mutual self-help.

> 'You cannot speak in private. We're not allowed to go into another lassie's room. We can't even borrow a paper off a lassie. You cannot give another lassie a smoke. Even a lassie who had come in from Dundee and didn't have any tobacco. Surely to God I could be allowed to give that lassie a fag. I've worked for it and it's my money. But you cannot do it, you're on report for that as well. It doesn't make sense, that.' (Olive O'Brien)

Ann Archer agreed with Olive:

> 'You're apt to get selfish in prison too. If you get tobacco
> or people's got sweets, they're not allowed to share it out
> with each other. Well I'm not like that outside and I don't
> see why I should be like that in here. So I don't think
> prison helps anybody, it just makes you more selfish and
> bitter.'

And Kirsty King claimed that so much normal sociability
and communication is suppressed at Cornton Vale that it
is more like a hospital than a prison: 'It is more like a hospital, you know. You're all separated and you don't know
half of what is going on. In the real prison you had much
more social life.' Yet the real prisons of the nineteenth century also operated with the principle of 'divide and rule'.
It is ironic, but not accidental, that features and effects of
the nineteenth-century separate system should reappear in
new form in the much-lauded 'family unit' system of Cornton Vale.

Some women, like Thelma Thompson, admitted to experiencing an extreme tension. Others said that they could keep
a tight rein on their emotions, that in particular they would
not allow officers to 'wind' them up. Olive O'Brien, Daphne
Daniels and Melody McDuff commented on this phenomenon,
a common and sinister feature of institutions where the
power of one group is both arbitrary and total:

> 'They try to wind up some of those lassies until they are
> in a terrible state.' (Olive O'Brien)

> 'Some of the officers, when they see a girl's nerves are
> kind of bad, they'll try and pick on her.' (Daphne Daniels)

> 'One girl said something to an officer which she didn't like
> and the officer says "We can always make it a hundred
> times harder for you in a hundred different ways."'
> (Melody McDuff)

Melody is a photographic model by profession. She told me
how the prison officers constantly goaded her about certain
aspects of the job:

Melody: 'When I came into reception they started making remarks like "Oh, here she comes, here come Paris models now." Then when they told me to strip and put this sheet round me, I went to turn my back and she says "Turn round, you've shown it all before."'

Pat Carlen: 'And did this continue?'

Melody: 'Yes. The other day I was down on my knees doing the floor and this officer comes along and says "Oh, look, everyone, it's rear end we've got now, not topless."'

After this very conversation I myself was jokingly told, 'Oh, you interviewed the model this morning, didn't you?'

In a more serious context I witnessed what must surely count as an outstanding instance of 'winding-up'. It involved a woman in Sierra. This woman, let's call her Cleopatra, was by all accounts one of the most disturbed women in Cornton Vale. The following report is mainly of a conversation (which was noted down verbatim as it occurred) and of the circumstances in which it took place (which were noted down about ten minutes after the end of the episode). I was rather surprised that such an episode could occur in front of someone known to be an 'official' researcher sponsored by the Scottish Office.

Ms X, a prison officer, introduced me to Cleopatra. 'Cleopatra is our star. When she misbehaves she's horrible. Now don't go near Mrs Carlen because your breath stinks.' We sat down in the sitting-room together with a new inmate who had not as yet been given any work to do. The conversation turned to illness and Cleopatra said that she was scared of getting cancer. Ms X said to her, 'Perhaps Mrs Carlen would like to contribute to buying you a copy of *Exit* for Christmas.' Cleopatra said, 'What's that?' 'The book of the Euthanasia Society . . . you could go when you like then.' After some further desultory conversation, Cleopatra announced that she was going to comb her hair and put on some make-up. Ms X responded with, 'Well, don't do those silly bunches you did the other day and don't make yourself up like a circus clown.' When in reply to these injunctions Cleopatra began to shout, Ms X caught hold of her by the lapels and shouted threateningly 'Are you starting again?' Cleopatra cried, 'No, Miss, I'm not starting. It's just all this aggravation, all this antagonism.'

When Cleopatra had left the room an extremely thin woman came into the sitting room. (I was later told that she was suffering from anorexia.) Ms X now turned her attention to this lady and introduced her to me with 'Now, look at this one Mrs Carlen. Watch out for this one, she's a handful. Looks horrible, too, doesn't she? It's because she won't eat.'

Sierra Block is occupied mainly by the women who are said to have 'personality disorders' and whose behaviour can be very strange indeed. It also serves as an induction unit for all convicted prisoners over the age of twenty-one, all of whom remain in Sierra for at least the first six weeks of their sentences. The reason for combining the initial observation unit with the secure unit for very disturbed offenders is punitive. The bizarre behaviour of some of the women in Sierra terrifies new prisoners and, as one officer said, 'it makes them realise they're in prison.' The Governor herself said that 'it is good for women to go into Sierra when they first come in as it makes them feel guilty. It makes them feel that they are in prison.' And other officers also expounded on the positive disciplinary advantages accruing from Cornton Vale's overlarge proportion of severely disturbed offenders: 'All admissions have to go to Sierra and they think they are in a madhouse' (Prisoner Officer No. 4).

'Being in Sierra can have a good effect on first offenders. Some get very frightened of people like Cleopatra. One woman was in with two who were worse than Cleopatra. They threatened to take her food and to beat her up. And we can't be there all the time. . . . At least it did frighten her.' (Prison Officer No. 7)

The staff *want* Cornton Vale to be experienced as a prison.

'It is good for them to realise they're in prison. One woman, an embezzler, told me that when she came into Sierra she cried all night because women were screaming and she was so frightened. She said she thought "Oh my God! What have I let myself in for?"' (Prison Officer No. 5)

In Sierra, too, new prisoners learn that all powers of definition are the officers'. The 'good' prisoner 'opens up' to the officers and doesn't think that she is any better than the other women. Camilla, for instance, was a new prisoner who had not yet learned this, as the following dialogue (held in the presence of a half-dozen prisoners) demonstrates:

> *Prison Officer (to Pat Carlen)*: 'They're just like bairns. If you sit in here with five of them you've got five competing for your attention. Yesterday I was in here and they were all trying to talk to me at once.'
> *Camilla*: 'I wasn't, I didn't say a word.'
> *Prison Officer (snaps)*: 'And that's just as bad as the other way. You were keeping too much to yourself. You'd been here two days and it was only last night that you began to open up.'

Once, however, the women have opened up, have made their private lives into public property, they are reprimanded if the officers think that they talk too much! Phyllis Prince summed up the double-bind in which many of the women found themselves: 'They tell you that you should be yourself, just be natural and be yourself. If I was myself in here I'd never be off report.'

There is resentment and suspicion of the women developing a private realm of consciousness, yet at the same time there are bars to sociability which prevent them developing a public realm of consciousness. Though, therefore, the women are *physically* locked into small family units which might appear to provide secure rehabilitative settings, the superimposed prison discipline ensures that they are mentally and emotionally straitjacketed into the same debilitating tension and isolation which they have already experienced in nuclear family situations outwith the prison. When many of the prisoners subsequently indicate that not only are they outwith the family physically but that emotionally and mentally too they are committed neither to family relationships nor to domesticity, the prison officers find it difficult to endow their charges with any kind of legitimate social being at all. The women who have stepped outside family and domesticity are also seen to be beyond femininity and without adulthood.

Imprisoned — within and without femininity

'But she's not like a woman, is she? Smelling like that! Ye canna say she's a woman. She's lovable enough — more like a bairn, but she's never a woman.' (Prison Officer No. 6 talking to me about Kirsty King)

'You're not allowed razors or Immac for your arms nor tweezers for your eyebrows. It's most uncomfortable when you've been used to it. Some of the officers would be willing to bring in their old make-up but they're not allowed. I mean, why can't they bring in their own make-up and put it into a box so that the lassies can use it? It would make the women feel better, and make morale better anyway. There's nothing worse than feeling down in the dumps. Even at home if you're feeling a bit down — you go and have a bath, do your hair and put make-up on. There are lassies in here that are good at putting make-up on and good at hairdressing. And I think they should be encouraged to do that kind of thing. Still . . . maybe they *like* to see you walking about like something from the Dark Ages.'[1] (Clare Carlton)

Familiness is one dominant conceptual axis along which women's imprisonment is conceived by the Scottish judicial and penal authorities. Femininity is another. Together with the insistence that deviant women should be interpellated as members of a family and reconstructed as lifelong candidates for domesticity is the insistence that, because prisoners in Cornton Vale are treated as women, they should behave accordingly. Sometimes when the officers contended that 'at least they're treated as women' they were merely referring to the fact that Cornton Vale has standards of sanitation far superior to most British prisons. At other times they were making reference to some innate female 'need' for familiness catered for by the small 'family' units. On other occasions again they were referring to the higher standards of cleanliness and decorum expected of women. At the same time, however, officers continually pointed out to me that few of the women had acquired the ordinary 'female' accomplishments of baking and sewing, whilst the women themselves complained that the prison authorities denied to them most of the sartorial and cosmetic props to femininity which they were accustomed to enjoying outside the prison. Lest, however, it is thought that talk of femininity exhausted the discursive parameters within which the women themselves talked of their bodily and psychological confinement, it must be noted that the women were equally concerned about the generally degrading aspects of the prison regime, aspects common to most British prisons and stubbornly and surprisingly (or not) retained even in a modern institution such as Cornton Vale. For, despite the reiterated claims of the officers that women are not degraded at Cornton Vale it has to be remembered that at any one time about a third of the adult women there may be accommodated in closed units, thereby being forced to use the hated chamber-pots whenever they are locked up, whether it be during the day or at night. Netta Nelson thought that the system was both generally degrading and particularly distressing to women:

> 'It's degrading, women of our age having to use a chanty. And a lot of people here have got diarrhoea too. There's a girl in my unit she's got piles and she's got these tablets off the doctor but she's scared to take them in case they make her go to the toilet after lock-up time. Hardly anyone uses the chanties, most of them just hold it in. And when you've got your periods, some people are heavy, you know, there's no way you can get out to change the towel or anything.'

Several of the women spontaneously made the point that prisoners received little sympathy regarding pre-menstrual tension and even less recognition of their need for increased access to washing facilities during menstruation.

'I took my periods one day on a Monday. I had bled a lot and I asked if I could go over and get changed and get washed. I was told "No." And that was me from early afternoon to quarter to five when I had to come over and take a bath.' (Ingrid Ingham)

Further (and despite the sheriffs' belief in the quality of the medical provision at Cornton Vale) one of the greatest complaints of the women concerned their lack of unmonitored access to the doctor. Ten of the women spontaneously complained about the system whereby all requests to see the doctor have to go through a person with no medical qualifications at all, i.e. a prison officer. That the initial diagnosis of their complaint was made by a lay person was, however, the least of their worries. What the prisoners were more concerned about was, first, the lack of privacy in which they had to make their requests to see the doctor, and, second, that once the request had been made they sometimes did not see the doctor for a week or, in some cases, if the officer had so decided, not at all. Olive O'Brien was angry about this lack of privacy:

'There was a lassie had piles up in her thingy. That's a sore thing, that. And the officer was asking her "What do you want to see the doctor for?" And she didn't want to tell her 'cos everyone was sitting round the table. So the lassie said "It's personal." Well, she's never got to see the doctor yet.'

And June Jones also pointed out that refusal to give a reason for requesting to see the doctor could result in not seeing him at all.

'If you're requesting to see the doctor they'll say, "What's it for?" So you say "Well, it's personal." Next thing you're in the office and the Principal Officer is asking what you want to see the doctor for. And if you don't tell her, you don't get to see him.'

The officers, for their part, justified this official screening of the women's requests to see the doctor by claiming that some women would always be seeing the doctor about trivial or even non-existent complaints if they had absolutely free access to him. Against this, both Melody McDuff and Bernice Bradley pointed out that if the doctor was so overworked then it was surprising that 'when it suited them' the officers could invoke the doctor's authority for the granting or not of requests which need not have been seen as being medically related at all. Thus when Melody and Bernice separately requested an extra blanket for their beds on the grounds that their rooms were particularly draughty they both received the same reply; that they would have to make an appointment to see the doctor to seek his authorization for the issue of an extra blanket on *medical* grounds! As neither of the women felt that she could make out a *medical* case for an extra blanket both of them went without.

In addition to the general complaints about degrading sanitary conditions and the denial of privacy in relation to medical matters, most of the women mentioned that they felt 'degraded' by the ill-fitting wrapover dresses which they were forced to wear for work. Further, they were limited in the extent to which they could improve their appearance by make-up. Only three pieces of make-up are allowed to each woman and when it is used up they are not allowed to have any more sent in but, instead, have to replace it out of their weekly earnings of 82 pence. Prisoners are never allowed to wear their own clothes and the clothes issued for association and visits (and locked away after each occasion for which they've been issued) are often as ill-fitting as the wrapover dresses issued for work. Women are not even allowed to wear their own shoes! As for tights . . . 'Now,' said Bernice Bradley, 'You know what ordinary tights are like — how they get holes? Here, you've to wear them sometimes until they're literally falling off!'

Regulation of dress has traditionally been a major mode of control in total institutions and particularly in girls' schools (see, for example, Okely, 1978), but the rigid sartorial control of women prisoners at Cornton Vale is hardly conducive to repair of their already-fractured self-images. Once again, therefore, there is a bifurcation between the official and discursive claims that women are 'helped to regain their self-respect' and the extra-discursive institutional conditions wherein the self-respect is further battered and bruised, if not altogether destroyed.

Institutional control of the women's self-presentation does not stop at sartorial control. Although, as Freda Franklin said, prisoners are not allowed 'even the simplest of things that would help a woman feel more female' there is, at the same time a rigid control of the washing of their hair, their clothes and their bodies. Clare Carlton, a woman in her late forties, gave an instance of the type of control which she and others found most humiliating.

> *Clare*: 'I don't think they should tell normal grown-up women that they've got to change their underwear every day. It's just a matter of course. I mean I wouldn't be putting on pants that I'd had on yesterday. Yet you get officers saying "Now don't forget to wash your knickers."'
> *Pat Carlen*: 'To you? They've actually said that?'
> *Clare*: 'Aye, oh aye, you get this a lot. And lassies just turn round and say "Aye, I'll wash them," and walk away.'

Clare had added that she could understand that women who had been 'skippering' might need to be told about such matters of cleanliness. However, Melissa, who had been skippering for over ten years, was equally annoyed about the indignity of being told when and how to wash, saying angrily, 'I've skippered, but I've always kept myself clean — always.' My continued scepticism about the claims that officers regulated *all* adult prisoners in this way was in fact destroyed by a prison officer who herself offered a spontaneous and sympathetic comment on the effects of such bodily control:

> 'They have *no* independence here. And the majority do mind. They hate being told when to take a bath, when to wash their hair. I wouldn't like it myself, though of course I don't think about that when I have to do my job.' (Prison Officer No. 6)

The accommodation of the women in small family units means that their every move is monitored. How they dress, how they eat, what they talk about, who they talk with, their mental and physical health — it is all screened by the prison officers for reasons of rehabilitation and security. Just as the women are denied sociability in the name of the social, just as the development of a public realm of communication is denied them in the name of the public good, so too in the name of femininity are they denied the physical and psychological props normally attendant upon the celebration of the feminine myth. Such concomitant celebration and denial of the myth causes confusion and bitterness. As Phyllis Chesler, writing of Goffman's *Asylums*, put it:

> [Goffman] is primarily thinking of the debilitating effect — *on men* — of being treated like a woman . . . . But what about the effect of being treated like a woman when you *are* a woman? And perhaps a woman who is already ambivalent or angry about just such treatment? (Chesler, 1974)

'I'm awfully, awfully bitter' was indeed the one phrase most commonly used by the women to describe their feelings about life in general and their prison experience in particular. Yet their bitterness did not stem solely from the ways in which their femininity was engaged, played upon and then denied. Their major complaint was that, in being treated like 'wee lassies' they were also being denied full adult status.

Imprisoned — within and without adulthood

> 'I think of myself as a mother to inmates and officers. Down in that office, I'm the mother.' (Prison Officer No. 10)

> 'They're very childish. They're just like bairns. You wouldn't speak to a four year old how we have to speak to some of them, sometimes.' (Prison Officer No. 9)

One effect of Scottish women's imprisonment is that it turns 'grown women into wee lassies'. Ann Archer summed up what happens when she claimed that 'they're awfully, awfully childish in here. See, when you come in you're grown up, but I feel I've got awfully childish since being in here.' Explanations for this phenomenon varied. It has of course been noted previously in descriptions of penal institutions. Bettelheim (1960) in particular has described how prisoners' infantile dependency was the dominant factor in the interaction between guards and prisoners in a concentration camp. Both officers and women at Cornton Vale could likewise give specific examples of the childishness which inseminated all aspects of prison life. Some of the officers thought that women prisoners *are essentially* childlike, that it is their lack of maturity, their inadequacy, etc. which has landed them in prison in the first place. The more analytical officers and women blamed the hierarchical organisation of the prison itself for the childishness which permeated it. Other women thought that many of the prison's disciplinary and security measures were *actually designed* to induce feelings of infantile dependency in the prisoners.

That British prisons are hierarchically organised is well-known (see for example, Thomas, 1972); that such hierarchical organisation also permeates the whole system, having adverse effects on staff and prisoners alike, was borne out by both staff and women at Cornton Vale. When I remarked to one officer that the women complained that they were too often treated like children she replied:

'We are treated like children, too. Why do you think we have such a turnover of staff? They come in at that gate and are out a few months later and people wonder why. I'll tell you why. I'll give you an example. I once phoned the Deputy Governor and asked if I could have an appointment with him sometime. Within half an hour my Principal Officer and Chief were on to me: "How dare I contact the Deputy Governor without contacting them first, without telling them what it was about."' (Prison Officer No. 11)

The lack of lateral channels for the transmission of information was confirmed by both the prisoners and the Governor. The women complained about a system set up to ensure that all their requests to see the doctor, the social worker, the

Governor and anyone else, had to go through a prison officer. They all complained that this inhibited form of communication was often, in practice, no form of communication at all. Only Melody McDuff, however, speculated about why prison officers themselves might favour such blocked forms of communication. Speaking of one principal officer in Papa Block, Melody said,

> 'If she can deal with it herself, she will. Rather than say to the Governor "There's five girls to see you this morning." She'd rather say "Nobody to see you." So the Governor thinks "Oh, it's all nice and quiet," whereas in fact the girls are getting refused everything right, left and centre.'

I myself asked the Governor if the women had any kind of forum where they could put forward requests and suggestions. She replied:

> 'No, not as such, if you mean the type they have in certain Scandinavian countries and in Canada, an actual prisoners' committee. There's nothing like that. What you do find is that in the small units they often possibly have a spokesman who talks to the staff and that comes up through the principal officer . . . . But nothing formal.'

The Governor thought that from her point of view this hierarchical transmission of knowledge was successful: 'You have your chief officers and through them you get to know everything. They're often surprised at how much you do know.' A prison officer dissented — as people at the bottom end of an hierarchical structure often do! 'The Governor walks round with rose-coloured spectacles. All the information she gets is controlled by the chiefs. She hears only what they want her to hear.' (Prison Officer No. 13).

However, whether or not the hierarchical structure affects knowledge transmission within the prison, it certainly ensures that those at the very bottom — the prisoners — have no space in which to develop any positive forms of independence. Again and again when I asked prisoners if they knew *why* a certain procedure or rule was in operation I received replies like:

'I don't know, I've never really asked them why. It's just one of the rules and I just do what I'm told.' (Clare Carlton)

'You get to the stage where you sort of don't bother to ask reasons because you never get a direct answer back anyway.' (Bernice Bradley)

Clare Carlton claimed that the prison officers wanted the prisoners to react like 'automatons' and for her part a prison officer explained that she always had to let women know 'who is wearing the uniform' even when they were attempting to be totally helpful. Talking of Eliza Eastwood, Prison Officer No. 10 said:

'She's no trouble, but she's just really funny sometimes. She says to me "All right then, I'll do it for you, I'll do this, Hen, and then I'll do that." And I have to say "Wait a minute, who's wearing the uniform?" Then she says "Oh! Sorry Miss."'

The instances discussed in this section so far are general to prisons and to other establishments where a hierarchical discipline is enforced. They are not peculiar to Cornton Vale. At Cornton Vale, however, the general features of the hierarchical discipline combine with the domestic work programme, with the denial to prisoners of sociability and adult womanhood and with the organisation of the women into small family units, to ensure a mental and bodily surveillance which denudes the prisoners' daily life of all dignity and independence.

Several women were scathing about the type of work on offer to them. It is not surprising that Melody McDuff, who had had more formal education than the other women interviewed, should be most vocal on this score.

'People who are bright get treated like wee girls. They don't want to know you've had an education. You can go to the canteen; you can go to the laundry; you can work the machines; you can go to the cookhouse; you can go round and empty the bins; or you can just stay

here and clean the unit. But you're not going to get a
job you could put your mind to.'

Some of the prison officers were also of the opinion that
there was no interesting work for the 'more intelligent'
women, though both Melody McDuff and Thelma Thompson
claimed that even access to education classes and discussion
groups themselves was monitored too closely by the officers.

'I'm treated like a four year old. There's classes over there
but before you can get that far you're taken into the
office and it's, "Now, are you sure you can manage this?"
I mean, it's just like being a wee girl.' (Melody McDuff)

'Last night, for instance, I was at the Bible Class. The
purpose was to have a discussion when the film finished.
Myself and another girl spoke up and at the end of it, one
of the officers says to me "Give some of the other girls a
chance." I felt really bad about it and actually last night
is the first night I've cried since I've been in here.' (Thelma
Thompson)

Yet, even when women had become resigned to the fact
that imprisonment in Cornton Vale means a constant round
of routine domestic and machine work interspersed with
contrasting periods of isolation and enforced and monitored
sociability, they still resented the enforcement of minor
rules relating to forms of address, deportment, conversation,
etiquette and other forms of self-presentation in general.
When they repeatedly made the point that 'men wouldn't put
up with this carry-on, this rigmarole' they were more often
than not referring to the type of discipline that is usually
only enforced in schools, young people's training centres or
the armed services. But there are striking differences. When
these modes of behaviour are enforced in the armed services
the whole organisational edifice and ethos is consistently
militaristic and impersonal. In Cornton Vale, by contrast,
a dominant official discourse invokes the concepts of familiness, domesticity and self-regulation, principles at odds with
the elements of partly school-girlish, partly militaristic discipline actually imposed. One could also argue that *all*

prisoners, male and female, suffer humiliation through the arbitrary enforcement of innumerable petty rules. Male prisoners, however, being less isolated one from another, are usually able to develop a mutually supportive counter-culture which militates against male prison officers regulating the minutiae of their charges' personal presentation and style to the same degree that women prison officers, imbued with notions of womanly propriety, regulate the minutest details of the women prisoners' self-presentation.

The prisoners address the officers as 'Miss'. This in itself is a hated reminder of schooldays.

> 'We've got to say "Yes, Miss," and "No Miss," sort of "three bags full, Miss," this sort of thing.' (Thelma Thompson)

> 'I work in Reception. If I want to go to the toilet, I have to say "Please, Miss, can I go to the toilet, Miss?"' (Ann Archer)

In their turn the officers monitor the women's deportment and personal cleanliness. At the age of fifty-nine Mandy MacDonald was resentful of being told by a young officer that she must keep her hands out of her pockets; Clare Carlton felt that she did not need a young officer to tell her how to keep her cell clean and tidy:

> 'We're all grown women in here. I'll be forty-seven on Saturday and when I get a young lassie of twenty-one telling me how to polish my floor, how to make my bed, it gets right up my nose.' (Clare Carlton)

Women, like Clare, whose whole life has been steeped in the ethos of maternal responsibility, experience a very specific and painful loss of status when they themselves are treated as the children of a paternalistic regime which denies them their adulthood.

> 'I think most grown women know how to keep themselves and their room clean. Perhaps it's different with men . . . or with very young girls, but I think that most women

who've had a home and reared a family don't need to be told.' (Clare Carlton)

Thelma Thompson thought that it was *because* she was treated like a child in prison that she had deteriorated into a 'rambling' chatterbox!

'If they would treat us more like adults we would feel
better. Sometimes it's hard to be an adult if you're getting
treated like a child. . . . You know . . . going in twos,
"Take you hands out of your pockets." You talk like
that to children, you don't talk like that to married
women with children, or grandchildren.' (Thelma Thompson)

But it was the close surveillance of leisure and meal-times which the women particularly resented and which they felt would not be so docilely accepted by male prisoners. Altogether eleven women spontaneously claimed that although the women in Papa Block were supposed to be the more stable and responsible of all the adult prisoners, they were, in fact, 'treated like kids'. The following catalogue, made up of remarks made by a few of the women covers the main complaints which were repeatedly made as I talked with the prisoners. They are all concerned with the extreme degree of control which is exercised over the bodies of women prisoners.

'Even if you want your toe-nails or your fingernails cut
you've to go over to the Health Centre and ask to get
them cut (Ingrid). You're never allowed to sit on the
floor of the sitting room, you've always to sit on chairs
(Melody). See, even if you don't want anything to eat
you've still got to sit at the table until they say (June).
They tell you what you're going to eat, when you're
going to eat and how you're going to sit. They practically
spoon-feed you. You're treated more like a kid than a
grown woman. Bed at eight o'clock, told what to do all
the time and when to do it. Even on a day when you
don't want your jacket on you're made to put it on. We
went to the pictures last night and it was "Get into twos,

hands out of pockets; first ten step forward, next ten."
Even if you go up to medication you're told to walk in
twos, not to talk, to take your hands out of your pockets'
(Phyllis Prince).

So much for the sheriffs' notion that Cornton Vale isn't
really a prison!

This chapter has provided a conventional picture of a
conventional prison, a prison without the brutal physical
conditions of the old Victorian prisons, but a prison none
the less. This description of Cornton Vale should astonish
no-one. The prisoners admitted that, just as the physical
conditions are in themselves lacking in brutality, so too are
the officers. Most of the women saw most of the officers as
being 'pretty fair in the main', and as 'just doing a job'. The
prisoners complained less about the officers, more about the
'system'. And their complaints were not just about the prison
system but about the various 'systems' via which they had
arrived at Cornton Vale. For the astonishing thing about
Cornton Vale is the composition of its prison population.

It is often assumed that a reduction in the prison population will result in only the most 'dangerous' offenders, or
maybe the most persistent of the serious offenders going to
gaol. The concept of 'dangerousness' is a tricky one when
applied to almost anything, particularly so when applied to
offenders, but, on none of its possible definitions would the
majority of women at Cornton Vale be seen as dangerous. As
reported in Chapter One, approximately a third of all adult
women received at Cornton Vale under sentence in 1980 had
been convicted of breach of the peace, and, altogether, 54
per cent had been convicted of Class VII miscellaneous
offences. Another third had been convicted of crimes against
property without violence. Half of all the women in prison
were there because of failure to pay a fine. So why maintain
an extremely secure, technologically complex establishment
at a cost of approximately £100 per week for each woman
for these few petty offenders? The reasons are many and
complex — and, as will be seen in the following chapters, are
only obliquely connected with the punishment of crime.

Part four
The women that nobody wants

'There is nothing . . . glamorous about those who drink too much. In men it is crude and embarrassing: in women it is plain sickening.' (Mr David Ennals, Secretary of State for Social Services, quoted in Camberwell Council on Alcoholism, 1980)

'I look at *them* with disgust, and I feel like going up to them and saying: "Come here, come with me and I'll show you how the other half lives." I'd show them the skippers, the gutters . . . and I'd say "How long would *you* survive in this?" *They* wouldn't survive two minutes.' (Melissa Malcom, Scottish Woman Prisoner, 1981).

6   The dismissive society

'If you don't know nothing, Hen, nobody will tell you. They don't
care whether you're dead or alive. It was the same in the court. The
whole court was a farce. No-one told us anything, not even where to
sit. The lawyer didn't tell us anything and you can't get up and say
anything in your own defence. The lawyer says it all (and he doesn't
say what you want him to say) and they call it justice! Och, Hen,
the world's all topsy-turvy. Those who have, get more, those who
haven't, get more taken away. I wish someone would shoot this
Government.' (Mother of a Scottish woman prisoner, Glasgow, 1981)

'Crime amongst the unemployed and working class is not a new
thing. It has nothing to do with this Government. *Some people* will
always sink to the bottom of the pile and when they do they commit crime.' (Edinburgh Sheriff, 1981)

'At the same time, you've got to think, "*These people* are going to
be professionals and for a little prank they could get a conviction
of theft."' (Procurator Fiscal, 1979, explaining why he had NOT
prosecuted some students who had taken a boat without permission (Moody and Tombs, 1982).) (My emphases in all quotations.)

The female petty offenders who, at the moment of prison,
become Cornton Vale's short-term prisoners are those women
who have already been in trouble so often that they are seen
as being outwith family, sociability, femininity and adulthood. Consequently, too, they are also seen as being beyond
the help of the legal and caring profession. In court they are
usually without legal representation; upon their release from
prison they are seen by the welfare authorities as being beyond
care, by the medical authorities as being beyond cure (see
Chapters 7 and 8).

There have been numerous studies which have described in careful detail the lack of welfare and after-care provision for rootless petty offenders (see Davies, 1974, Fairhead, 1981 and Prins, 1980 for Britain in general and Strathclyde Regional Council 1978 for Scotland in particular). In this chapter, therefore, I shall only describe first, how the women at Cornton Vale had experienced the courts and second, how both they and Scottish judicial and penal personnel perceive contemporary Scottish social-work provision for female offenders. For, although it is the magistrate or the sheriff who actually passes the sentence which either immediately or (in the case of fine-defaulters) eventually results in the imprisonment of a petty offender, it might not be inappropriate to identify the legal and welfare personnel as being the main penal gatekeepers — that is, as being those whose intervention (or not) plays a major part in determining whether (or not) a female petty offender goes yet again to prison.

Courts, lawyers and female offenders

'The district court's a farce. You can either laugh or weep at it. It's tragic or comic, whichever way you look at it.' (Court Liaison Officer No. 2, Edinburgh)

'The district court's a joke.' (Court Liaison Officer No. 1, Glasgow)

Eight of the twenty women interviewed in Cornton Vale said that their last case had been heard in a district court, eight that it had been heard in a sheriff's court and four that it had been heard in the high court.[1] Ten claimed that they had been represented for whole or part of the judicial proceedings which had preceded their current term of imprisonment and ten said that they had not had a lawyer for their last case. All of the unrepresented ten said that they had been represented by lawyers at some previous stage of their penal careers. Thus all of the women interviewed had had experience of some kind of legal representation in court. Ten of them had very specific criticisms to make of the whole system of legal representation. At the same time they often developed these criticisms into an attack on the adversarial process in general: 'They should let people know exactly how they stand — there should be a book brought out on it and given to people in court so that they know what's going on' (Freda Franklin). In a discussion of proceedings observed in both the Scottish and the English summary courts Doreen McBarnet has recently observed that 'to enter the lower courts is to be taken aback by the casualness and rapidity of the proceedings' (McBarnet, 1981:123) and it has by now been well-documented that the lower courts' 'casual and rapid proceedings' do indeed mystify and exclude defendants to such an extent that they very often have no idea at all of what is happening (see Bottoms and McClean, 1976, and Carlen, 1976 for descriptions of proceedings in English magistrates' courts; Erikson and Baranek, 1982 on Canadian lower courts; and Dell, 1970 on the position of women defendants in court). All the court liaison officers whom I interviewed thought that the majority of defendants have no idea of what is happening in court. Moreover, some of them added, they were not entirely satisfied with the quality of the legal representation which women receive. Two court liaison officers suggested that often lawyers find some women's courtroom style embarrassing or distasteful. Court liaison officers from both Glasgow and Edinburgh were able to give examples of what can happen when a woman either misunderstands the court proceedings or gets very upset during them.

'With females, the worst thing is the inadequate or weak woman who may be shouting about her baby in court but doesn't really understand what's going on.' (Court Liaison Officer No. 1, Glasgow)

'We have an interesting case on now concerning a woman. She has a nine-month-old child and accused her husband of assault which he denied. In the middle of the case she changed her mind and said that he didn't assault her. So she was then charged with wasting police time, perjury, etc. She spent the night in the police cells — we had to mind the baby so to speak — and yet the lawyer who had been in court and seen her commit perjury advised her to plead 'not guilty'. All the other agents disagreed. So then, of course, she was remanded in custody and sent to

Cornton Vale to await trial. She created hell, we could
hear her. Now it could have been cleared up that day;
the sheriff wanted it, *we* wanted it, but the lawyer refused
to go and take new instructions because she was in such a
state — really high by then. That was five days ago. She
should have come up for trial today but the lawyer *still*
hadn't been to Cornton Vale to see her. So there she is
still, a week in Cornton Vale for her at £100 per week,
the baby in care, and all because a lawyer didn't fancy
talking to a woman who was in a state.' (Court Liaison
Officer No. 8, Glasgow)

'A large proportion of female offenders are totally unaware
of their rights and of what is going on in court. Sometimes
a clerk will jump up and down if a woman says, "I did it
but I'm not guilty", and he will say, "You can't say that"
and put the case back for another month; when if someone explained it to the woman it could be sorted out on
the spot.' (Court Liaison Officer No. 6, Edinburgh; cf.
Carlen, 1976: 111)

These comments, besides indicating that the lower courts
continue to be as big a shambles as they've always been,
raise a further point about the legal representation of Scottish women offenders: that because Cornton Vale is the
only prison for women in Scotland, lawyers are often faced
with long journeys if they wish to visit a woman remanded
in custody and that for that reason they sometimes choose
not to visit their female clients at all.

'Because there is only one prison for women there are
problems of visiting at Cornton Vale. Problems for visitors
in general, and for social workers and lawyers too.' (Deputy
Principal, Scottish Prison Service College)

'Sometimes lawyers will come, more often they won't.
And when they do come they usually don't let the women
know that they are coming.' (Social Worker, Cornton Vale)

The women prisoners themselves made many critical
points about their own experiences of legal representation

and judicial process. Their main targets of criticism were: the haphazard way in which legal representation and knowledge of legal rights is acquired or not; the very small amount of time which they had with their lawyers prior to the court appearance; the plea-bargaining which they saw as a perversion of the course of justice; the *very* summary way in which recidivist petty offenders are dealt with by the police and the courts; and lastly, the way in which the adversary process prevents the defendant from putting her own point of view, often excluding her to such an extent that even when she has committed the crime and feels deserving of punishment she none the less feels that justice has not been done.

It was not possible to assess how many women had been represented at their first court appearance for their first offence. For some of them it was too long ago, others thought that *someone* had intervened on their behalf but said that they had not known at the time, and certainly had not found out since, whether the intervention had been by a lawyer or a social worker. Two of the women, however, spontaneously mentioned that things might have turned out a bit differently for them if they *had* been represented on the occasion of their first court appearance.

'I was so silly and stupid at the time of my first prison sentence — and I'd nobody to talk to and advise me — that I ended up in court with no solicitor nor nothing.' (Bernice Bradley)

'If I'd had a lawyer that first time when I took the money he might have spoken better for me.' (Kirsty King)

Netta Nelson had eventually acquired a lawyer though not until *after* she had pled guilty:

'I knew I was entitled to a lawyer but then for some reason I never got to see any because I was remanded in custody. After I'd been in court the turnkey came up to my cell and says "Have you got a lawyer?" and I says "No" and he says "Do you want to see a lawyer?" and I says, "Aye" and he took me down to a lawyer. He must have just been a court lawyer, for people who've got no one. I didn't even know his name and never had a chance to find out. I don't think court lawyers are much cop. You're better getting a lawyer you've been recommended.' (Netta Nelson)

How do women set about getting their own lawyer, though? Most of the Cornton Vale women said that they had only acquired knowledge of the legal aid system after several court appearances. Others said that they had only known how to go about getting a lawyer because they had friends or relations who had been in some kind of criminal trouble. Freda Franklin knew that she would have been in the same position of powerlessness as Netta Nelson if she had not had relatives with knowledge of the system:

'I was quite lucky when I was arrested — it was my brother and sister that actually phoned the solicitors and told them I'd been arrested otherwise I wouldn't have got one so soon. I'd asked for a lawyer and they says to me, "You'll see one in court." Know? Usually they tell you that you'll "see one in court".' (Freda Franklin)

It is, moreover, interesting to note that, of the ten women who had had legal representation at the last court appearance prior to their imprisonment, five had taken a lawyer already known either to a male co-defendant or an already-imprisoned male relative. However, even though all twenty women said that it was better to have a lawyer than not, all of the fifteen women who were either persistent petty offenders, 'drinking' women and/or homeless women said that lawyers could not in fact do much for defendants like themselves, whilst the remaining five women, i.e. Clare Carlton, Freda Franklin, Ingrid Ingham, Melody McDuff and Phyllis Prince, all had complaints about either their lawyers or the courtroom proceedings.

The women's most common complaint was that their lawyers had not given enough time either to the preparation of their cases or to explaining to them what was happening at each stage of the proceedings. As a result the women had felt that what had gone on at the trial had had very little to do with either them or their offence. Melody McDuff, for instance, had been amazed when her lawyer had erroneously stated in court that, at the time of the alleged offence, Melody had been on holiday in Glasgow, her permanent address being in *Luton*! She had felt further irritation when, after she had interrupted her lawyer in order to correct him — 'No, I stays with my Mum in Glasgow' — the sheriff had jocularly commented to the lawyer, 'She doesn't seem to know whether she's coming or going.' Melody believed that if her lawyer had spent more time with her prior to the trial that he would not have been so confused:

> 'I was supposed to have this one guy — he was costing us a fortune, and he was doing this other case so they got me this other guy I'd never seen before. And I only saw him for about twenty minutes before I walked into the Appeal Court.' (Melody McDuff)

Bernice Bradley had also been confused by the various solicitors and barristers involved in her case:

> 'I don't know what went wrong in the end but something went wrong. I was in here on remand without a solicitor and I wrote away at the last minute for a solicitor and he came. He seemed really genuine and really like he was going to help me. Then when I went to court there was this other man in a suit, kind of standing there sniggering (and that's a fact, I'm not just saying that) and he was the man that was going to be representing me and he just wasn't interested. He couldn't have cared less. He just waved a couple of bits of paper in front of me and off he went.' (Bernice Bradley)

Once the conduct of their cases had already been appropriated by professionals towards whose personal style the women often felt antipathetic it was not surprising that the female defendants had been suspicious and sometimes disgusted when it had been intimated to them that their lawyer had been engaging in plea-bargaining with the prosecution. Ingrid saw it as blackmail, Freda saw it as just sheer trickery.

> 'The lawyer was trying to get my charge dropped from attempted murder and assault to severe injury with endan-

ger to life and a serious assault. But if I'd have pled not guilty it would have been the high court. This is just a form of blackmail and I don't agree with it. To me, that was: "If you're going to save us money, we're going to give you less sentence." My father wanted me to take my chance and plead not guilty but you're at their convenience really.' (Ingrid Ingham)

'Pleading guilty when they tell you to doesn't really make it better, it makes it worse. When I was arrested on this charge there were two other charges along with it. They said that if I pled guilty to the harbouring and the assault that they'd drop the firearms charge, but I refused. And when I did get into court they'd actually dropped the firearms charge — I was getting off that anyway but they were trying to kid me on they were making a deal. They knew they couldn't get me on the firearms charge anyway. Yet my QC says to me, "If you'd pled guilty to that you would have got a lesser sentence" — but that doesn't make sense.' (Freda Franklin)

Freda, Ingrid and Melody were relatively well-versed in courtroom procedures and yet they had felt powerless within the courtroom. How very much more alienating is the summary justice dispensed to the persistent petty offenders, the homeless and the alcohol offenders.

The majority of the women interviewed thought that legal representation could not significantly affect their sentences as they were at this stage being regularly sent to prison as incorrigible offenders. Factors such as their alcoholism, their recidivism, their homelessness and the relationship between the local policemen and the local magistrates and sheriffs were seen as being more important than whether or not they had a lawyer in court.

'I had been left penniless before I committed the crime. The lawyer put some of it forward, but not all. The judge just wouldn't have wanted to listen, 'cos I'd been in trouble before.' (Thelma Thompson)

'Actually', said Kirsty, 'I had a lawyer last time. But then, see, I had no fixed address. When you have no fixed address you usually do get imprisonment because they can't fine you.' 'And', said Melissa, 'After you've been in court several times they just shove classes on you, they don't see you as an individual anymore.' (See also the explanation of why psychiatrists refuse requests to write repeated reports on recidivist offenders, Chapter 8, page 209.) It was Olive O'Brien who summed up what the problem-drinkers and alcoholic women thought of their regular parade through the courts:

'Police don't apprehend men as quick as they do a woman. A woman's easier to lift. They'll not lift a man in a bar unless there's five or six of them because they'll not get away with it but two can lift a woman so it's a sort of easy job for them. Then it's all right for them to black and blue you top to bottom but not for you to retaliate. In court the sheriff's not interested in what you say to him anyway and if it's about the police he says that they're just doing their job. He doesn't ken the *way* they're doing their job. And you've just got to plead guilty. For if you plead not guilty what could you do then? You've got policemen in the box swearing their lives away and you've got convictions anyway so they just look on you as if you're a bit of dirt with no brains and no feelings. According to them, you're NOTHING.' (Her emphases)

Yet although the persistent petty offenders were prepared to explain their own feelings of powerlessness in court in terms of their homelessness, drinking problems and recidivism, both the unrepresented petty offenders *and* the represented women charged with more serious offences had felt that the court had sentenced them on the basis of very little knowledge about their actual circumstances.

The primary concern of the drinking women was with their total lack of credibility in the courts, the way in which the policemen's version of events was always believed whilst they themselves were allowed little opportunity to present an alternative version. A secondary concern was with the way in which magistrates and sheriffs characterised Cornton Vale as a 'rest home'. 'He says,' said Eliza Eastwood, '"I'm going to send you to prison because you need a rest." Some rest! The governor needs us here to get the work done.' Finally, they pointed out, few of them had had social work help in the courts as most were seen to be beyond the help of welfare. Ann Archer summed up the persistent petty offenders' general consensus of opinion about social workers when she said to me, 'I've had probation, but I don't like social workers. No. They pry into your business but they cannot do much to help you, can they? Just talk.'

The women charged with the more serious offences were, as we have already seen, primarily concerned with the small amount of time which their lawyers had spent with them. Freda Franklin believed that this had resulted in the court hearing such a very muddled and contradictory defence that her own version of events had completely lacked credibility.

> 'I never got much consultation with the lawyer. I could say that I was with the QC for about three-quarters of an hour in all. Things were just coming out in the dock as I remembered them. Actually, the court case should have been cut off, so it should have, to give that QC time to find out what my views were and what I did.' (Freda Franklin)

Bernice Bradley thought that the lawyer had been more interested in putting her man's case than hers and that he had failed to see her as a defendant in her own right:

> 'He read out what my man had put up for his defence. My defence wasn't read out. So the judge says to my man first, "Quite frankly I don't believe the story that's been told in your defence, and as for you, Mrs Bradley, the same goes for you." And he had never been given a story about me.' (Bernice Bradley)

Clare Carlton and Melody McDuff had both felt that they could have put forward a better defence than the one presented by their lawyers. Melody felt that her lawyer had got so carried away with his own rhetoric that he had put forward a most unflattering (and inaccurate) picture of her.

'I was cringing when I heard the lawyer stand up and say the things he said. He says, "She was put into an adult world too soon with too much money and no responsibilities and she thought she could just do anything." And I says to myself "My God, this just isn't true," but I think it's because of what he said that I got such a hammering.' (Melody McDuff)

Clare Carlton and Bernice Bradley simply felt that the system of professional advocacy was self-evidently silly (cf. Christie, 1976).

'When I was at the trial itself there were things that I knew the witnesses were lying about and I feel I should have been able to question them. What would the QC know about it? I mean, I only met the man once, for about twenty minutes and all he was asking me about then was about what was on the papers he had already read. No, that man didn't know anything about me nor if it was true what they were saying. Even my solicitor wasn't in court that day, it was a young bloke they sent up to court and I'd only met *him* twice. I mean, if you have something to say in court you should be allowed to say it, not these QCs.' (Clare Carlton, her emphasis)

'The Procurator Fiscal himself told a load of lies. He says, "Your Honour, the reason we've not got any background reports on these two is because they refused to give any to the Crown", and we'd never been asked. Nobody ever came to ask us. And that was that. What could we say? I couldn't jump up in the court and say anything because this QC who was standing there was meant to be doing it all for me — and he didn't.' (Bernice Bradley)

Neither Clare, Melody, Ingrid nor Bernice claimed that they should have 'got away' with what they had done, and they certainly did not hold their lawyers responsible for their present incarceration in Cornton Vale. What had embittered them was their exclusion from the judicial process. They felt that they had never had their day in court, that rather, as Clare Carlton put it, 'the Court went on as if you weren't there.' Such exclusion can embitter all defendants, male or female; it can cause particularly acute anxiety to the woman defendant who is worried as to whether anyone in the court even knows that she has dependent children to look after at home.

In Chapter 3 we heard sheriffs claiming that they are always most punctilious about investigating the domestic circumstances of women with dependent children. Yet three of the seven women who had dependent children still living with them felt that the court had not fully understood their domestic situation. Melody thought that her lawyer's defence had given the judge a totally false impression both of her material circumstances and of her relationship with her child.

> 'The judge didn't even know I had a son. When the QC put it to him the judge just goes, "Oh, I'm sure they'll manage, she can put the child into a private home."'
> (Melody McDuff)

Freda and Ingrid thought that the fate of their children was never seriously considered by the court:

> 'It was hardly ever mentioned that I had children. At the very end the lawyer stands up and says, "Mrs Franklin's married and she's got two kids," and the judge says, "Oh, *two* children, I thought she only had one," and then the lawyer turns round to me and says, "How many kids have you got?" I says, "Two" and he turns back round and says, "Mrs Franklin's got two children" but the judge was never under this impression, nor was the jury.' (Freda Franklin)

> 'On the Monday I was taken to the sheriff court and I was remanded for a week. On the Monday night I came to Cornton Vale and it was when my lawyer went back in front of the sheriff and explained that I had a wee boy that I was released on the Friday, after five days.' (Ingrid Ingham)

Lawyers cannot be expected to act as surrogate social workers (though, because of possible difficulties of regaining custody, women prisoners should NEVER allow their children to go into local authority care or 'fostering' without consulting their solicitors). Some people, however, might, none the less, be surprised to find that, in the last quarter of the twentieth century, mothers (and no doubt fathers too) can still be hauled off to prison without anyone in the court inquiring about the present whereabouts of their dependent children. To understand how this can happen we need to examine the organisation of Scottish social work provision for offenders.

Scottish social work provision for offenders — the official tale

Prior to the Social Work (Scotland) Act 1968 Scotland had a separate probation service. It never did develop the same range of back-up facilities (such as probation hostels, day centres, volunteers), which for a long time have been connected with the service for England and Wales, but, none the less, until 1968 Scotland, like England and Wales, had a court-related service whose officers were especially trained to prepare reports for the courts and, at the order of the court, to supervise offenders. According to the Howard League (Policy Review No. 2) moreover, the service improved considerably after the Morrison Committee's 1962 report of their inquiry into the probation service. In 1968, however, when the Social Work (Scotland) Act was passed, the probation service ceased to exist. The legislation still allowed courts to make probation orders but in future probation supervision was to be undertaken by the newly integrated and generic local authority social work departments. Their duties to the courts and to offenders were, formally and generally, to have been much the same as those of the former probation service but in addition they have gradually been expected to shoulder a whole new range of offender-related duties, onerous duties which were either included in the 1968 Act (e.g. fines supervision) or added later (e.g. supervision of community service orders and social work in prisons).[2] The interpretation of these duties and the actual range and quality of services provided to the courts and to offenders have varied from authority to authority, but in both the Strathclyde and Lothian Regions the social work departments provide a specialist service to the courts as well as some specialist services to offenders. However, it was those few social workers in both regions who *do* specialise in working with offenders who were most concerned to emphasise to me the skeletal nature of the social work provision for offenders in general in Scotland. In the remainder of this chapter I shall describe the type of social work provision which, according to judicial, prison and social work personnel and the prisoners themselves either might or might not have been available to the women I interviewed at Cornton Vale. I shall describe first the social work 'presence' (or, more often than not, according to all reports, absence!) in the courts. Next I will examine the facilities for probation supervision and after care. Then I will describe the work of the local authority social workers employed in HM Institution, Cornton Vale. Throughout, the implication is that certain female offenders could be kept out of Cornton Vale altogether if better social work provision were to be made for ALL Scottish offenders.

Scottish social work provision for offenders — the unofficial tale

1 Scottish social work and Scottish courts

As the majority of the prisoners whom I interviewed told me that they usually resided in either Glasgow or Edinburgh[3] and as the only court liaison officers and sheriffs whom I interviewed worked in either the Glasgow or Edinburgh courts the discussion which follows will be limited mainly to a consideration of social work and the courts in those two cities. What follows is not, therefore, claiming to be a survey of court liaison officers' views of Scottish social work provision for offenders. The views of a few court liaison officers were sought only because the picture of Scottish social work provision for offenders painted by *all* other concerned parties was such a black one. As the chapter unfolds I hope that the story which emerges will be seen more as an indictment of central government policies than as a criticism of the very few people who *do* concern themselves with Scotland's persistent petty offenders.

In both Glasgow and Edinburgh I interviewed specialist social workers (hereafter called court liaison officers) whose basic function was 'to service and liaise with the courts, the parole board and penal establishments' (Strathclyde Regional Council, 1978:135). However, because of acute staff shortages the work in Glasgow tended to be mainly administrative (e.g. chasing up social inquiry reports for the courts and contacting local authority social work departments to inquire about the possibility of supervision for a potential candidate for a probation order); whilst in Edinburgh the court liaison officers claimed that they were able to spend a bit more time assisting defendants in the court. But although the court liaison officers of both cities said that 'if asked to by the turnkey,' they would visit a woman in the cells before the court appearance they also said that they very seldom interviewed women prior to their court appearance. The court liaison officers in Edinburgh said that they would usually interview a woman *after* sentence had been passed but although the court liaison officers in Glasgow agreed that this would be a desirable practice they also pointed out that, as each of them was usually the only officer on duty for several courts sitting at the same time, it was impossible for them to see many women after sentence.

> 'Someone who needs us may appear in a court other than the one we're attending and if the police think we're needed the sergeant sends for one of us. What happens to women who might need us depends on the luck of the draw.' (Court Liaison Officer No. 1, Glasgow)

Recidivist petty offenders in the Glasgow district courts, however, are, by and large, to be considered lucky if they speak with a social worker at all.

> 'We hardly speak to the regulars at all.' (Court Liaison Officer No. 7, Glasgow)

> 'In this court people are appearing with no clear idea even of what they are being charged with. It's a sausage-machine. They may see a solicitor for only three minutes before he goes in and makes his spiel. I would hope the time comes

when a social worker in the courts automatically sees homeless women. *But it's not happening yet.*' (Court Liaison Officer No. 3, Glasgow, his emphasis)

'The district court may have people we could help, but I don't know because I go to the sheriff court where we think there are more people we can help. I think "Why should I start with them — you know, people with drink problems — when I can't follow them through?" What can you do with them, there's nowhere for them to go. There are no hostels to take emergency referrals.' (Court Liaison Officer No. 8, Glasgow)

Edinburgh court liaison officers confirmed the Glasgow officers' point: even if they do speak to women with drinking problems there is not much they can do: 'We talk to alcoholic vagrants because we know them, but the provision here for alcoholic offenders is nil, nil, nil' (Court Liaison Officer No. 5, Edinburgh). In fact this last court liaison officer had, over many years, worked regularly with Kirsty King and, according to Kirsty herself, had done a lot for her by helping with medical and accommodation problems. Yet, notwithstanding all her skills and concern, in the absence of any kind of back-up facilities the social worker could not keep Kirsty out of prison. 'What you have to understand' said Court Liaison Officer No. 2 (Edinburgh) 'is that here the district court is locking people up for homelessness.' And Kirsty, unfortunately, having her flat vandalised each time she went to prison, was often at least temporarily homeless. Eliza Eastwood had been through the same mill in Glasgow. 'Social Services did get her a flat', said a Cornton Vale social worker, 'but she never lived in it! Instead she came in here and lost it — as well as two months rent paid in advance.'

The majority of the women who pass through the courts, however, are neither alcoholic nor homeless. Many of them have conventional home backgrounds and are mothers of dependent children still living at home. One might therefore have reasonably expected that, in the interests of the children at least, *someone* in the courts would have inquired about the present whereabouts of, and (in the event of a custodial sentence) future arrangements for, the children. Of course, as I argued in Chapter 3, and as the sheriffs affirmed, women from conventional homes and families are the least likely to end up in Cornton Vale. The fact remains, however, that seven of the twenty women interviewed in Cornton Vale *did* still have dependent children living at home with them at the time of sentence to their current term of imprisonment, whilst nine more were of an age when it might reasonably have been expected that they might have care of dependent children. Yet six of the seven mothers (all from Glasgow) said that at no time had anyone in the courts inquired after their children and the other nine women said that they had certainly not been seen by a social worker whilst in the court building.

'No-one asked about the kids. It was about three days later I saw a social worker in here and she asked me — but it took three days, so it did.' (Freda Franklin)

'I was just brought straight here. My wee boy could have been with *anyone* — a twelve-year old girl, for instance, watching him — they don't bother. In fact, my Mum had Alasdair but as far as they were concerned he could have been anywhere.' (Melody McDuff)

'There was one girl up at the court with me, she'd her baby there and her mother. And when she was sent here it was my husband who offered to run the old lady and her son back to Glasgow or she'd have had to find her way back to Glasgow with that baby in the train. And the wee one was ill, you know.' (Thelma Thompson)

It could be argued that, given that the majority of prisoners whom I interviewed were regulars in the courts, the magistrates, policemen and social workers are already so well appraised of these women's circumstances that it is unnecessary for them to make new inquiries at each court appearance. Alternatively, it could also be argued that the more rootless an offender is the more changeable and precarious are her circumstances likely to be. As Court Liaison Officer No. 3

(Glasgow) said, 'Women have problems about children but the ones we have here have all other kinds of problems as well.' And he went on to give an example of just how a custodial remand or sentence can jeopardise the best attempts of single, 'separated' or homeless women to get themselves settled — even when, as in this case, they do receive some social work assistance.

'Here's a case I've been dealing with today [January 12th 1981]. A woman in court on Friday was remanded to Cornton Vale. She is separated from her husband and he has the baby. When she left him and was homeless she went to social services and the only place they could get her was in a home for battered wives. She hasn't been battered, she was there because it was the only place they could find for her. When she left there to come to court on Friday she didn't tell them where she was going — for reasons of her own. I've just phoned there because she gave that address, but they are so hard-pressed for accommodation — they've always got someone waiting — that when she didn't return they gave the place to someone else. So now she's homeless again! That's what can happen when someone's remanded in custody.' (Court Liaison Officer No. 3, Glasgow, his emphasis)

Let it be noted too (especially by sentencers) that this woman fulfilled many of the conditions which sheriffs and magistrates had listed to me as being those which would make a woman a very likely candidate for either a custodial remand or a custodial sentence; she was separated from her husband, she was not presently looking after her child and she was homeless. At least the plight of this woman was brought to the attention of the court liaison officer. All four Glasgow court liaison officers, however, thought that many other women in similar situations slip by, unremarked by the various agencies with which they come into contact, until the snowballing effects of homelessness, imprisonment, marriage breakdown, alcoholism, failing health and mental and emotional impairment once more bring them to the crisis point where either their behaviour or their state of health yet again *forces* itself upon the notice of either welfare, medical or, too often, the judicial and penal authorities. Whilst the Edinburgh court liaison officers were slightly more sanguine about the type of coverage which they could give to the courts they, like their colleagues in Glasgow, said that there could be difficulties of liaison with the social workers from an offender's home area; and they stressed, too, that Edinburgh, like Glasgow, has very few facilities for alcoholic and/or homeless offenders. Yet once the court liaison officers of both Glasgow and Edinburgh (as well as other interested parties) got round to discussing the general attitude of the Scottish generic social workers to the courts and to the offenders, it became slightly more apparent why it is that so many women defendants find their way through the courts without benefit of welfare advice. It is because so few Scottish social workers attend the courts with their reports.

In England and Wales it is common practice for probation officers to attend court in order to support the recommendations which they have made in their social inquiry reports. In some cases, too, they practically act as surrogate lawyers for their clients. Thus, in addition to the probation officer on court duty there are often other probation officers going in and out of the court. The result is that in many courts there is often quite a strong welfare 'presence' — a 'presence' which though 'objecting' to being taken advantage of, is none the less often successfully invoked by both magistrates and police when they perceive a defendant to have a social problem — and no social worker. And, many English and Welsh probation officers do give help in these situations. But there is no comparable social work 'presence' in the Scottish courts. As the reasons for this absence are not unconnected with the ways in which local authorities have interpreted their other statutory obligations both to the courts and to offenders in general, they will be discussed in the next section.

2   *Social workers, probation, through-care and after-care*
'People can come out on after-care and probation and no-one looks after them at all. I send a copy of offences and

offenders in this court to all social work offices daily. But it's back to the same old story — social workers are now jack-of-all-trades and masters of none. You wouldn't believe how many newly qualified social workers have never been to a court. If you're a social worker and you're going to recommend borstal, detention centre, etc., you need to know what the places are like that you're sending them to — and many of them don't know. Quite a number of social workers don't know how to do a breach of probation and it's quite amazing how many have no idea of what the inside of a court is like or a prison. I've arranged visits to Cornton Vale but some social workers just aren't interested.' (Court Liaison Officer No. 1, Glasgow)

'The working of the 1968 Act is a bloody scandal, there's no other way of describing it.' (Senior Lecturer in Social Work)

The main complaints about social work provision for offenders in Glasgow and Edinburgh centred around: first, social workers' 'invisibility' in the courts; second, the apparent reluctance of social work departments to supervise offenders on probation; and third, the paucity of after-care provision for ex-prisoners. These criticisms were made by court liaison officers, prison social workers, prison officers and sheriffs. Administrators acknowledged that the complaints had substance. *All* of the court liaison officers interviewed regretted the non-attendance of social workers at the courts.

'Only about 25 per cent of social workers are well-versed in court matters. They tend to be put off by the amount of time taken in the district court.' (Court Liaison Officer No. 6, Edinburgh)

'Not an awful lot of social workers know much about courts and they very seldom come to support their reports. I try to tell them how to behave in court, how to write a report but some only want to identify with the offender. Others don't want to know about offenders at all.' (Court Liaison Officer No. 7, Glasgow)

In 1978, Strathclyde Regional Council, having reported that social work liaison arrangements were generally good in the high courts and the sheriff's courts, also concluded that 'the service given to District Courts is less consistent and in some Districts is only provided when the court specifically requests that a social worker attends in relation to individual offenders' (Strathclyde Regional Council, 1978:5). Some of the interested parties whom I interviewed saw the social workers' non-attendance at court as being indicative of a general lack of interest in offenders:

> 'They don't attend court because the helping or super-vision of offenders has a very low priority in Scotland.'
> (Senior Lecturer in Social Work)

> 'If social workers cared at all about this kind of super-vision they *would* be in court to see what happened.'
> (Social Worker, Cornton Vale. Her emphasis)

But the main concern of the court liaison officers was related to how the absence of the social workers from the courts might affect the general standing of social workers with the sheriffs. Their very particular concern was with to what extent the lack of a social work presence in the courts had been responsible for the recent decline in the use of the probation order in Scotland.

Between 1966 and 1977 there was a 16.3 per cent fall in the number of probation orders made by the Scottish courts for adults aged seventeen and over (Chambers, 1979:28-9). In 1978, 2,136 probation orders were made on adults aged seventeen and over in the Scottish courts. Although this was a 14 per cent increase over 1977 when 1,874 orders were made, sheriffs and magistrates may not have been heartened to learn from Strathclyde Regional Council that one social work team had been able to allocate only 44 per cent of its probation cases (Strathclyde Regional Council, 1978). In 1979 only 1,733 probation orders were made on adults aged seventeen and over, and 1,997 orders were made on adults in 1980. When I was interviewing court liaison officers, sheriffs and magistrates in 1981 they all made the point that it was still difficult to get supervision for offenders on probation. Despite their best efforts at liaison, court liaison officers in Glasgow found that again and again there was a refusal by local authority social workers to undertake probation supervision.

'I run an induction course for social workers to meet sheriffs, police and court staff, to try to give social workers, who have little interest in the legal side, some knowledge of how the court works — see the sheriff with his wig off. Yet it's becoming more frequent for social work departments to say that they cannot supervise an offender. I'll give you an example. Yesterday there was a phone call from Sheriff No. 9 who wanted to know if a young man *would* be supervised if he were given probation. I said that I would speak to the social work team involved. When I telephoned, the Senior said, "We have 100 per cent supervision here", and she passed me on to the person who was supposed to deal with offenders. He then said he couldn't take him because he had too big a case load. So I reported all this to the sheriff who was very annoyed and said, "What *are* they doing if they never take offenders?" And I had to explain to him that it's a matter of priorities. But really, they're not very interested in offenders. Often probation cases are what they call 'unallocated' — and that's why sheriffs are reluctant to consider probation.' (Court Liaison Officer No. 3, Glasgow. His emphases)

In Edinburgh it was claimed that the situation there was slightly better:

'We have a bit more credibility about probation than Glasgow. We do have some unallocated cases but we do at least write back and say that we can't allocate them. We don't just *not* allocate them.' (Court Liaison Officer No. 2, Edinburgh)

But Court Liaison Officer No. 4 modified this claim:

'In this area it is assumed that *if* someone is given probation they *will* be allocated. But no, probation isn't *really* available and that's a disgrace to Scotland.' (Court Liaison Officer No. 4, Edinburgh, her emphases)

How does this situation affect women offenders? According to the two Glasgow stipendiary magistrates and some of the sheriffs it means that women have sometimes been fined on occasions when, if probation supervision had been available, a probation order could have been made.

'We make very few recommendations for probation now because the social work departments maintain they can't find anyone to supervise. I had a case a few weeks back where the woman was an obvious case for probation but the social worker doubted whether supervision could be carried out.' (Glasgow Stipendiary Magistrate)

Then, when the women have been unable to pay a fine, they have been sent to prison.

'With the current situation in Strathclyde proper probation facilities in Glasgow are not really available so probation is not really an available alternative to prison or a fine.' (Sheriff No. 10)

'Social workers decline ideal social work cases and so we're driven to sending young females to prison. Social workers don't want them because they can't face the responsibility of having a failure.' (Sheriff No. 2)

It is likely that this situation had adversely affected the prisoners whom I interviewed in Cornton Vale. For although eleven of the fifteen sheriffs whom I interviewed had said that they would be more likely to ask for a social inquiry report on a female offender than on a male offender they had also said that it was unlikely that they would be able to obtain probation supervision for a persistent petty offender, especially if it were already known that she had drinking problems. The sheriffs did not criticise social work departments for not offering supervision to this type of offender; rather they implied that it was understandable that social workers should give priority to offenders who were either seen to be still amenable to social work intervention or who, because they were caring for dependent children still living at home with them, were seen to be worth keeping out of prison. Like Chambers I found that, in the main, sheriffs tended to see women as being particularly suitable for probation because they thought 'that other disposals are unsuitable rather than [because] women have positive characteristics which make them particularly appropriate candidates for social work intervention' (Chambers, 1979:23).

Most of the women interviewed in Cornton Vale had either had probation long ago or had never had regular contact with local authority social workers at all. Only two of the non-drinking women said that they had ever had probation, whilst present relations between the drinking women and social workers were rather wryly summed up by Mandy MacDonald when she said, 'I never get much of a welcome from social workers now.' This is not to say that all of the women with some kind of drink problem claimed that they were completely cut off from any kind of helping agency — on the contrary, several of them spoke highly of the Salvation Army and other voluntary agencies which offered tangible help rather than talk — just that such contact as they had experienced had been sporadic and not of much practical use. Once imprisoned, therefore, they usually had no-one outside who could look after their affairs (e.g. accommodation, belongings, fines, legal help); upon liberation their chances of any kind of concerned after-care were minimal.

The social work practised within Cornton Vale was praised by everybody with whom I discussed it outside the prison. It was stressed to me on more than one occasion that the social workers at Cornton Vale were interested in the prisoners' practical problems, that they were interested, moreover, in *doing* something for prisoners rather than *'just talking'* to them. Even Strathclyde Regional Council's very critical *Who Cares?* excepted Cornton Vale's social workers from their general criticism that prison social workers had failed to get themselves accepted within penal establishments (Strathclyde Regional Council 1978:20). The social workers at Cornton Vale agreed with the general opinion that they had very good working relationships with the officers and I myself found that the officers' evident interest in the women's welfare extended to a sympathetic interest in the task of the prison social workers. 'Through-care is practised here,' said the Governor, 'and we try to make sure that they have somewhere to go when they go out. However, we just have to let some go out through the gate with nowhere to go.' This latter group is likely to be composed almost entirely of the short-term recidivist adult offenders.

In 1963 the Advisory Council on the Treatment of Offenders defined through-care as 'a process which starts on the offender's reception into custody, is developed during his sentence, and is available for as long as necessary after his release' (Davies, 1974:5). In 1978 Strathclyde Regional Council reported that:

> Parole and after-care is an area of work which places
> increasing demands on social work services but does
> not receive corresponding priority in terms of resource
> allocation. Many of those who should have been receiv-
> ing after-care supervision and support were given little or
> no service. (Strathclyde Regional Council, 1978:23)

Strathclyde Regional Council is here referring to social work departments' statutory duties towards ex-prisoners. In fact, social work departments have no formal after-care duties towards adult offenders serving less than eighteen months. In view of the failure of social work departments to fulfil their statutory after-care duties it is not surprising that no informal after-care is available for the majority of women prisoners passing through Cornton Vale.

Prison social workers are so short-handed that they have to give priority to those categories of prisoners whom they expect to have the most problems. In Cornton Vale the major commitment was to seeing all newly-remanded prisoners, they being the ones who most often present a 'crisis situation', especially in relation to arrangements to be made for their children. Once the social worker has sorted out the new prisoners' initial practical problems (frequently a lengthy and almost impossible task in itself due to the often convoluted nature of the women's usual family and living arrangements!), the women must make their subsequent requests to see a social worker to a prison officer. This officer will then ask them what they want to see the social worker about and decide whether the request is to be granted or not.

Most of the short-term prisoners interviewed in Cornton

Vale said that prison social workers could be helpful on
occasions when prisoners wanted 'little things done'. At the
same time they said that social workers could not help them
with their 'real' problems concerning drink, money, continuous thieving, homelessness, battering husbands, etc. They
did, however, distinguish quite clearly between those areas
of their lives where they felt that it was up to them to help
themselves and those other, more material, areas of their
lives where they felt that a bit more welfare intervention
might have enabled them to come to grips with their drinking problems, personal relationships and general difficulties
in living.

Melissa, Olive and Kirsty stressed that as far as their excessive drinking was concerned they had to help themselves.
Ann Archer and Thelma Thompson recognised that only they
could make the decision not to steal again. And June Jones
thought that she could keep out of prison if she avoided
alcohol before her future shoplifting expeditions! When it
came to more material problems, however, the women knew
from experience that however hard the prison social worker
might try to get them accommodation or other immediate
help upon liberation she was unlikely to be successful.
Several women thought that the social worker responsible
for the short-termers was just too hard-pressed for time to
make the numerous telephone calls needed to obtain even
one hostel place. Others, like Melissa, felt that they themselves had let people down so many times that it was difficult
for the prison social worker to present their case for accommodation with any conviction at all.[4] Then there were those
prisoners who did not seek social work help because they
did not feel that prison social workers guaranteed to their
clients sufficient confidentiality. Others were frightened that
if they were to disclose some of their fears about the welfare
of their children the children would be taken into care and
removed from their present homes. The major complaint of
the women who were not persistent offenders was that they
had found it difficult to gain information about the financial
and other welfare entitlements due to the people looking
after their children while they were in prison. Whatever the
women thought of the prison social work service, however,
they all knew that their problems would 'still be all piled-up,

waiting at the gate' for them until they were liberated. It was generally recognised, too, that, once they were beyond the prison gate the women would yet again be on their own.

Ingrid Ingham had certainly had no idea of which official agencies she could turn to upon her release from prison. The sheriff who had sentenced her had not requested a social inquiry report prior to imposing a custodial sentence and Ingrid had never previously had contact with the local social services. The prison social worker had performed several small services for her whilst she had been in prison and Ingrid had been duly grateful. The notes in her file indicated that the prison social worker had assessed Ingrid as being a competent woman who would serve her sentence with no trouble before resuming her normal life. And most likely Ingrid was one of the most competent women interviewed. She did none the less face many problems upon liberation (see Chapter 4, page 84). In the end she went to, and obtained advice from, a local authority social worker. Yet she had only done this after some hesitation. On the one hand she had thought she was not eligible for local authority social work assistance because she 'had never had any contact with them before', on the other, she had not contacted the prison social worker because she had believed that 'you're not allowed to contact them once you've come out.' And a prison officer had already indicated to me how such a belief could arise when, remarking on the inadequacy of the present piecemeal reality of 'through-care', she had said,

'In here we have very good relations with the social workers; and, maybe, a social worker outside could work wonders with some women. But it's difficult sometimes to get those outside to be interested in after-care. Women say, "I'd like you to get me a social worker," but it's a low priority in Scotland, after-care.' (Prison Officer No. 9)

While social work provision for offenders in Scotland continues to be so haphazard that even the few offenders who *do* come into contact with social workers continue to be faced with different social workers at each stage (probation, court, prison, after-care) of their penal careers, it is difficult to see how the concept of 'through-care' can be effectively realised.

The dismissive society?

It is unlikely that anyone has ever called Scotland a permissive society. Though the Scots' ambivalence towards alcohol might lead one to suggest that at least in that area they are at one and the same time both boisterously permissive of over-consumption *and* contemptuously dismissive of those who suffer its unwanted ill-effects (see Chapter 7), all recent commentators have indicated that, as far as offenders in general are concerned, Scotland is a dismissive society. The Special Unit at Barlinnie (Boyle, 1977) and the innovative juvenile panels are merely two of the less unacceptable faces of Scottish criminal justice (see Brown and Bloomfield, 1979; MacDonald and Sim, 1978). Beyond them lie the mass of persistent petty offenders who, *as persistent petty offenders*, are seen as being irrevocably beyond the pale of the welfare state. How has such a situation arisen?

In 1979 an article in the *Scotsman* commented that:

> Whatever the successes in other areas, work in the offender field has not won for social work any plaudits; instead it has been the target of attack from the Bench, the Parole Board, Visiting Committees and the voluntary organisations concerned with penal issues. (Moore, 1979)

The author of the article, George Moore, was pointing to a situation which, the denials of some higher-level administrators notwithstanding, was still apparent in early 1981. However, although I found little dissent to the prevailing notion that social work provision for offenders in Scotland is poor to non-existent, the reasons given to me to explain the situation were wide-ranging.

The majority of people with whom I discussed the matter of social work provision for offenders made very specific criticisms which highlighted particular instances of how the poor working of the 1968 Social Work (Scotland) Act had resulted in a general lack of confidence in social workers' competence to undertake probation and after-care duties. The next largest group of critics was composed of those who thought that the concept of 'generic social worker' was essentially an unworkable one. Finally, a minority of critics argued that the more fundamental causes should be sought, and their explanations of contemporary Scottish penal policy tended to relate to their assertions about either the fundamental nature of Scottish society in general or the fundamental nature of the British criminal justice system in particular.

Whatever the *deeper* causes of the parlous state of Scotland's social work provision for offenders, most critics were content with isolating as an *immediate* cause the fact that the Scottish generic social worker (unlike the English probation officer) is not an officer of the court. This fact was identified as the primary cause of a downward spiral of secondary and follow-on effects and causes culminating in the total decline of Scottish social work provision for offenders. Different groups of officials tended to identify the initial secondary effective cause at different points in the spiral. All the sheriffs and magistrates for example claimed that they had made fewer probation orders as a *result* of either the non-allocation or non-supervision of offenders by social work departments; the social workers themselves, on the other hand, tended to claim that they had initially been deterred from working with offenders by the low priority accorded to such work by the courts, as evidenced by the decline in the number of probation orders, and by the society, as evidenced by the lack of community facilities for offenders. For all of the downward-spiral critics, however, the spiral's basic elements were the same: lack of confidence in generic social workers, leading to fewer probation orders being made, leading to fewer social workers wanting to work with offenders, leading to either the reluctance or the inability of social work departments to supervise offenders, leading to the courts' lack of confidence in social workers ... and so on.

The critics of genericism tended to see the 'downward spiral' situation as an almost inevitable effect of the genericism which, since 1968, has formally been the major organisational principle of the social work departments and the social work training courses. These generic critics claimed that, at the level of the colleges, genericism has resulted in the production of social workers who have no *specific* skills and certainly very few of the practical skills of organisation which are often necessary for untangling the material and emotional problems of recidivist offenders.[5]

> 'Training in social work is training in nothing more than talking. The system of multi-service training means that *practically* social workers are good at nothing except sitting around having meetings.' (Lecturer in Social Work)

> 'Social workers like to sit around and talk about what they *should* be doing. I wonder if it's the colleges, but they seem to be turning out a lot of social workers who aren't interested in the practical affairs of the client.' (Deputy Principal, Scottish Prison Service College)

In the local authority social work departments genericism was seen as inevitably involving the continuous ranking of needs and the identifying of priorities and, consequently, it was seen as being equally inevitable that, in such a situation, offenders' needs would always be put at the bottom of the list. Phyllida Parsloe well described the situation in Scotland when she wrote:

> Here, former prisoners compete for service not only with those subject to compulsory after-care and probation, as do their English equivalents, but with all the multiplicity of human need which comes to local authority area teams. Against children at risk and old people liable to die of cold, a prisoner seeking voluntary after-care has low priority. (Parsloe, 1979)

Others, however, did not see this ranking as being a natural one and were prepared to speculate about the ways in which social workers *choose* their priorities. A court liaison officer thought that the social workers themselves simply find offenders too difficult:

> 'My own personal view is that social workers have bitten off too much. The young girl who has previously only dealt with young children cannot necessarily deal with the tough offender — and often doesn't want to.' (Court Liaison Officer No. 1, Glasgow)

This being so, argued other critics of genericism, it was to be expected that the generic social worker who, unlike the old probation officer, is free to reject offenders as clients, should choose to work in those areas which are expected to yield both the deeper personal satisfactions and the greater career rewards. Social work within the prisons, it was emphasized, is *not* seen to be 'good for anyone's career.' Against these latter critics who tended to suggest that ultimately it was the social workers' own self-interest which determined their professional priorities a sheriff thought that social work priorities merely reflected the priorities of the society as a whole:

'If you ask a social work department why they can't supervise someone they will say that it's a matter of priorities. That is perfectly fair. Society can choose its own priorities . . . but it does mean that I cannot assume that a person given probation will receive adequate supervision.' (Sheriff No. 10)

Yet some of the critics of genericism blamed neither 'the Society' nor 'the Social Worker', rather they thought that the concept of genericism had resulted in Certificate of Qualification in Social Work courses which produced social workers who defined the social work task in a way which is totally at odds with the needs of offenders, the courts and the prisons. These critics were not only saying that the social workers have few practical skills, they were also saying that social workers have developed ideologies by which they can also *justify* the taking of a non-interventionist stance on criminal justice. Two major ideologies were identified: the revolutionary political ideology, the propagators of which fear incorporation into the criminal justice and penal systems; and the existential, democratic self-help ideology, the propagators of which fear being charged either with paternalism or with being 'agents of social control' and who justify their unwillingness to supervise offenders on the grounds that clients must retain their independence of being. The irritation of the critics with these two social work ideologies can be heard in the comments of two ex-probation officers.

'A lot of our young social workers are anti-court, they are more interested in the Revolution. I tell them that the Revolution won't be made by criminals.' (Court Liaison Officer No. 7, Glasgow)

'The kind of people we've got coming into social work here like to think about *being*, not doing. The emphasis is on "being" a social worker. And they would say they couldn't do anything for people with drink problems in any case. But drink isn't the only cause of crime. There are plenty of other factors, for example, unemployment and deprivation in general. Admittedly, social workers would find these problems intractable, but just because they can't sit around and *talk* them away doesn't mean that these people have to be denied welfare and put into institutions.' (Social Work Lecturer)

Although there is little evidence to suggest that the Scots need fear that a revolution will be led by either their social workers *or* their criminals, there is substantial evidence that both social workers in Scotland and probation officers in England and Wales fear that their involvement in prisons is contrary to their major task of keeping people *out* of the custodial institutions. Certainly Scottish prison social workers might have reasonably feared 'incorporation' and an unwelcome reformulation of their welfare task when they heard a speaker at a 1978 seminar on 'Social work in prison establishments' recommend that they be selective in their work and prove their usefulness *first* to the institution and *then* to the prisoners! And here, too, it should be noted that the prison social workers at Cornton Vale, whose own relationships with the uniformed discipline staff were so universally commended, themselves attributed much of their success within the institution to the fact that they were prepared to share confidential information about the prisoners with the prison officers! On the basis of this evidence and the contention of Strathclyde Regional Council that, 'with the exception of the Women's Institution, there is no indication that social work staff are either fully accepted or integrated within penal establishments' (Strathclyde Regional Council, 1978:20) it could be argued that the price of Cornton Vale's excellent prison officer-social worker relationship is paid by the women prisoners who, unlike their male counterparts, have no 'alternative' nor 'independent' voices to speak for them within the institution. Such arguments, of course, could be (and are) countered by claims that it *is* only by 'fitting in' to the prisons that social workers can hope to achieve *anything* for prisoners; and, furthermore, that social workers should not be so concerned with saving their own souls that they cannot suffer the ambiguities posed by the transposition of the generic social work task to the specifically custodial setting. None the less, whichever way it is argued, the tensions remain, and, claim the critics of genericism, while there are no officers specifically trained to cope with the contradictions between the welfare and control elements in social work provision for offenders, these tensions will continue to be elevated into a justification for absolving local authority social workers from their failure to provide supervision and support for ex-offenders and ex-prisoners.

According to their critics the propagators of the democratic self-help ideology claim (a) that the majority of petty persistent offenders do not want help; (b) that even if they think they need help the majority are so far 'gone' as to be beyond help; (c) that even if they want help and are still deemed to be helpable, then the best help is the self-help which will enable them to regain their lost self-respect. I never heard this ideology expressed in its 'pure' form but I often heard it partially expressed, e.g.: '90 per cent of recidivists don't want help' (Court Liaison Officer No. 5); 'Often sheriffs put women on probation so that a social worker can sort out her money problems — things that she could do perfectly well herself' (Court Liaison Officer No. 6); and, 'We won't do *too* much for them. We see ours as an enabling role, to get them to do things for themselves' (Prison Social Worker). Most frequently, however, the democratic self-help ideology was incorporated into those circular explanations in which each official agency first blamed every other agency for failing to provide 'back-up' to each other's non-existent initiatives *vis-à-vis* offenders, and then rounded-off the explanation by pointing to the very *existence* of recidivists as evidence that they were already beyond the pale of the non-existent welfare provision! Typical of these buck-passing statements was that of a senior social services administrator in Edinburgh:

> 'It's all a matter of priorities and it could certainly be argued that short-term prisoners should have top priority, that you could do more with people who go in and out of prison. But you could also argue that they've had all the help and the fact that they *do* go back shows that they *don't* want to change. Whichever way you made the argument you'd have to remember that there's not much court facility and not many facilities in the community either.'

As will be seen in Chapter 7 the existential democratic self-help ideology is at its most rampant in relation to alcoholic offenders. It is noted in this chapter too, however, because it is *in general* a most persuasive official justification for the non-relief of problems which have, at least in part, already been exacerbated by an almost totally punitive criminal justice system.

It was the almost totally punitive nature of Scottish criminal justice which the 'fundamentalist' critics set out to explain. One group focused on what they claimed to be the fundamental nature of Scottish society, the other on the fundamental nature of British criminal justice. Those who claimed that Scotland was basically a punitive society rather predictably pointed to the stern doctrines of Calvinism to explain why Scotland has not had a strong tradition of voluntary work with offenders — the kind of tradition which in the south gave birth to the probation service. But it was the second group, those who made a link between the lack of a voluntary social work tradition in the Scottish courts and the nature of British criminal justice in general, who provided some of the most interesting pointers as to why Scottish social work provision for offenders is so inadequate. Their argument was constructed around three sequential propositions.

First, they argued that it is because the Scottish public has not been given an accurate picture of the nature of law-breaking and imprisonment in Scotland that it continues to take a traditionally punitive line towards offenders. This point, made most vividly by George Moore in his 1979 *Scotsman* article, was put to me by many people.

> It would no doubt come as a considerable surprise to that
> ubiquitous creature, the man on the top of a No. 10 bus,
> that Scottish prisons are not, on a day to day basis filled
> with violent men and women serving long sentences
> for sensational crimes. On the contrary they are chock
> a block with petty inadequates, the majority of whom
> ought not to be in prison — costing as they do something
> in excess of £100 per week per [person] to say nothing
> of the ancilliary costs of maintaining families during
> their enforced sojourn. (Moore, 1979)

Second, they argued that the closed and secret nature of the British criminal justice and penal systems in itself does nothing to educate either the public or the legal and judicial officials in the possible advantages which might be gained from opening up these systems to extra-legal and extra-judicial scrutiny (see also, Carlen, 1982). As illustrations of this dimension of the argument I did indeed come across many examples of court officials expressing hostility and suspicion of social workers. The fear most generally voiced was that the provision of increased welfare aid either to accused or to convicted would mean that they would be the recipients of greater resources and concern than the complainants and the victims. Furthermore, several procurator-fiscals said that they did not 'trust' social workers and one even claimed that he thought that they were 'just empire building'. It was, in fact, put to me again and again by social workers themselves that the inner circle of the courts' personnel make no secret of their hostility towards social workers nor, indeed, towards any outside influences which seek to penetrate their domain.

> 'The courts are very inward-looking. The police have a
> field day making fools of social workers who don't know
> what they're doing.' (Court Liaison Officer No. 8, Glasgow)

> 'It's a closed trade. You and I know a bit of it but the
> general public knows nothing and it's not encouraged to
> either. The public is interested if given the chance, though,

the response to advertisements for the juvenile panels
shows that.' (Court Liaison Officer No. 2, Edinburgh)

Familiarity with both the exclusiveness and exclusionary
processes of courts in general led the fundamentalist critics
to their third proposition: that, given such a traditionally
retributive and closed criminal justice system, the post-1968
absence of probation officers from the courts has made it
extremely difficult for Scottish generic social workers (themselves by definition denuded of the 'officer-of-the-court'
status of the probation officer) to develop a position from
which they might authoritatively and effectively argue the
advantages to be accrued from dealing with the majority of
offenders by way of non-custodial social work intervention.
So . . . back to the 'infamous' Act!

The unravelling of contemporary discourse on social work
provision for offenders in Scotland has been designedly
circular, for I do not believe that it is either useful or possible
to isolate one single cause of the present situation. Instead
of providing a unicausal explanation I have tried to show
how certain elements of statutory change (i.e. Social Work
(Scotland) Act 1968) have combined with some peculiarly
Scottish cultural conditions and some generally British
judicial conditions to constitute an image of contemporary
Scotland as a *dismissive* society, a society where penal policy
is retributive rather than rehabilitative and where, ironically,
either despite or because of the ideology of generic social
work, a rigid distinction is still made between criminal justice in particular and social justice in general.

And where does this leave our petty recidivist female
offenders? In Cornton Vale, of course. But they are not in
Cornton Vale *purely* because of the welfare-void. The welfare void itself is not accidental. Nor is its existence made
possible only by the legal, ideological and cultural conditions
described above. Additionally, therefore, in Chapters 7 and 8
we will see how the notions of 'the alcohol-related problem'
and 'the personality disorder' *positively* buttress the welfare-
void so that certain petty, recidivist prisoners are system-
atically and authoritatively being reproduced as being always-
already ineligible for non-custodial supervision.

7 Down, out, alcoholic and in prison

'She's the Miss Piggy of the Grassmarket — red face through drink and badly scarred by her boyfriend who's also an alcoholic.' (Policeman No. 25, Edinburgh)

The principles of definition and penal organisation which co-ordinate a woman's prison-worthiness are largely negative. The imprisoned women are in no-woman's-land. When the court's appropriate knowledge of their domestic lives and incorporate it into a public and apposite history of maternal failure and dereliction of duty, the offending women are seen as being outwith family, sociability, femininity and adulthood (cf. Litman *et al.* 1976). Although in penal discourse they are often seen as being outwith 'real' criminality too, they are also: rejected by hospital alcoholic units as being outwith motivation; rejected by social workers as being outwith reform and beyond help; and rejected by psychiatrists as being outwith treatment and beyond cure. 'Our people' said the Governor of Cornton Vale 'are often the people that *nobody* wants.' The prison does not want them, either, but, unlike the other agencies, the prison cannot refuse them. The refuse of other agencies provides the prison's *raison d'être*. Something has to be made of what has already been defined as being beyond recognition. The 'alcohol-related-problem' and the 'personality disorder' are two positive notions which officially and discursively co-ordinate the moment of prison with a concomitant recognition and denial of the prisoners' always-already written-off futures and pasts. Under the auspices of these two concept-

155

ually dispersed notions, programmes of rehabilitation can be inaugurated *within* the prison at the same time as their predicted failure can be justified by reference to the women's lack of material chances *outwith* the prison. What sticks out awkwardly from the plethora of knowledges and official and voluntary expertise which attempt to harness the 'alcoholic', the 'drinker' and the 'disordered' to the logics of sobriety and normality is what the 'saving' professions call the 'lack of motivation' of the women themselves. In the place where they are beyond recognition *some* of the women have achieved an imaginary independence — an independence which, though imaginary, can neither be denied nor made realisable by conditions outside the prison. Thus when these isolated and destitute women commit their alcohol-related crimes — for example, the infrequent serious assault, or, more often, the breach of the peace which is embarrassing, say, to the tourists at the Edinburgh Festival — there is neither a discursive space nor a physical space in which they can be contained. A note in Mandy MacDonald's file by a prison social worker explained why Mandy could not be a candidate for either treatment or welfare:

> Mandy has reached the stage when no-one has anything left to offer her — she is not ill, therefore she cannot be treated for anything. She is not without intelligence, therefore, she should be able to cope with her own life.

At fifty-nine, Mandy was the eldest of the women I interviewed but several others were aware that they were on the same road. The *Report on Prisons in Scotland, 1979* indicates that in fact more and more alcoholic women are being imprisoned:

> The relationship between over-indulgence in alcohol and anti-social behaviour is well-recognised and it is, therefore, no surprise that Alcoholism is a condition frequently requiring treatment in admissions to penal establishments. It is also apparent that this is an increasing cause of morbidity. During the year 800 (724) cases were recorded 635 (548) male and 165 (140) female. 61 (49) inmates, 34 (16) male and 37 (33) female required treatment for Delirium

Tremens. Many others received treatment for varying degrees of withdrawal symptoms. . . . The upward trend in alcohol-related problems in female offenders is obvious. (Scottish Home and Health Department; 1980:22, figures in brackets are for 1978).

In 1980 diagnoses of alcoholism were made for 169 women prisoners (see the *Report on Prisons in Scotland, 1980*:21). Yet from the official statistics alone it is not possible to gain even a rough estimate of the numbers of women imprisoned for alcohol-related crimes. For in addition to the old crime of drunkenness (now no longer an imprisonable crime in Scotland) and the ubiquitous breach of the peace (usually drink-related), there are many alcohol-related crimes which appear in the statistics as crimes against the person and crimes against property. Some male prison officers go so far as to claim that 99 per cent of all Scottish crime is drink-related, and the prison officers at Cornton Vale frequently told me that I would find that *all* the short-term recidivists had a drink problem. In fact, of the twenty women whom I interviewed in Papa Block only three were currently in prison for breach of the peace, though the evidence of the official records of eleven of the others, combined with their own testimony, supported the prison officers' claims.

Seven of the women interviewed claimed to have no drink problems at all. Six of these seven were serving sentences of more than six months. One of them, however, admitted that the 'attempted murder' charge to which she had pleaded guilty and for which she had received a year's imprisonment had resulted from a stabbing which *had* occurred during a heavy drinking session. The other women had drinking problems of varying degrees of seriousness. Eight women (seven of whom were homeless) said that they were alcoholics and all but one of them had, at some time, received in-patient treatment for their alcoholism. Three of the women said that they were not alcoholics but that they had real problems with drink, had repeatedly been convicted for offences committed when drunk and were beginning to wonder if they should stop before it was 'too late'. Finally, two of the youngest women interviewed said that they always had to take a drink before they went shoplifting and that they wished they could shoplift without drinking beforehand because they thought that they would then be more efficient. For these two young women at this stage the main problem with alcohol was that it had too often proved to be a necessary but totally unreliable partner in crime! Thus eleven of the women interviewed realised that their relationship with alcohol was either already out of control or was going that way, while the remaining two whose crimes were drink-related felt that although they had a degree of control over their instrumental drinking its effects were to be regretted. The crimes and sentences which had led to the imprisonment of the eleven women who admitted to having some kind of problem with alcohol were as follows:[1]

Bernice Bradley (homeless alcoholic) had been convicted of 'assault to severe injury' when she had attacked and injured three men during a drunken brawl at a dance-hall. She had been sentenced to eighteen months imprisonment.

Daphne Daniels (drinking problem) had previous convictions for drink-related offences though her present (and first) term of imprisonment was not drink-related. She had on this occasion been sentenced to two years imprisonment for perjury, a charge to which she had pled not guilty and which offence she still vehemently denied at the time of interview.

Eliza Eastwood (homeless alcoholic) had been found guilty of breach of the peace and was serving thirty days in lieu of payment of a fine. She was liberated during the research period and three days later was back in prison — for breach of the peace!

Hermione Hall (self-defined alcoholic) was serving 'thirty plus twenty' days in lieu of payment of previous fines for 'theft, prostitution and assault', though she was not quite sure how the 'thirty plus twenty' had been calculated!

Kirsty King (homeless alcoholic) was serving a three-month prison sentence (direct) for theft. (She had gone into a Chinese restaurant, had a large meal, several brandies, some beers and three half-bottles of beaujolais before telling them that she had no money!)

Lisa Lobell (self-defined alcoholic) was serving three months for theft. She was liberated during the research period and four days later was back in prison having been found guilty of being drunk and disorderly.

Mandy MacDonald (homeless alcoholic) was serving sixty days for breach of the peace.

Melissa Malcom (homeless alcoholic) was serving thirty days for assault. She was liberated during the period of the research and twelve days later was back in prison to serve ninety days for breach of the peace.

Olive O'Brien (drinking problem) was serving ninety days direct for 'police assault', i.e. hitting a policeman with her handbag when she was drunk.

Thelma Thompson (drinking problem) was serving nine months direct for a theft committed when she was drunk.

Vivienne Vincent (homeless alcoholic) was serving thirty days for breach of the peace.

Yet though the *Report on Prisons in Scotland*, 1979 is probably justified in claiming that the problem of alcoholics in prison 'may well be a small part of the national problem of alcoholism' (p. 22) it should not be assumed either that the prison population of alcoholics merely mirrors the distribution of alcoholics throughout the total population of Scotland, nor that alcoholics in prison are there entirely because of their alcoholism. The imprisoned alcoholic is too often the living embodiment of a myriad of social problems and injustices which, having been both socially and psychologically distilled as 'alcohol-related' are then discursively displaced on to drink. Given that few officials in the criminal justice and penal systems are prepared *formally* to justify the imprisonment of alcoholic female offenders it is necessary to look at the actual workings of these systems to understand how certain women with drink problems fall: first, through the interstices of a *dismissive* society; then, through the interstices of competing professional discourses; and finally through the enormous craters in social and welfare provision — into the ever-adaptable and ruminant maw of the prison.

As long ago as 1853, Mary Carpenter, writing of women prisoners, remarked:

Once in prison, many of them are continually going and coming. . . . What a mockery of justice is this, for a bench

of magistrates to be constantly inflicting a punishment
which is thus publicly stated to produce no impression.
(Carpenter, 1970:104-10)

As early as 1910 the Commissioner of Prisons and Directors
of Convict Prisons were bewailing the continued use of
imprisonment for the 'drunkard', the tramp and the imbecile
(Gunn *et al.*, 1978). Since then it has become commonplace
for official reports to recommend that alternatives to impri-
sonment should be developed for offenders whose main
problem is drink (e.g. Scottish Health Services Council, 1965;
The Home Office *Working Party on Habitual Drunken
Offenders*, 1971 the 15th Report of The House of Commons
Expenditure Committee, 1978, *Report of DHSS Advisory
Committee on Alcoholism*, 1978, The *May Report*, 1979;
Parliamentary All-Party Penal Affairs Group, 1980; and
Fairhead, 1981).

Clause 5 of the Criminal Justice (Scotland) Act 1980
which came into force in 1981 empowered the police to take
a drunken person 'to any place designated by the Secretary
of State . . . as a place suitable for the care of drunken
persons.' However, as the Glasgow police commented in early
1981, at that time there was only one such place in Glasgow
(with six beds) and in the event of her 'cutting up rough' and
not being able to pay fines imposed at any subsequent court
appearance, the recidivist alcoholic was likely to end up in
prison in exactly the same way as she had prior to the act.
It is the same in Edinburgh and Glasgow as it is in London:

The more rootless the woman alcoholic, the more likely
it is that she will be in poor health, that she will be arrested for drunkenness and that she will not have easy access
to hospital for treatment . . . for many of them [the
prison] serves as a substitute for a shelter in which to dry
out. . . . The setting up of detoxification centres and other
non-punitive facilities as an alternative to the courts would
present a means of breaking the trap in which the woman
alcoholic finds herself as she moves through a treadmill of
drunkenness, arrest and imprisonment. (Camberwell
Council on Alcoholism and Campaign for the Homeless
and Rootless, 1976)

'The women who are floating round the Sally-Ann and the Vicky are not really offenders but they are very likely to appear in court for shouting and bawling or some other offence, and, because they have nowhere else to go and no money to pay a fine will also spend the odd month in Cornton Vale.' (Edinburgh Social Worker)

Certainly the alcoholic women whom I interviewed were pessimistic about their chances of staying out of prison. To understand why, it is necessary to examine the world that awaits the liberated prisoner with drinking problems.

'Prison made us children again and, when our term was ended, let us loose into an adult world.' (Turner, 1964:8)

The world into which alcoholic women prisoners are liberated after they have been sobered up by the prison is indeed an adult world; it is also an uncaring world (see Davies, 1974; Strathclyde Regional Council, 1978). The women who, though experiencing an enforced sobriety have been helped in no other way by their incarceration, are totally unfit to cope with it. In fact, the first thing that many of them do is to take the 'wee drink' which will rescue them from the sobriety in which they see even more clearly the hopelessness of their position in a society which rejects them. Once the ex-prisoners are drunk again the police are the main arbiters of the next stage of their careers. However, this is not because of any police enthusiasm for the job of 'minding' drunks — it is because no other agency is prepared to cope with them except on a very selective basis. Let us therefore examine first the world into which the alcoholic/problem-drinking woman is liberated and then the agencies which, though their official mandate is to alleviate the difficulties of that world, in effect both aggravate and deny them.

The main problem facing the eight alcoholic women and two of the problem-drinkers was the need to find accommodation (see Otto, 1980). Seven of the women had been classified as being of 'no fixed abode' when they had begun their sentences, one had lost her home since she had been in prison and two more did not want to go back to their wife-battering husbands. Most of the women with severe alcohol problems went straight out of the prison gate and (via the off-licence) back to the streets.

Several of the alcoholic women had not had any permanent accommodation for several years, but this state of affairs had not in every case been precipitated by their alcoholism. Melissa, Bernice, Lisa and Kirsty, for instance, had been moved from home to home from early childhood onwards, as Melissa was quick to point out. In reply to my question, 'Why did you leave home?' She replied, rather tartly, 'I didn't leave home, I was in a children's home.' In other instances the women's homelessness had been contributed to either by the violence or alcoholism of their husbands or by their husbands' or their own prison sentences. Lisa Lobell was only twenty-four but already she was experiencing the effects of her several prison sentences.

> 'You lose a lot even when you come in a place like this.
> I mean, I've lost a house and a flat when I've come in
> here. You just can't afford to keep the payments up. So
> you lose your flat and the landlord takes your stuff.
> When you get out you've got to look for another flat.'

Not that the council hadn't offered Lisa a flat:

> 'They offered me a flat, but in a bad area. And with my
> record that's all they'll do. But why should I bring up
> the wean in a bad area because of my record?'

However, getting a house is one thing, keeping it, another! After several years of homelessness Mandy MacDonald had at last obtained a house, but before she could move into it she had once more been imprisoned for breach of the peace (squabbling with her elderly aunt about a hair dryer!) and had lost the house again — as well as three-months rent paid in advance! Kirsty King had managed to keep a precarious hold on her derelict council flat in central Edinburgh but she so often spent periods in Cornton Vale that her house had recently been in an almost continuous state of squalor, vandalised by male vagrant alcoholics who had known that she was 'away'. As a result, Kirsty divided her time between Cornton Vale, the Salvation Army hostel and her own house

— when it was in a habitable state.

Once they have lost houses the ex-prisoners find that there are many obstacles in the way of them getting another. Bernice Bradley, for instance, had made up her mind while she was in prison that she wanted to leave the man who had so badly disfigured her.

'In here I was thinking about leaving him and I went to
see the welfare officer. I was wanting to see if she could
get me a council house for Dundee and she says "Oh no,"
she says, "They won't have that at all because you're outwith their jurisdiction — the only thing I can offer you is
hostel accommodation or the double grant."'

In the reports prepared on Melissa during the time she had been imprisoned on the attempted murder charge doctors had always stressed that without a 'structured' environment she would not be able to withstand the 'pull of alcohol' upon liberation. When she was paroled in February 1980 she was found unconscious in the gutter on the same day — and was unconscious for fifty-six hours. She was recalled to prison and then, next time upon release, went along to the council to see what were her chances of getting a flat.

'I told them I was in here for two and a half years and they
asked me the reason. I said, "Attempted murder," and I
could see from the expression on their faces that they
weren't interested. Also, I was skippering at the time, I
was living rough, and they said, "If you're in a hostel the
chances of getting a house are better, but as long as you're
skippering you'll get nowhere." Which I think is a lot of
bullshit. *Now* when I leave here on Saturday I don't know
what's waiting in front of me. If I got the chance of a
house I would be able to cope with life a lot better.'

For Melissa, and *all* the other women, a house represented independence, from the 'hostel', the 'man' and the 'street'.

None of the homeless women had a good word to say for hostels. True, Eliza Eastwood had been banned from all the Edinburgh hostels, and, because of her violent behaviour, their wardens had few kind words to say about her either!

But when I visited the Glasgow and Edinburgh hostels I found that although the homeless women I had met in Cornton Vale were well-known in the hostels of their respective home towns, they had not caused them any kind of bother. Hostels are unpopular for many reasons but one is simply that to the person who has chosen, or become accustomed, to live outwith family or institutional discipline the rules and regulations of the large hostel are anathema.

> 'I don't like hostels. I'd rather stay out altogether. You get a lot of rules and all that, you know, and I get fed up. Well, I do. I've had rules and regulations all my life.' (Melissa)

> 'I don't want to go into those hostels because I was in one down in London and it was terrible. It was a place for down and outs, there was all types — it was terrible. Honest, I couldn't stay one night. I'd have rather walked the streets. In fact that's what I did do.' (Bernice)

Even if a woman *is* prepared to 'try a hostel', alternatives to the large Salvation-Army type common-lodging house are almost non-existent. As for private lodgings, it was generally agreed that it is even more difficult to get ordinary lodgings for a single woman than for a single man. As the Governor at Cornton Vale said 'It is most difficult to provide for women — any women — not just ours. Landladies just won't touch them.' A senior social worker agreed with these remarks, adding: 'I would be unwilling to take a woman myself. Women go in for dumb insolence. Also, I think men are cleaner than women.' I asked my landlady in Stirling how she felt about taking women guests: 'I'm not against women as such, but you noticed that I asked you a lot of questions. If you don't mind me saying so, you wonder about a woman who comes looking for a room for a short time.' And Melissa made explicit what my landlady had thought it better to leave implicit: 'A lot of people are not keen on taking single women in because they think they'll maybe start bringing in men.'

Certainly SACRO (Glasgow) had been driven to attempting to obtain their own house for women ex-prisoners after the failure of earlier attempts to place women with private landladies. The Director of the Edinburgh and District Council on Alcoholism thought that the general dearth of residential provision for alcoholic women resulted from the fact that their problems were 'invisible':

> 'You'll find that in Scotland in general there is not such an awareness of women's problems. Drinking is associated with maleness — so is crime. So, in a way, women's crime and drinking problems are not taken seriously. Not that I want women sent to prison, but at least there should be some recognition of their problems. It does not mean that because they are not going to prison that they are getting any other kind of help.'

Melissa agreed, and thought that women were much harder done by than men.

> 'You go into George Square any night in the week and you'll see the women. The women's that skippering in Glasgow is amazing. It's atrocious to see them. Half of them are only young and they look ten years older than their age. Aye, they drink, they have to. It's just to forget their problems and what they've got to go home to at night. Because you can't skipper on sobriety, it's impossible.
>   It's rotten what is happening to women. That's why a lot of women turn to what they do. They're not getting a fair deal, that's the cause of it. The Glasgow Corporation got up the money to build a hostel for men but when one was suggested for women — "we don't have the money."'

A prison social worker pointed out that the situation had been worsened by the pulling-down of old houses: 'The official vandalism of the last twenty years has involved pulling down the old slums which provided shelter for the "no fixed aboders".' Additionally, many areas, like Edinburgh's Grassmarket, for instance, have increasingly been taken over by middle-class shopkeepers, have become public amenity areas like Clyde Walkway, or have otherwise been gentrified. One result has been that traditional street communities of alcoholics have become more visible to the 'respectable' public and there has been a greater demand for the police to 'do something' about them. But what can the police do? In early 1981 Glasgow had 131 beds for homeless women, Edinburgh 92. Glasgow had drying-out facilities for six female alcoholics, Edinburgh had none. There were no beds in either city specifically for women with drinking problems or for ex-offenders in general. Furthermore, with the heavy demand for beds for the single homeless, hostels are not prepared to take bookings in advance from prison social workers attempting to smooth the path for prisoners about to be liberated. The ex-prisoner has to take her chance with the others — and if she has been black-listed by the hostels she has no chance at all. But most of the women who are turned away are refused shelter because the hostels are full, rather than because they themselves have previously been excluded for 'extreme' behaviour; for instance, between 1 January 1980 and 31 October 1980, 120 women were turned away from the 37-bedded Victoria Hostel in Edinburgh, 'the vast majority because the hostel was full, only one or two because they had been blacklisted' (Warden). Once they have been turned away from the few hostels there are, the women can either 'shack up with a man for the night' (Warden, Common Lodging House) or, if sufficiently sober, attempt to find a place in some old building, safe from other vagrants, men in general and the police.

It was suggested to me by several concerned individuals (including the police) that many homeless women never come to the notice of the public at all because, being too proud casually to share a man's bed for the night and being too frightened of people in general and men in particular to join the more gregarious vagrants, they literally hide themselves away. The drinking woman, however, has to mix to some extent with others in order to get alcohol — and a social life — and at the least she has to traverse the streets to get to the pub or to the off-licence. When she does she is prey to all kinds of male-predators — thieves and rapists in particular. Melissa had been assaulted and raped often enough to know the score:

'I wouldn't sit in George Square at night. I'd rather get

in somewhere (out of the road) where you feel safe — even though you're not safe. At least you're not sitting about and you're not an easy target for these men that are going about: "Well, come on, then, I'll gie ye a bed for the night." No way, that doesn't work with me. No.'

And if a woman known to be a homeless alcoholic is attacked in view of the police, they, according to Melissa, often turn a blind eye, seeing the affray as being nothing more than yet another of the drunken squabbles for which the vagrant alcoholics are notorious. 'That's the way some of them [the police] look at it' said Melissa 'because there *are* always fights and quarrels about this and that, whose turn it is to buy the drink, who's lying, that kind of thing.' Once the police *do* intervene the only agency that stands between the insensible or injured alcoholic and the police cell is the hospital.

'If they're drunk and incapable and not in the care of a proper person we wake them up and try to send them to hospital. They're no more willing to have them than we are. The problem is that there are no detox. centres in existence. Until someone else looks after them we will have to.' (Policeman No. 15, Glasgow)

'Often young doctors can't deal with them because they're very difficult to deal with, these people.' (Policeman No. 1, Glasgow)

'The Royal Infirmary won't take them if they're violent.' (Policeman No. 23, Edinburgh)

'The hospital doesn't want to know. We have to take them to hospital if they are unconscious but they just examine them and say, "Well, it's just drink" and they won't take them in.' (Policeman No. 8, Glasgow)

'Hospitals are good if they're quiet, but often drunks cause a lot of trouble. After treatment, if they're still drunk, the hospital phones us and asks us to take them.' (Policeman No. 16, Glasgow)

'A few years ago we had a detox. scheme, Ward 3 at the
Royal Edinburgh. The drunks used the detox. scheme as
a place to flop down so the hospital blacklisted them.
They blacklisted so many that it was a self-defeating
scheme.' (Policeman No. 26, Edinburgh)

So the police have to take in the unconscious, the violent
and in many cases the completely unhinged. Whether they
eventually decide to let them go or whether they present
them at court, the whole cycle soon starts up again. The
police I spoke with seemed resigned to the fact that in the
case of alcoholics they have once more been left to shovel
up the problems of a hypocritical and uncaring society.
Said Policeman No. 7 from Glasgow:

'I think too much is done to cover it up, to sweep it
under the carpet. Why not let them sit in George Square
if they're not causing any trouble? They're human beings
and they feel the basic human need to socialise. They're
as much entitled to sit there as anyone else.'

'A lot of people think we shouldn't bother with them but
it's the only protection they've got. I've been through all
this [research] before — it's just a paper exercise, they
won't do anything about it. You can't do anything about
the drink unless you look at their other problems, but
it's still a terrible indictment on this society that the police
have to lock them up in a cell and bring them to Court
because there's nowhere else for them to go.' (Policeman
No. 24, Edinburgh)

'Most of the females are detained for one or two hours —
for sobering-up, and then they're let out. The case is
reported to the Procurator Fiscal but we try not to keep
them if they have an address. Fourteen per cent of women
coming in for drunkenness are NFA and will drink themselves insensible, but others are more likely to commit
other offences. They have been in police custody so much
that all decency and morals have gone. If they're released
by the court they're back in the station within fourteen
days. At the end of the week they are getting money and

even if they get over the first time without drinking, they don't get over the second time of having money, and then they're back. In fact, if we don't see them after fourteen days we assume that they're either dead or back in Cornton Vale.' (Policeman No. 9, Glasgow)

Yet, at the 'moment' of prison the imprisonment of these women is neither an inevitable conclusion to an entirely penal process nor is it the ill-chance of a haphazard process. Despite official deprecation of the repeated imprisonment of recidivists with acute or chronic drinking problems there remain at least four major obstacles to their removal from the penal system:

(1) The complete absence of detoxification centres or other non-penal sanctuaries means that when a drunken woman is either endangering herself or being a nuisance to the public at large there is nothing for it but for the police to put her in a cell. Once they have taken her in, the police cannot detain a drunken woman overnight without charging her.

(2) There are still some officials in the criminal justice and penal systems who believe that prosecution and imprisonment can have a beneficial effect on recidivist alcoholic offenders.

(3) The women themselves have often been physically, emotionally and mentally debilitated to such an extent that they appear either incapable of, or unwilling to, fulfil the contractual conditions which most non-penal 'saving' organisations impose.

(4) The 'saving' organisations themselves have confronted the challenge of very limited resources by developing discursive and classificatory strategies which both constitute and discriminate between the 'treatable', the 'saveable' and the 'lost'.

The police do not want to deal with homeless drunks. It is neither a pleasant nor a rewarding job:

'Their clothing is cloaked with the excreta, drink and vomit of months. You wonder, "Is she going to choke on her vomit, or die of hypothermia?" If they die in the street no-one cares; if they die in the cells it's bad publicity.' (Policeman No. 1, Edinburgh)

'Drunks create problems and produce Meacherisms — you know, Michael Meacher and his figures of police-cell deaths which make it sound as if the police are killing people.' (Policeman No. 15, Glasgow)

Despite these disincentives to arrest, the police listed four main types of situation where they feel obliged to take some interventionary action against drunks.

(1) If the woman is unconscious or endangering herself by, for instance, walking about regardless of traffic danger.
(2) If the woman is interfering with 'respectables' or children.
(3) If there are complaints from businessmen or householders.
(4) If the woman has 'wandered' into a 'good' area, a tourist area or a railway or bus station.

Other factors which could affect the arrest rate are:

(1) the time of year, e.g. there are more complaints during the tourist season in Edinburgh; in Glasgow during the summer there are more 'drunken garden parties' amongst the alcoholic vagrants congregating at Glasgow Green.
(2) the 'tolerance' of individual police officers. Older and more experienced police officers claimed that they are less likely to arrest a drunk than their younger colleagues either because (a) they know it will do no good, or (b) being less nervous, they can more easily 'talk-round' the obstreperous drunk.
(3) the disturbances centring around 'the few wee shopkeepers who keep in large supplies of hair-lacquer and sell it to the winos.'

Seven of the thirty police officers interviewed said that they thought that in general the public were more shocked at seeing a woman drunk than a man but added that the public tend more often to think that a woman is just ill when in fact she is drunk. Regarding the apprehension of drunks the police were divided in opinion as to how much trouble they cause. Twelve of the police officers said that alcoholic offenders are no trouble at all but eighteen claimed that they cause a great deal of trouble, thirteen of the latter maintaining that generally the female inebriate causes much more trouble than the male. They complained that drunken female offenders are:

(1)   more likely to be verbally abusive;
(2)   less easy to 'talk round';
(3)   more likely to incline towards sexual exhibitionism;
(4)   dirtier than drunken men;
(5)   more likely to make accusations against the police;
(6)   more likely to 'become breaches of the peace'.

Two of the policemen mentioned that they are less willing to 'take language' from a woman and the only two policewomen interviewed also thought that women are more difficult to handle.

> 'I, personally, will accept language more readily from a man than from a woman, even if that is a bit sexist.' (Policeman No. 15, Glasgow)

> 'Women are bitchier. There are some bad, bad buggers about. I'd rather deal with a male drunk any day.' (Police-woman No. 21, Edinburgh)

If the woman is kept in the police cell overnight a report is made to the procurator fiscal. If the woman is then taken to court, the stipendiary magistrates and sheriffs find that, in the absence of drying-out facilities and of social workers willing to supervise them, Cornton Vale is the only place of safety for the female inebriate continually and publicly drinking herself into a state of either insensibility or incapacity. One of Glasgow's stipendiary magistrates (before whom ten of the drinking women interviewed had appeared at some time) gave a very concise statement of his sentencing policy in relation to alcoholic female offenders.

'We gaol women if they've had three alcohol-related convictions within a year. We do it then for their own health. At least in Cornton Vale they're off alcohol and really it's an act of charity to put them somewhere they'll be looked after. It keeps them alive, although the regulars come straight back and are in the court every two or three weeks. I can't see that the new Act [Criminal Justice Scotland Act 1980] will make much difference either. Whether they go to prison or not, they still won't be able to pay the fine which, incidentally, has been raised to £50.'

On the assumption that the number of female prisoners with drinking problems is unlikely to get smaller in the near future an Alcohol Project was inaugurated at Cornton Vale in 1979. The project lasts for four weeks and is attended on a daily full-time basis by women who are not deemed to be beyond help. During the first week the women and staff form small groups with the aim of 'gaining each other's trust'. They each make a frieze telling their own story and later act out situations involving someone who is drunk. The main emphasis in the early stages of the project is on what alcohol does to the body. After receiving talks from doctors and nurses they have group discussions on different aspects of alcohol-abuse. Towards the end it is hoped that deeper discussions will take place. Throughout the group discussions prison officers are encouraged to join in fully by talking about their own problems too.

Prisons are often criticised for not doing much for prisoners with drink problems. For prisoners serving short sentences of thirty, forty or sixty days, however, it is difficult to see what the prison *can* do other than provide the forum for discussion and information currently being provided by the Cornton Vale Alcohol Project. The main focus of criticism should be the *fact* of imprisonment rather than the prison regime itself. Prison officers can justifiably claim that they are the only ones who do anything for the alcoholic women whom nobody else wants. They are (also justifiably) resentful of suggestions that they should do more to 'rehabilitate' homeless offenders.

'We keep them alive, when no-one else will. That's what
we do.' (Prison Officer No. 10)

'How can we be expected to rehabilitate people who have
never had any background at all?' (Prison Officer No. 3)

'What have they got outside? They've got nothing. What
do we rehabilitate them *to*?' (Prison Officer No. 4)

Young prison officers involved in the Alcohol Project were
appalled to learn that after all their own intensive work on
the project there would be no back-up once the prisoners
were released.

'The officers in Cornton Vale have begun to ask what will
happen to the women when they go out. And we have to
tell them that there is absolutely nothing — no drying-out
facilities, no back-up facilities. The officers are becoming
very concerned.' (Director of the Edinburgh & District
Council on Alcoholism)

And well they might be. Lisa Lobell completed four weeks
on the Alcohol Project and was liberated during the period
of the research. Having nowhere else to go she returned to
the man who have previously beaten her up to such an extent
that she had lost an eye. Four days later she was convicted
for breach of the peace and returned to prison.

The policies of certain agencies, e.g. some DHSS officers
and social services departments, also militate against a change
of lifestyle for those who, during their prison sentences,
have decided at least to make an attempt to come off the
drink. At the end of a previous term of imprisonment Vivienne Vincent, for instance, had decided that a first step to
sobriety would be to leave her cohabitee. Her local social security office, however, refused to make separate payments to
her. Some social services departments refuse to allow women
places in hostels wholly or partly supported by them if the
woman is deemed to have come from outwith their area.
Thus, when after a score of telephone calls — ten in the day
before Melissa was released — the prison social worker had
eventually obtained Melissa Malcom a place in a 'dry' hostel,

the prison authorities had to agree to liberate her officially from Glasgow (rather than from Stirling) before the Strathclyde Social Services would allow her to take up the place.

Even when the woman is settled in suitable accommodation there is still sufficient police harassment of drunks, still a sufficient number of procurator fiscals, magistrates and sheriffs who believe that prison *is* the best place for the vagrant alcoholic offender to ensure that the slightest lapse into inebriety will lead once more to Cornton Vale. Both prisoners and prison officers were adamant in their beliefs that a change of police policy would be a key element in any concerted attempt to clear the prisons of vagrant alcoholics:

> 'If you want them to stop coming in here you would have to instruct the police to stop lifting them. Some of them have only to walk down the street to get lifted.' (Prison Officer No. 10)

Once the alcoholic women have been arrested, however, there is some evidence that certain fiscals still believe that imprisonment is the *best* way to deal with them. Mr XYZ, a procurator fiscal in central Scotland explained how he himself had come to accept this view:

> 'We have a person [whom] we have made it a rule to prosecute and she is up . . . if not three times a week at least once a week for "drunk and incapable". When I first came, I saw the list and I said to the other depute, "Look, what is the point?" And he said, "The point is that she gets fined and gets less money to do it. We're not interested in her record, nobody's interested in her record. She's got a record, we all know it, but the fact is, if we bring her in and fine her £6, that's £6 less and in a way we are stopping her from drinking." Now, that might sound harsh but that's the way to look at it. That's £6 less for her to get drunk on and ruin herself even further.'

Mr ABC, a fiscal from just outside Edinburgh, felt both defeated by, and punitive towards, alcoholics:

'To be perfectly honest, the drunk and incapable I get
have been drunk and incapable for a long, long time and
will be drunk and incapable for a long, long time. As far
as I can see the only thing they really don't like is going
to prison because they will not get drink there and they
will not get any sympathy when they don't get drink.'
(Moody and Tombs, 1982:74)

Yet I met very few officials who felt distinctly punitive
towards recidivist drunken and alcoholic offenders. The
police themselves most frequently claimed that their own
response was determined by two main considerations: a
humanitarian concern for the incapable; a duty to respond
to public complaint about nuisance. At each stage of the
penal processing of drunken and alcoholic offenders, however, the agencies concerned pass the buck — they either
blame someone else or claim that the next agency in line
will be able to remedy the situation. Again and again sheriffs
justified the imprisonment of alcoholic vagrants on the
grounds that imprisonment would bring these women to the
attention of the social services whence they would receive
help. And again and again, also, both prison officers and
prisoners indicated that they were better appraised of the
reality of the situation; they knew that for the alcoholic
offender imprisonment is but one moment (though a not
inconsequential one) in a downward spiral.

'You can watch the short-term recidivist going right
down. We know through experience that she won't be
able to make it on the outside. The down and outs go
on until their sixties, when old age takes its toll.' (Prison
Officer No. 1)

At fifty-nine, Mandy MacDonald also talked from experience:

'If you're "no fixed abode", it's prison. You come out,
you're still "no fixed abode"; it's prison.'

No fixed abode! Without motivation! Inarticulate! Disordered! Down and out! Beyond help! These are the terms

that were used again and again to describe Cornton Vale's habitual drunken offenders. Outwith family, sociability, femininity and adulthood, the women were also seen to be both beyond the help and outwith the remit of the welfare and saving professions. It was in this No Woman's Land, this space where the women were seen to be beyond recognition, that some of them had constructed an imaginary independence, an independence constructed from the debris of the competing and contradictory demands which had assailed them since childhood, an independence ironically dependent upon a deep bitterness and contempt both for social hypocrisy and their own peculiar response to it. It was this imaginary independence which effectively defined the space wherein they were beyond the reach or remit of welfare — without motivation, disordered, down, out and beyond help. It was within this space also that they were most without hope, for it was there where they most felt themselves that they were most often seen as being beyond recovery both by themselves and by others.

Again and again the women expressed a puzzlement that their best attempts at self-help were continually being thwarted. Housing departments were unsympathetic, hospitals were sceptical about their claims that they wished to dry out and hostels were full of people 'no better' than themselves. At the same time, however, many of the women also saw quite clearly that the perennial exhortations to reform were made under material conditions which made the likelihood of a change of life-style improbable. In private, prison officers agreed. Indeed, even the prison officer who told me that she was prepared 'to try religion on women who are at rock-bottom' added, almost in the same breath:

> 'Though of course most of them are very unrealistic and will keep on about wanting a house and a job when they get out.'

The women's responses alternated between amused astonishment and contemptuous astonishment at the sheer inappropriateness of some of the help offered. Vivienne Vincent saw the funny side:

'This elderly woman came — they come to see the Catholics. Well, *I'm* partially deaf, and *she* was partially deaf and she couldn't hear me and I couldn't hear her either. Then, in my circumstances, the position I'm in, I don't want to hear all this carry on about God. We all know there's somebody up there — but there's someone down here and all — know what I mean? She says to me "Vivienne, you've lost your faith." I thinks, "I'll lose my head if you keeps this up."'

Likewise Olive O'Brien had not been very impressed by her doctor's advice about her drinking problem. She told me: 'He said, "Open the window, lay on the bed and move your arms and legs about." I think he's daft himself.' Others were bitter, debilitated and confused. Vivienne Vincent explained:

'There's no way out. Put it this way, we're down and outs. You've no address, or you're in a model lodging house — or there are only two hostels, you canny get into them. Then there's the Sally-Ann. I was taken down there years ago when they thought I was an alcoholic. To this day I still don't know what I am.'

Others were harsh in their self-knowledge, their self-criticism, and their self-contempt. Listen to Melissa again:

'We're in here because we haven't got the guts to face-out what's in front of us outside. The biggest majority of the women drink because they cannot cope with their problems outside and they come in here. It's all right for a wee while but when it comes to going out that gate they're terrified. It's all right sitting and laughing and joking: "Oh! the morrow night, I'll be sitting in the pub having a couple of Carlies," but you know within yourself "that lassie's feared." That's why I want to get back into society, to live as a normal human being, not a zombie.'

But prison degrades even further. Kirsty King and Mandy MacDonald saw a direct relationship between their 'down and out' status outside the prison and their jobs as garbage collectors within the prison:

'Us who're in for drink, we're in the bins.' (Kirsty)

'They treat us like dirt. They are degrading us even more.
It's degrading looking in bins for dowts because you're
worried if you haven't got a smoke at night.' (Mandy)

As they talked, the women oscillated between blaming
themselves and blaming others. But the others were gradually
being ousted from the women's world. Only by building up
barriers against others who might reject them could Melissa
and the other women maintain any self-respect. After all,
the drinking women saw themselves as being outwith criminality:

'Personally, I'm not interested in what the general public
think of me because there's far too many serious offences
being let off.' (Mandy)

'If anyone says to me "where are you staying?" I just say
"Glasgow". I don't tell them I'm skippering or anything
like that. I don't care if they know or if they don't know,
it's immaterial to me. 'Cos one day it might come to them.
I'd like to see them bloody coping with it. They're not all
bad people who're skippering. There are worse than us
staying in fancy houses.' (Melissa)

At the same time the drinking women were too proud to
court criticism from those others who either did not 'know'
or did not 'understand about this side' of their lives. This
isolated them even from those who might want to be friendly:

'I've let lots of people down. Then I don't go back. I
never show anyone any embarrassment. I keep my distance from the door when I've got a drink in me. I put
the barriers up again.' (Melissa)

Eliza Eastwood expressed the same sentiments:

'I don't bother with friends. I've never told them about
this side, you see. I think that if your mind's strong
you're better to keep this side to yourself. I'd never

go near my daughter or my sister with a drink in me.'

On the other hand not one of the women claimed that their drinking pals were congenial to them. I asked Melissa:

Pat Carlen: 'Do you like the people you mix with when you're drinking?'
Melissa: 'I don't. I hate the sight of them. I don't know why I go back and talk to them because half the time I can't be bothered having a conversation with them. I feel I shouldn't be in with that class of people. You get so you don't trust anyone, not even yourself.'

Kirsty expressed a similar distaste for the company she kept:

'I'm alone outside. I've no friends. You don't get a chance to meet people properly. You don't go to the right places. We go to all the dingiest pubs you can find and you meet people like yourself that you don't get on with. Of course, you start argy-bargying with them. *You* don't like *them* and *they* don't like each other, anyhow.'

Viewing themselves like this the women saw little reason why others should view them differently either:

'It's not so easy getting a job. They wouldn't want someone who's got a record of being a thief and drinking every night running round their home, would they?' (Bernice)

'People start wondering, "Well what's wrong with her, that she can't live in a normal house?" You look odd in the street. And it's true. People will not put up with you. You want to live the way you want to live and people's not going to accept that; they want you to live like *they* live.' (Melissa)

Homeless, the women *cannot* live like other people; wanting their freedom from the contradictions wherein others have continuously tried to contain them, the women refuse to go into hostels, to compromise their imaginary independence. For they have not gained the independence for which they yearn — the freedom from the competing demands of others. The others continually crowd back. Sometimes family intrudes:

> 'I'd like a wee house of my own because of my daughter; when she's old enough she might want to come to see me and I don't want to be lying in any old building, being drunk or anything like that. I want to be able to open my door to her.' (Melissa)

Sometimes intimations of the lives of others intrude:

> 'At night, when you're in your cell you think about what other people's doing, how others are making it — working, a bit in the bank, going away on holiday. And you think "Och! I was made for something better."' (Kirsty)

And, always, the bottle intrudes. In the place whence the others have been ousted stands the drink which, once, in the beginning, merely signified an independence from male-related domesticity. A hopelessness sets in, a hopelessness ameliorated neither by public policy towards habitual drunken offenders nor by the contradictory discourses within which the Scots have always celebrated their ambivalence towards alcohol (see Burton, 1983). So, said Kirsty, 'When I say my prayers at night I say "God Almighty! *Is* there a God?"'

In its 1978 *Memorandum to the House of Commons Expenditure Committee* the Howard League wearily remarked that 'the arguments against sending habitual drunken offenders to prison are so well-known that we do not intend to repeat them.' The fact remains, however, that, notwithstanding the familiarity of the arguments against the imprisonment of habitually drunken offenders, many of them still finish up in prison. Officials are so familiar with both the arguments against imprisoning them *and* the regularity with which they *are* imprisoned that they see a certain inevitability in the process. Indeed, so familiar are prison officials with the disjunction between the rhetoric and the reality that, in the same year as the Howard League declined to document yet again the arguments against the imprisonment of these

offenders, the *Report on Prisons in Scotland 1978* remarked
that 'Alcoholism, *as one would expect,* is commonly diagnosed in admissions to prison' (my emphasis). Yet there *are*
officials who believe that in the 1980s the public would *not*
expect to find the prisons still crowded-out with vagrants,
alcoholics and other physically and emotionally debilitated
people. Policemen and prison officers, for instance, were
united in their condemnation of a social system which,
seemingly, can only make a punitive response to the alcoholic
and the psychologically or emotionally disturbed person.
Prison Officer No. 13 summed up the general view when
she replied in answer to my open question, 'Is there anything
else you think should be known about the situation of
women offenders?'

> 'Yes, that alcoholic and mentally ill people *have* to come
> to prison because that's the best we can do. It's a terrible
> slur on our society.'

Yet the judges have not supported the notion that the 'penal
system should take over where treatment fails' (Hancock,
1977). Contributing to the book *Alcoholism: New Knowledge
and Responses* (Edwards and Grant, 1977), D.N. Hancock
described the 1976 appeal court case of the 'Flowerpot Lady'
(*R.* v. *Clarke*, 1976).

> A young woman from a deprived background and with a
> history of violent offences had an eighteen-month prison
> sentence quashed and a £2 fine substituted. The woman
> had thrown some flower pots at the police when they were
> called to a hospital and she refused to leave. The doctors
> said she had a gross personality defect but could not be
> treated in hospital. The Probation Service said it could not
> cope with her. . . . The Appeal Court said in over-ruling
> the original sentence:
> 'There is some evidence that the attitude of the social
> services was, "We cannot cope with this woman, let the
> courts cope with her." The first thing to be said, and said
> very firmly indeed, is that her Majesty's courts are not
> dustbins into which the social services can sweep difficult
> members of the public. . . . The National Health Service

and the Social Services cannot cope with a woman of
this type who does not require treatment (so it is said). . . .
This court has no intention of filling that gap by sending
people to prison when a prison sentence is wholly inappropriate. We ask ourselves, "What was the appropriate
sentence for breaking a flower pot?" The answer is a fine
of £2.' (Hancock, 1977)

Maybe so. But with all due respect to the learned judge, it
is necessary to point out that an 'appropriate' judicial disposition in terms of classical justice is only 'appropriate' if it is
accepted that the defendant should have been in the court
in the first place. After all, as the Director of the Edinburgh
and District Council for Alcoholism pointed out, 'It does
not mean that because [these women] are not going to
prison that they are getting any other kind of help.' Rather,
as we saw in the last chapter, once women have suffered loss
of job, home, friends and family they are on a downward
spiral of less and less eligibility — for housing, hostel accommodation and hospital treatment. The strangeness of manner
and behaviour which at this stage so often signals the now
complete independence of the drinking women from the
contradictory definitions of femininity, sociability and adulthood imposed on them by institutional others signifies to the
saving organisations that not only are the women without
motivation to give up drink but also that they are unsuitable
both as social work clients *and* as hospital patients. A very
specific terrain of professional discourse enables the welfare
agencies to justify the allocation of their slender resources
to the cases from which they can expect the greatest returns
in terms of the social gains to be gleaned from the client's
personal regeneration. In fact, as is only to be expected
during an economic recession, the saving organisations
become more interested in saving money than in saving
people. Said the Director of the Edinburgh and District
Council on Alcoholism: 'Only if you could say that it would
cost less to the ratepayers would you get the full range of
facilities for those with alcohol problems. It's money that
talks up here.'

Such limits to social philanthropy are, of course, neither
new nor unexpected. As Karel Williams (1981) has recently

argued: 'from the 1860s onwards the theme of "splitting" the deserving from the undeserving is to be found everywhere.' But what is interesting about the contemporary classification of persons with alcohol and/or emotional problems is that the immediate evaluation is not simply a moral one. What is constructed is not a calculus for reckoning welfare eligibility in terms of moral *desert* but a calculus for measuring either welfare or clinical worthiness in terms of the defendant's/client's/patient's moral *capacity* to respond to welfare intervention or medical treatment. And it could be argued, of course, that doctors *should* only treat those for whom they can reasonably expect the treatment to be beneficial. But, in the case of the women defined as either 'alcoholics without motivation' or as 'women with personality disorders' the saving professions are not only saying that their condition defies *treatment*, rather they are saying that their condition defies *recognition*. Where then can the women go? In asking for medical reports the courts have indicated an unwillingness to credit them with criminal intent. The clinic will not credit them with a recognisable illness. 'These are the people that NOBODY wants' (Governor of Cornton Vale; Policeman; Social Worker). Degraded beyond recognition they are derelict. In or out of prison, they are living witnesses to the play of contradictory discourses which facilitate their exclusion from welfare and treatment.

Concomitant with the increasing costs of incarcerating the criminal, the mentally ill and the inebriate has been the growth in the numbers and powers of the saving professions. Nowadays, defence lawyers, doctors, psychiatrists, probation officers, local authority social workers and voluntary workers all have a mandated interest in saving at least *some* defendants from the penal consequences of the judicial stare. At the same time they all have a vested interest in defining *some* potential clients as being beyond their remit. Even policemen define alcoholic vagrants as being beyond both criminality and salvation. In police discourse there is neither a *custodial* nor a *saving* space for the habitual drunken offender.

'We don't want them. It's not really a crime, is it? They come in and take up space in police cells which could be taken up with criminals.' (Policeman No. 29, Glasgow)

'You can't think you've maybe stopped someone from getting into further trouble like you can with juveniles or the ordinary decent chap who's gone on a binge and needs a shock to stop him getting that bad again.' (Policeman No. 23, Glasgow)

We saw in Chapter Six how overburdened social workers reject some clients on a straight cost-benefit analysis, which process, ironically, ensures that those most in need become those least eligible for help. In the specific case of habitual drunken offenders the saving professions have developed clinical discourses which ensure that homeless and habitual drunken offenders are beyond *everybody's* remit. And the guardians of the treatment sanctuaries have perfected these principles of exclusion at the same time as they have enlarged their potential clientele by making the people of Scotland more aware that they are *all* potential victims of the sacred bevy. The result is not unexpected. The charitable organisations and the statutory agencies that once focused their gaze upon the wayward and debauched working classes have now found that the 'problem drinkers' of the middle classes (though they can indeed be equally debauched) are more likely than their working-class counterparts to contact the saving agencies whilst still having the material means which are seen as being desirable prerequisites to salvation. For not only are they more likely to make contact while they still have jobs, homes and friends, the middle-class 'problem drinkers' also have easier access to the educated language which is seen to signify 'insight' and 'motivation'. Furthermore, because they are materially better off, the middle-class 'problem drinkers' can concentrate on gaining 'insight' and 'motivation' in comfort. The lower working-class drinker or the already-homeless alcoholic, however, will have more material problems. When *she* pesters the social worker about practical problems such as accommodation, treatment, etc., it is much more likely that she will be defined as being 'unrealistic' rather than as having 'insight', as being 'manipulative' rather than 'motivated'. The Governor of Cornton

Vale summed up the current position when she said:

> 'Nowadays everybody is much more aware of the dangers
> of drink. Now that more and more people in every sphere
> of life are having drink problems the danger is that those
> are the people that are going to be dealt with and our
> people are just going to be left out again.'[2]

Certainly general agencies argue that the presence of habitual drunkards offends other, non-alcoholic clients. The very
sight of drunken people hanging around an agency can deter
other potential clients from approaching that agency at all.
SACRO (Edinburgh) was particularly aware of the problem.
Situated in Edinburgh's Grassmarket, traditional meeting
place for alcoholic and other homeless people, it always has
its doors locked, so that the sobriety of unknown callers can
be assessed before they are admitted. Said Sacro's community
worker:

> 'We can't cope with them — no-one wants them. There
> are hostels for them but even they don't always want
> them. That's why the new Director of Sacro is looking
> for new premises — so as to get out of the Grassmarket
> altogether.'

Other agencies cannot hope that they will be able to distance
themselves physically from habitual drunken offenders. When
the police take unconscious drunks to the hospital, when
desperate people with either acute or chronic alcoholic conditions present themselves at the welfare agencies, the hostels
and the hospitals, the institutions' main defences are discursive ones. Gradually, the failure of the institutions to treat is
in itself seen as evidence of the alcoholic's lack of motivation
to be cured; the failure of the hospitals to diagnose — that is,
their failure to impose order via classification — is in itself
seen as evidence of a pre-existent *disorder*, a disorder which
is, none the less, recognisable through the professional lens
of psychiatry as 'personality disorder'.

If the 'alcoholic' or 'disturbed' offender is to be saved,
reality has to be faced — but it has to be the reality of the
experts and the saviours! Realities presented by the clients

themselves are seen as 'manipulation', adherence to their own point of view is seen as evidence of 'lack of motivation'. The warden of an Alcohol Recovery Unit in Edinburgh explained the policy:

> 'We cannot take people straight from prison. They have to have a period outside to show that they're motivated. Alcoholics are very manipulative. If they listen to any reality that we present, then they're motivated. If they storm out of the door then they're not motivated.'

When the material realities of individual offenders are so extreme that they are more often than not opposed to those of the experts, *then* these offenders are likely to be categorised not only as being 'alcoholic' but also as being 'disordered'. Once seen as being 'disordered' they are by definition beyond the place where they can have motivation. A recent Scottish survey (Woodside, 1976:29) described the reasoning:

> 'The survey demonstrates that the main problem both for the Court and the psychiatric service is the psychopathic offender, usually incorrigible and unresponsive to any form of treatment. Next came the social inadequates, often of limited intelligence, who form the hard core of petty offenders regularly appearing before the court. For individuals in both categories alcohol abuse depletes what little self-control and judgement they may have. It is not surprising that the psychiatrists were sparing with their treatment recommendations.'

Additionally, it is also thought by some that, in those cases where the candidate for treatment is already known to the screening agency, higher and higher standards are required as evidence of 'motivation'. Certainly this seemed to be suggested by the case of Mr Nildefind, a homeless alcoholic whom I accompanied to the Royal Edinburgh Hospital on 21 November 1980.

Mr Nildefind was an alcoholic who had been calling regularly at SACRO's headquarters in the Grassmarket for a

period of three weeks, asking them to get him some
treatment. The community worker had made him several
appointments at the Royal Edinburgh Hospital but although Mr N. had kept them (no small thing for him —
community worker) the doctor who had seen him had
said that on each occasion he had been drunk and that
she couldn't *'make head nor tail of him'*. On November
20th the doctor had told the community worker that
once Mr N. presented himself in a sober state at the
hospital consideration would be given to the possibility
of his being admitted for treatment. Each time Mr N.
had been told by the doctor that he was drunk he had
returned to SACRO protesting his sobriety and the community worker there told me that in her opinion Mr N.
was not drunk, 'certainly stinking of drink, vomit and
urine, but not drunk.' After her telephone conversation
with the hospital doctor on November 20th SACRO's
community worker had told Mr N. that if he presented
himself sober at the SACRO offices at 9.30 the following
morning he would be taken to the hospital and would
indeed be produced as sober. At 9.30 on the 21st November I was at SACRO when Mr N. turned up to keep the
appointment. The community worker said that she wanted
to keep him there a few hours to assess his state and we
therefore arranged that I should take him in a taxi to the
hospital at 12 noon. (After several telephone calls to the
hospital it was established that Mr N. would be seen upon
arrival — though not by the doctor who knew his case.)
When we arrived at the hospital we were seen almost
immediately. (Mr Nildefind insisted that I went in with
him for both interviews with the doctor.) Mr N. was
questioned by the doctor about his medical history and
at the end the doctor said, 'We have no spare beds in any
case but as I haven't got your notes here I will go off and
make some inquiries about them.' After a twenty-minute
absence the doctor returned and addressed Mr Nildefind
thus: 'I've found out that you've been an in-patient before.
You've had several chances and at the moment, even if I
wanted to take you in, I couldn't as I have no bed free.
Go home, come back in three days and show me that you
really want to keep off the drink and I'll reconsider your

case.' I explained that Mr N. had no home, that if I took
him out I would have to leave him on the Grassmarket
and that he would be bound to drink. I pointed out that
Mr Nildefind had, after three weeks of trying, actually
arrived at the hospital sober. How could he now be put to
further test? Doctor: 'But he's got to show motivation.
He's had many chances. Now he's got to show that he
really wants to change.' We all sat in silence for five
minutes. Doctor: 'All right, I'll take him in.' (To Mr N.)
'But it's only because these people have shown so much
concern . . .' It was arranged that the doctor would leave
Mr Nildefind in reception until 2 p.m. when he would
take him to the ward. Because I had another appointment
I had to leave the hospital, having been assured by the
receptionist that she had seen Mr Nildefind there, 'nearly
every day for the last three weeks. He's no trouble. No,
he's always sober.' I reported my 'success' to SACRO. On
January 15th 1981 I visited SACRO again. Community
Worker: 'They didn't admit Mr Nildefind after all. He
arrived back here at 3 p.m. on the same day and said that
they had decided NOT to admit him. He said that on his
way back he had decided that he might as well have a
drink and get on the road again.' At 5 p.m. on the same
day a doctor at the Royal Edinburgh Hospital had telephoned to say that they had decided not to take Mr Nildefind because the nurse had smelled drink on him when she
was getting him ready for bed. [My emphasis]

Later I recounted the story of Mr Nildefind to the Director
of the Edinburgh and District Council on Alcoholism who
remarked:

> 'I'm glad you saw it like that. "It is a matter of priorities."
> Is that what they told you? They used to operate a black
> list (denied, of course!) of alcoholic vagrants whom they
> wouldn't see.'

And her reply fitted in with what Edinburgh and Glasgow
policemen and the women in Cornton Vale had already told
me. Women prisoners had said that 'there is no way you can
get into hospital once you're homeless'; policemen had

remarked that 'you cannot force treatment on people who do not want it'; and the Governor of Cornton Vale had said that 'at a certain stage the only way they can regain their dignity is in a discipline setting.' As the officials of the saving agencies talked further the lynchpin of the specific discursive formation which effects the continued imprisonment of the habitual drunken offender became more apparent — the conflation of the notions of civil liberty: 'You cannot force treatment on people', with the professional assessment of motivation: 'if they do not want it'. However, this teleological assessment (based on the women's 'down and out' condition), that habitual drunken offenders do not really want treatment has effects. It instantly disposes of the obstructive dissymmetry between civil liberty and welfare intervention: the person who, being free to choose, appears to be incapable of choosing sobriety, puts herself beyond the social domain where civil liberty and welfare are deemed to have constitutive effect. Thereafter only a discipline setting is deemed appropriate for the 'puir creeturs' — officially outwith society, officially outwith motivation and, ultimately and officially, outwith personality.

By way of conclusion listen to Melissa:

'My adopted mother died when I was eight and that was it as far as I was concerned. I went to several children's homes, then back to my real mother when I was twelve. When my stepfather "interfered" with me I was sent to an auntie in Ayrshire. When I ran away from there I was put in an approved school. I didn't get into any trouble with the police until I was twenty. I had two children by then, and I'd a corporation house. But one day I came home and some people I knew had broken in and stolen all my things. I was so disgusted I just went and threw my keys in the Clyde. I didn't drink then, either. I didn't drink until I was twenty and that was what landed me in trouble. I wanted to join the police force, then I wanted to join the army. Well, when I got into trouble with the police, that was me knackered, the boot. In fact, I finished myself for good. I was constantly in trouble, all the time. I was only out of prison three days at a time and then I was back in, doing thirty days; back in, doing sixty days; back in, doing three months. And I was skippering all the time. Even when I was out of trouble I was skippering.

I'm a bit of a loner, you see. I'm not a woman who goes about hunting for men. You might see me drinking in their company but that's as far as it bloody goes. I don't pop into bed with them. I've met a lot of men who want you just for the one thing. They want to make a cunt of you. I know. I was raped when I was twenty and I was raped a couple of years ago by a lot of men; two of them got sent to gaol for it. You can take just so much violence towards your own person, then you retaliate. I'm fed up with getting battered, and when you get fed up with it you retaliate.

I see no end to this road I'm on, no turning, no crossroads even. I didn't leave home. I was in a children's home. If, when I go out, I could get a wee house I think this would solve a lot of my problems and get me my independence. Nobody to ask you where you've been and what you're at coming in at this time, and who was you wi'? It's not a lot to ask for in this world, but it's like asking for a million dollars.

Three weeks after I left here last time I was in Intensive Care in the Royal Infirmary. I was unconscious for fifty-six hours. You see, they've no after-care place when you leave here. They've got more for men than women. You go into George Square in Glasgow any day of the week and you'll see women skippering. The number of women skippering in Glasgow is amazing. Aye, they drink. They have to. It's just to forget their problems. You cannae skipper on sobriety, you cannae, it's impossible, you'd be insane. You've got to have that drink to get oblivion. The least wee thing keeps you awake, so there's no relaxation, no security.

At the first half of a sentence you don't bother so much. But when it comes to the end, that's when you start worrying. Half the lassies in here cannae face what's waiting for them when they get out. Reality is out there, not in here. You wonder what's out there for you and, I don't know, you've got a feeling that you don't want to leave this place. You've got to go, though. I wouldn't want to make this my home. I want to stay away from this place as much as possible. They only send you here for a bath.

I've got to think about somewhere to stay the night I get out. The Social Security's not giving you money as a down payment on a flat. Where in hell are you going to get a flat with £17 a week? You're supposed to perform miracles! There's only three hostels for women in Glasgow and I'm supposed to get into the Simon House. It's run by wee lassies. They came here to see me and said I could go there when they have a vacancy. It might be this year, next year or the year after. I could be dead and buried by then. That would solve a lot of problems, wouldn't it?

Women's got a raw deal. It comes down to that. A lot of people give up the fight and they depend on this place. There's still fight in me. I don't need this place. I don't depend on it. Believe you me, I've starved and all that outside and I've done without, but no way would I give my body away to a man for money. Maybe that gives the impression I couldn't care less whether I'm skippering or not but, deep down inside, I'm really sick of it. I started very young at skippering and I was ignorant. Now I'm thirty-one and still ignorant. Christ knows where I'll be at forty! . . . if I see forty.'

Melissa's story is an individual odyssey of the gradual transformation of severe social problems into psychological and physical problems (and vice versa) until problem overlays problem in a pastiche of ungraspable cause and effect. Melissa's story is also microcosmic; the same distillation, transformation and displacement occurs at the national level too. In contemporary Scottish discourse, the most contradictory and dispersed elements of Scottish culture can be conflated, distilled and displaced on to the bottle. The following extract, from a booklet published by the Scottish Health Education Unit, indicates that even in an official discourse the historically ambivalent attitude of the Scots to their drinking can result in the 'bevy' being elevated to the realms of the sacred.

It is only necessary to consider the widespread use of alcohol for ceremonial purposes to realise how fundamental its symbolic function is in our society. Almost all really important events (births, christenings, weddings, funerals) tend to be linked to the deliberately ceremonial consumption of alcohol. Our cultural heritage puts more than a utilitarian value upon drinking on such occasions. It is not merely to increase sociability, but to bolster, sustain and revitalise the sense of integration of the family unit. Perhaps even more important than the open acknowledgement of the pre-eminence of alcohol on such ritualised occasions, is the way that a host of symbolic functions relating to its use have permeated all spheres of our life. Alcohol . . . can reach across boundaries of race, colour and creed, or it can create new boundaries where none existed before. . . . There are many reasons why drinking should play such a disproportionately important part in the cultural life of Scotland. It has been suggested [Neill, 1975] that alcohol consumption rates tend to be particularly high where there is (a) social pressure to imbibe (b) inconsistent or non-existent social sanctions against excessive drinking (c) drinking outside a family or religious setting and (d) ambivalence towards moderate drinking. All these conditions are fulfilled in Scotland today. When they are viewed in the context of a rigorously enforced protestant ethic, a fierce and sometimes embittered patriotism and a comparatively inimical climate, it is easy to see how the functional aspects of drinking behaviour have become inextricably tangled with a host of compensatory and guilt-provoking feelings. These have acquired separate symbolic associations and have served to make drinking an activity qualitatively of considerable importance to the self-esteem of the individual and of the nation. *When you take a drink, you are not simply consuming a measurable quantity of ethanol, which will produce a predictable pattern of bio-chemical and behavioural changes. You are also participating in an act which society, and you, have invested with a myriad of special meanings.* . . . Drinking, like sex, is a very special kind of activity. Its symbolic value and the importance that the individual attaches to his performance is in direct proportion to the value and importance accorded to that activity by society itself.' (Scottish Health Education Unit, 1976, emphasis in original)

There are however increasing signs that Scotland's economic and symbolic investment in drink is having diminishing social returns:

> 'It has been estimated that at least one in ten families in Scotland suffer from the ill-effects of alcohol dependence . . . probably 120,000 people suffer *directly* from a drinking problem and 500,000 indirectly.' (Edinburgh and District Council on Alcoholism pamphlet, 1980)

Furthermore,

> "threequarters of all men and half of all women in Scotland are regular drinkers." (Scottish Health Education Unit, Pamphlet, 1980) . . . and, although the stereotype of the skid-row alcoholic or meths-drinking vagrant represents only a tiny fraction of the total alcoholic population of Scotland, possibly as little as 2% . . . the number of women alcoholics presenting for treatment appears to be increasing at a proportionally faster rate than the men.' (Scottish Health Education Unit, 1976)

Given that there is nowadays in Scotland a marginally more permissive (though still ambivalent) attitude towards women drinking, and given, too, that there are so many women already bearing the burden of their men's drinking excesses, it is not surprising that the number of Scottish women who admit to drinking problems continues to increase. Indeed, if, as recent research suggests, women's physiological tolerance of alcohol is much less than men's (Bell *et al.*, 1968; Ghodse and Tregenza, 1980) then Scottish women, in a society which places so much value on the (now medically recognised) *masculine* feat of holding one's drink, are at a double disadvantage. It is now evident that, both for *cultural* and for *physiological* reasons, women in Scotland are severely disadvantaged in relation to, and by their men's relationship with, Scotland's sacred 'bevy'. Women, however, are trained to cope with disadvantage. Just as they cope with economic deprivation and their disadvantaged position in the family so — somehow — do most Scottish working-class women cope with alcohol and its related problems. Others fail — or rebel

— spectacularly. Those are the women who, of all Scotland's female drinkers, turn up at Cornton Vale again and again and again. For the authorities, and often for the women themselves, each return to prison signifies another failure, furnishes further proof that, as recidivist prisoners, they are 'without motivation' to change. The temporary classification, 'disorderly', gradually ossifies into the more permanent 'disordered'; the 'drinking woman' disappears and the emergent 'vagrant alcoholic' or 'derelict' is seen as untreatable. 'Disordered' and 'untreatable' the women are also seen as being beyond the remit of the treatment agencies, without hope and beyond recognition.

8 Down, out, disordered and *still* in prison

'Was she always mad, or did the world send her mad with its prudery, hypocrisy and unkindness?' (Fay Weldon, 1978)

Down, out and disordered

From the seventeenth century onwards the various categories of first madness and then mental illness have alternatively, and variously, resulted in the exclusion, the treatment and/or the disciplining of those whose behaviour has been seen to warrant medico-judicial intervention (Foucault:1976, 1978; Scull, 1979; Ignatieff, 1978; Mathiesen, 1980; and Williams, 1981). Contemporary studies and reports still regularly deplore both the continued incarceration of 'mentally disordered' offenders in penal institutions and the 'revolving door' syndrome (Pitman and Gordon, 1958) which shuttles them back and forth between mental hospital, common-lodging house and prison in a continuous round of treatment, discipline, dereliction and punishment (see, for example: Rollin, 1969; Butler Report, 1974; May Report, 1979 and Prins, 1980 — which is to name but a few!) In 1981 the national Chairman of the Prison Officers' Association for England and Wales stated in exasperation that 'there are a number of people in prison who should not be there ... the particular bug that I carry round with me [being] the people who are mentally-handicapped in one way or another' (NACRO, 1981a). In the same year, and stressing the applicability of that statement to Scotland, the General Secretary of the Scottish Prison-Officers' Association emphasised to me that 'it's now general throughout the service, the mental patient/prisoner question.' Throughout 1980 and 1981, in fact, there were numerous newspaper headlines about crises in the prisons. Those years witnessed, too, the unusual spectacle of prison governors publicly *demanding* that the prison population be reduced. In 1980, for instance, the Governor of Winson Green Prison, Birmingham, was interviewed for the *New Statesman* and claimed that (amongst many others who should not be there) patients from psychiatric units; 'social cripples and inadequates' definitely should not be in his prison (*New Statesman*, 19 September 1980). In November 1981 the Governor of Wormwood Scrubs Prison wrote his famous 'penal dustbin' letter to *The Times* and in the public debate which that letter provoked the plight of the 'severely disturbed' prisoner was once again highlighted.

Certainly at the 'ground level' of the courts and the prisons Scottish judicial and penal personnel were acutely aware of the problem of the 'mentally abnormal' offender. Eleven of the fifteen sheriffs interviewed stated that they were uneasy about having to send so many severely disturbed women to prison 'because there is no alternative'. Seven of the ten prison officers formally interviewed spontaneously mentioned that there were in the prison women who appeared to be so 'disturbed' that a lay person would most probably deem them to be 'mad' rather than 'bad', more deserving of treatment than of punishment. For, although the sheriffs and the prison officers had some difficulty in defining this group because they knew that their own lay descriptions were at variance with, and had already been denied by, those official and clinical ones authorized by psychiatry, they also knew that, at any one time, around two-thirds of the women in Cornton Vale are likely to have histories of mental illness. In 1979, for instance, of a total of 1,123 admissions, 881 had histories of mental illness (Govenor, in private communication). At the moment of prison, however, mental illness is denied. 'If they are diagnosed as being mentally ill' said the Governor, 'then no way do they come in here.' How, then, is it that these women, previously seen to be 'mentally ill', presently seen as being 'very disturbed indeed', arrive at the prison? How is it that, at the moment of prison, they are temporarily stripped of the excusing condition of 'mental illness' and, for the moment clothed instead with the *disciplinary* needs of the 'disordered'? The *enabling* discourse, that is the discourse which effectively transforms the diagnostic clinical gaze into the disciplinary judicial stare, is both a compression and a dispersion of all those definitional conditions and effects which cluster around the related concepts of 'personality disorder' and 'anti-social personality disorder'.

The General Register Office's *Glossary of Mental Disorders* (1968) defines *personality disorder* thus:

> This term refers to a group of more or less well-defined anomalies or deviations of personality which are not the result of psychosis or any other illness. The differentiation of these personalities is to some extent arbitrary and the reference to a given group will depend initially on the relative predominance of one or other group of character traits.

This definition, depending as it does upon a socio-medical distinction between deviation and pathology is presented as being morally neutral. Not so the same glossary's definition of *anti-social personality disorder*:

> This term should be confined to those individuals who offend against society, who show a lack of sympathetic feeling and whose behaviour is not readily modifiable by experience including punishment. They may tend to abnormally aggressive and seriously irresponsible conduct. (General Register Office, 1968:17)

Even more luridly moralistic is the definition of anti-social personality disorder which is offered by the American Psychiatric Association's *Diagnostic and Statistical Manual of Mental Disorders* (1968:43) — a definition which is quoted here because it encapsulates many of the phrases which I heard again and again as I went round the prison, the courts, the hostels and the common-lodging houses:

> This term is reserved for individuals who are basically

unsocialised and whose behavior pattern brings them repeatedly into conflict with society. They are incapable of significant loyalty to individuals, groups or social values. They are grossly selfish, callous, irresponsible; impulsive and unable to feel guilt or to learn from experience or punishment. . . . They tend to blame others or offer plausible rationalisations for their behaviour.

In connection with the diagnosis of 'personality disorder' it must be noted that the sheriffs and prison officers whom I interviewed were fairly cynical about the 'rationalisations' of the psychiatrists themselves! Certainly it is not immediately apparent to the lay person why it is that psychiatrists alone can recognise 'selfishness, callousness, loyalty', etc., etc. Rather, many judicial and penal officials hinted to me that they would agree more with the claim that 'the concept of psychopathic disorder is used as a dumping ground for a host of problems' (Gunn *et al.*, 1978) than with any more clinically sophisticated definition. Anthony Clare, a well-known psychiatrist, has summarised what can happen to the social-work client who is referred for psychiatric help:

> This difference in the manner in which psychiatrists approach personality disorders is of course well known to those agencies who regularly refer clients to psychiatrists for clinical assessment. Many a social worker has referred to a psychiatrist an especially disturbed and socially disorganised client with a history of repeated acts of self-destruction including drug-abuse, overdoses and wrist-slashing . . . only to be informed that as the client is not deemed to be suffering from 'overt psychiatric illness' [s]he is not thought suitable for psychiatric intervention. (Clare, 1980:20)

And maybe at this stage the effects of such psychiatric non-labelling can be benign — at the least the other, more material forms of welfare aid cannot be denied on the grounds of the client's mental incapacity. Yet, at the court stage, when the social worker's 'disordered' client has yet once again become the court's 'disordered' defendant, the psychiatrist's refusal to recognise a treatable malady too often results in imprisonment for the homeless middle-aged women or the rootless younger women who comprise the bulk of Cornton Vale's recidivist population. At this stage, too, as both sheriffs and prison officers (as well as a general practitioner who worked part-time in the prison) implied, both institutional and industrial interests may combine to be strategic in determining the psychiatric recommendation, if not the *diagnosis*:

'We go in heavily for psychiatric reports and we're rarely offered a constructive custodial setting.' (Sheriff No. 2)

'They [psychiatrists] tend to say that they have a severe personality disorder but that there's no treatment. And when psychiatrists talk about severe personality disorder I have my suspicion that what they're really meaning is that in the old days they would have taken them into what were then called asylums, but that under the new system they are turning anyone away that they don't like the look of or anyone who, once there, would stay a long time.' (Sheriff No. 15)

A prison doctor thought that the prison had to take the severely disturbed mainly because prison officers had less industrial muscle than mental nurses:

'The prison is becoming a depository for difficult people, for the most difficult people who can't be treated anywhere else — certainly not in mental hospitals with their "open-door policy". This itself is the result of the increasing power and unionisation of nursing staff. It is the result of an *industrial* decision not a medical decision. In this area we have psychiatrists who do have beds but who will not take people because they are frightened of becoming a depository for the very worst cases. They do not get more beds just because they have a prison in their area, so therefore they have to be very careful indeed not to become a depository.'

Prison Officer No. 10 summed up in one long diatribe what many other prison officers had said at least as forcefully, though sometimes only in part:

'Our psychiatric cases are so disturbed that the people at home can't put up with them. They go to the mental hospital first and then when the mental hospital can't put up with them they come here. Nobody in their right senses would send them here. It's a crying shame. We're not nurses. It's unfair to other inmates and unfair to the person concerned. . . . And now mental hospitals have this policy of looking after them in the community — but they don't. *We're* the community. They're emptying the mental hospitals by sending the worst ones to prison. Mental hospitals only want the ones they can *do* something with, ones they can *talk* to. We get the rest.'

'We get quite a lot who've been in mental homes and who should never see the inside of a prison. If someone hits a nurse in a mental hospital then we get them. Often they're picked up for lashing out when they're disturbed, remanded here, sent to court, sent back here for psychiatric reports, back to court again and back here for thirty or sixty days. It's a waste of time and money — especially putting them through the court when they're ill.' (Prison Officer No. 2)

Officer No. 13 showed me Sierra's 'strong room' and 'silent room'. The strong room, 'for those causing trouble', had no window and double doors. The 'silent room', 'more for the mentally ill' had a window, though the officer showing me round remarked: 'When I first came here I thought that putting them in here was cruel. But what can we do? And you get used to it.' I saw women in Sierra who screamed intermittently for no apparent reason, women who were anorexic, and women who were continuously scratching self-inflicted wounds. Others would not speak at all. It was in connection with Sierra's population of very disturbed women that I asked one of the prison's visiting general practitioners if he prescribed many drugs for prisoners. When he replied in the affirmative we had the following exchange:

Pat Carlen: 'What drugs do you provide?'
Doctor: 'You name it — we give it, depending on the case and what they've been prescribed outside. If a person has been on an anti-depressant for a medium term and

is telling us that it is doing them good then we'll continue it. If they tell me they've been on it for years and
it's doing them no good, then we try to stop them.'
Pat Carlen: 'Do you ever give drugs for control purposes
— for controlling violent prisoners?'
Doctor: 'Yes. We have to take the staff into consideration
when selecting a drug. Some people we've had in eight
or ten times in two years and you know they can be
pretty wicked without the drug.'

But the prison officers themselves expressed disquiet about
the situation:

'I think that it's disgraceful that the Mental Health Act
allowed courts to send mentally ill people to prison.
Because we just drug them up in here, they're hallucinat-
ing all the time. You see their eyes going right up into
their heads.' (Prison Officer No. 12)

'There's no drug *therapy* here, only drugs.' (Prison Officer
No. 8)

For, just as policemen resent the publicity and criticism
which attaches to them when unconscious drunks (with
whom no-one else will deal) die in police custody, so do
prison officers resent the criticism which they receive for
attempting to control by chemical means persons whom no-
one else is willing to cope with at all. Yet Sheriff No. 15, one
of the sheriffs who, as we have seen, was very cynical about
psychiatrists' usage of the term 'personality disorder' could
see no immediate alternatives to prison for the alcoholic and
'disordered' offender:

'I'm afraid that prisons will be housing these people —
alcoholics and people with a severe personality disorder —
for a long time. Prison officers will just have to put up
with them.'

Further consideration of the institutional practices and
penal discourses which have already been described in this
book will indicate how they overdetermine the imprisonment

of these categories of offender to such an extent that it is unlikely that this sheriff's bleak prophecy will be proved wrong in the near future.

And still in prison

The 1979 Committee of Inquiry into the United Kingdom Prison Services (commonly known as The May Report after its Chairman, Mr Justice May) was as bland and contradictory in its references to 'disordered' patients as it was in its references to nearly every other category of prisoner/prison problem. After commenting (interestingly enough) on the fact that in Scotland many beds for the mentally disordered tend to remain empty, the report defined the term 'mentally disordered' as referring only to 'those groups susceptible to treatment' (p. 48). However, it *then* went on to explain how it is that offenders who need psychiatric treatment go to prison — and, despite May's assertions to the contrary, the 'general argument' for England and Wales *does* also hold for Scotland:

> The general argument is that because changes in methods of treatment in mental hospitals have greatly reduced their original need to have secure wards these hospitals have over the years for various reasons become increasingly reluctant to take mentally disordered offenders. . . . This has had the effect that prisons have had to become institutions of last resort because the courts *have had no alternative but to send offenders who need psychiatric treatment to prison*. (p. 49, my emphasis)

And this contemporary policy of imprisoning 'mentally disordered' offenders (as well as the policy of hospitals towards recidivist alcoholics) is indicative of the concomitant dispersion and interpenetration of the two systems which, according to Foucault, developed in the eighteenth century:

> Two systems, the older elaborate system of medical/legal judgement and the newer, uniform system of confinement as implementation of that judgement existed side by side,

neither appearing to affect the other. The first saw the
person as legal subject made up of rights and obligations;
the second saw the individual as a social being. In the
first, there was recognition that various forms of insanity
affect the subject's freedom of moral choice; in the second
a simple awareness that 'unreasonable' behaviour itself
constituted an exclusion from the society of reasonable
men. (Sheridan, 1980:19)

Over the past two hundred years the dispersal and realign-
ment of these two systems has resulted in their insemination
of a variety of discourses, many of which are far removed
from the auspices of classical jurisprudence and conventional
medical practice. They are embedded not only in discourses
which define and demarcate areas of specialist knowledge
and competence (e.g. psychiatry) but they also condition
discourses which are concerned with general working conditions (e.g. the union militancy of the mental nurses), with
job protection (the prison officers) with civil liberties (the
anti-psychiatry movement), and with public order (the police
and sheriffs).

As we have seen from the complaints of prison officers,
and a general practitioner, the term 'personality disorder'
enables psychiatrists to refuse severely disturbed offenders
admission to hospital. Psychiatrists have taken the anti-
psychiatry movement's argument that the notion of illness
must imply the possibility of treatment and they have turned
it on its head. If they, *as psychiatrists*, do not *know* of any
way of 'treating' the 'disturbed' person who is also an offender then they will use their privileged position *as psychiatrists* to make a *judicial* judgment — the person knew what
she was doing, she needs a discipline setting; hospitals are
for treatment not for discipline, therefore the disturbed
offender must go to prison! A court liaison officer mentioned
Cleopatra (see Chapter 5) as being a case in point:

'Do you know, or has anyone mentioned to you, Cleopatra? We've had her here twice in eighteen months —
strips off in the cells, puts excrement on the walls. Her
behaviour is such that most people would consider her
insane. But no one can deal with her, no one wants her, so
she's considered sane.'

Some offenders who are referred to a psychiatrist never get to see one — and the professionals can engage in a fraternal respect for each other's work-load in order to explain why:

> In Scotland the difficulties of liaison between the court, the psychiatrists and the (then) probation officers have been compounded since the *Social Work (Scotland) Act* 1968 was implemented. The social work departments, still understaffed, and with many competing claims on their services cannot yet assign sufficient coverage to the supervision of probation cases. Nor is it easy for the hospital psychiatrists running busy general out-patient clinics to follow up reluctant probationers who fail to keep their appointments. (Woodside, 1974:342)

But, as we have heard, even when offenders are examined by psychiatrists, the latter are sparing in their recommendations for custodial treatment. The psychiatrists invoke 'civil liberties' in support of their 'open-door' policy, their critics intone darkly about the psychiatrists' professional self-interest. At a more fundamental level there is the battle to define the areas within which the law and psychiatry have their respective jurisdictions. There is some suggestion that sheriffs ask for psychiatric advice *after* they themselves have decided that an offender needs a judicial disposition other than imprisonment:

> 'We have the problem that hospitals refuse to say that there is a mental problem when it is obvious that there is.' (Sheriff No. 14)

Furthermore, some sheriffs suspect that psychiatric diagnosis more often than not serves to deny and close off problems rather than to illuminate them:

> 'What they write is, "psychologically disturbed, but not suitable for any form of treatment," which seems strange to me.' (Sheriff No. 5)

> 'One took off all her clothes. I asked for a psychiatric report and they merely said she was manipulating the

psychiatric services so I had to send her to prison.' (Sheriff No. 8)

'Psychiatric reports tend to compartmentalise — they come down on one side or the other. If there is no mental illness, but something else — something that most people would call madness — then it may mean prison because no-one knows what makes them tick.' (Sheriff No. 7)

In fact, there are strong indications that despite the powers that have been formally accorded to psychiatrists, people in all walks of life still assume that mental illness is what it always has been, i.e. what ordinary people think it is. Lord Justice Lawton certainly thought so:

Lord Denning and Lord Justice Orr have pointed out that there is no definition of mental illness [in *The Mental Health Act* (1959)]. The words are ordinary words of the English language. They have no particular medical significance. They have no particular legal significance. How should the court construe them? The answer in my judgement is to be found in the advice which Lord Reid gave in Cozens v. Brutus (*Appeal Court Cases,* 1973: pp. 834, 861) namely that ordinary words should be construed in the way that ordinary sensible people would construe them.' (*Weekly Law Reports,* 1973: 857-83)

The Governor of Cornton Vale, however, recognised a gap between legal definitions and the definitions of ordinary sensible people. When I asked her: 'who are the people with gross personality disorders?' she replied:

'People who to the layman behave as if they were mentally ill, but who in the terms of the Mental Health Act are not mentally ill — *they are not treatable.* And if they offend and they are over the age of twenty-five the prison is the place for them — I mean, *by law*, it is.' (My emphasis)

And, of course, the Governor of Cornton Vale had good reason to recognise what Lord Justice Lawton chose to deny — that psychiatrists have statutory powers to endow the words 'mental illness' with very specific meanings *which have institutional effects regardless of laymen's contrary definitions.*

The curious effects of psychiatrists' current usage of the term 'personality disorder' can, therefore be summarised thus: (1) that people whom policemen, sheriffs and prison officers think to be obviously mentally ill are refused admission to mental hospitals on the grounds that they cannot be treated, and therefore must need a 'discipline setting'; (2) that the judicial judgment made by the psychiatrist is made *after* the sheriff has (by virtue of requesting a psychiatric report) already made a lay-psychiatric judgment; and (3) that once these women, defined as being 'not mentally ill but needing a discipline setting' (i.e. as having 'personality disorders'), reach Cornton Vale they are once more contradictorily redefined as being both: 'mentally ill' (i.e. their mental illness history is invoked for the purposes of justifying their control by *medically* prescribed drugs); and as being 'not mentally ill' (for the purposes of their control by the normal penal methods of deprivation of liberty and the imposition of other forms of deprivation, e.g. deprivation of the normal channels and modes of communication, the normal modes of dress, etc. — all as described in Chapter Five). The response of the prison officers to this situation is, however, not *wholly* one of dismay. At a time when there is both considerable pressure on the government to reduce the prison population and an increasing degree of militancy coming from the two separate prison officers' associations of England and Wales, and Scotland, the refusal of the psychiatrists to recognise the 'disordered' as pertaining to the realm of psychiatry has opened up a space where prison officers can clamour for an increase in professional training *and* powers.

From the viewpoint of the people in management positions within the prison service there is a desperate need for some kind of official and public recognition that prisons are containing many people 'whom lay people would call mentally ill'. For, despite what psychiatrists may say, the people who actually work in the prisons do *not* see imprisonment as an appropriate mode of control for a 'disordered personality':

'The authorities should provide places for people who need
a secure setting but who are neither responsible for their
actions nor mentally ill *as the medical authorities define
it.*' (Sheriff No. 4, emphasis in spoken comment)

'Most psychiatrists would say that prison provides the
right atmosphere for them but you can't deal with very
disturbed prisoners in a discipline setting in a way that
makes them behave better. You have to give them more
latitude and they then get more objectionable. And the
other prisoners can't cope with it because they can't
understand why these people are getting off.' (Governor,
Cornton Vale)

Also, and as I have already mentioned, the prison officers
are resentful of being constantly criticised for using drugs
to control behavioural abnormalities 'from which every
other agency is copping out' (Deputy Governor, Cornton
Vale).

'At [the Special Hospital] the nurses may adminster a
limited amount of drugs and because they are nurses it is
not seen to be a bad thing. But prison officers can't do
that. Even when drugs are administered under medical
supervision there is a lot of criticism if it happens in a
prison.' (General Secretary, Scottish Prison Officers'
Association)

'There are many people with a previous history of mental
illness coming into prison. What we don't want in prisons
is to be seen as having psychiatric services available unless
we actually *do* have those services and have trained staff.
This is the next type of training we are going to get for the
staff, but it's all in the melting-pot at the moment.' (Governor, Cornton Vale)

A prison officer, however, was sceptical about her colleagues'
relationships with some of the disturbed women:

'There are so many amateur psychiatrists among the
officers that I think some of them prefer this type of

prisoner to those who don't get so dependent.' (Prison Officer No. 11)

The General Secretary of the Scottish Prison Officers' Association thought that the unrecognisable nature of 'personality disorder' would militate against such psychiatric training for prison officers. In its simultaneous identification of 'personality disorder' *and* its refusal to recognise it as a category of 'mental illness', psychiatry has succeeded in a masterly stroke of professional imperialism. Psychiatry has placed 'personality disorder' under a continuous erasure which ensures that at present there is neither a place whence it can be *ex*propriated, nor a place to which it can be *a*ppropriated by any other intending 'experts' or 'professionals'.

> 'We say, "If prison officers have to deal with them, prison officers need the training." Back comes the answer, "What type of training, if psychiatrists can't do anything?"' (General Secretary, Scottish Prison Officers' Association)

Instead of being offered a training which would necessitate that at least some of the functions of imprisonment be made more explicit the prison officers are obliquely reminded that their usefulness to the penal system resides solely in their general custodial skills, skills which must always remain sufficiently general and sufficiently adaptable to deal with the current penal product — *however* defined.

> '*We* say that alcoholics and other inadequates are not in prison mainly because of their crimes — they are there either because no one else can cope with them or because they have nowhere else to go. Or they're regular to-ers and fro-ers who go backwards and forwards between the mental hospital and the prisons just to give the staffs of each a break. *They* [The Prison Department] say that it's not the function of prison officers to say who should be accepted by prisons. Which it isn't.' (General Secretary, Scottish Prison Officers' Association)

And thus it is that the prisons continue to perform one of their traditional (albeit it sporadic) tasks, the minding of those who 'are treated neither entirely as madmen [nor mad women] nor entirely as criminals, nor entirely as witches, nor entirely as ordinary people' but who are cast, instead, into 'the void within which the experience of madness resides' (Foucault, 1976:76-7). The penal keepers of this void are those whose job must always be defined both generally and negatively; they are to be (amongst other things) the guardians of those residual deviants for whom the state and its saving and treatment agencies have no immediate use.

Once they are defined as having a 'personality disorder' the women have little chance of having the label removed. As Gunn *et al.* (1978) have pointed out, psychiatrists regard 'personality disorder' as a fixed category, with little hope of change. They therefore invoke economic criteria to justify their reluctance to meet repeated judicial requests to reassess cases of 'personality disorder':

> There were several instances where the court had sought repeated reports on an individual offender, whose persistent anti-social behaviour appeared unmodifiable either by therapeutic or correctional means. . . . When a question was put about the need for such series of reports, some within a few months of each other, it was explained that the court must have up-to-date information on which to base decisions. The offenders' mental state could have improved or deteriorated, or some new treatment measure be proposed. This policy may meet legal *desiderata*, but where such well-known offender-patients are concerned it could be thought an uneconomical use of NHS consultant time. (Woodside, 1976:29)

Here is the final contradiction: the women are *physically* located in the *prison* on the grounds that they are *physically* (and permanently) located within a *psychiatric category* whose pathology is always already denied! So, being seen as neither wholly mad nor wholly bad, they are treated to a disciplinary regime where they are actually infantalised at the same time as attempts are made to make them feel guilty about their double, triple, quadruple or even quintuple refusal of family, work, gender, health and reason (see Hutter and Williams, 1981:esp. 1-36). Further, and because of the contradictory definitions to which women in general are subjected, imprisoned women can be made to feel 'quite horribly at home' within psychiatric careers (Chesler, 1974) whilst both the history and the present organisation of psychiatric and penal internment in Britain are particularly suited to disciplining women into what is still regarded as being Scottish woman's most proper role, that of the child-rearing homemaker. And the Scottish female homemaker is also morally charged with the *guardianship* of familial and male-dominated domesticity. It is not surprising, therefore, that Michel Foucault's description of Samuel Tuke's nineteenth-century asylum at York so well describes the regime at the Scottish women's prison of the 1980s:

> The ideal asylum that Tuke created near York was supposed to reconstruct around the internee a family-like structure in which he would feel at home; in fact, he was subjected, by that same structure, to uninterrupted social and moral supervision; curing him was to mean reinculcating in him the feelings of dependence, humility, guilt and gratitude that are the moral backbone of family life. (Foucault, 1976:70-1)

The imprisoned women are not 'cured'. Prins (1980) has made the point that incarceration can make the 'mentally ill' much worse and the prison officers I interviewed certainly did not think that prison is the proper place for those with psychiatric histories. The petty restrictions of the penal regime can often 'wind-up' women prisoners to a point where they are screaming with the sheer pain of tension and frustration. When they *are* released from prison no-one wants them. Finally, after several years in the revolving-door syndrome they are beyond recognition:

> 'I keep saying that we don't have many ex-prisoners because I don't want to see the problem in those terms. In fact several of the women here *have* been in prison at some time or other — or in a mental hospital, but, whether they've committed a crime or are ill isn't the

main problem, at least, not the only problem. It's a circle of many things, housing, illness, drink, police attitudes, public attitudes, the stigma of living here [common-lodging house] no resources, no one interested and, in the end, what are you looking at? Crime? Mental illness? Or is it something else?' (Warden, Edinburgh Common Lodging House)

Overall, the dominant meaning of women's imprisonment in Scotland is that it is imprisonment denied: it is denied that the women's prison is a 'real prison', it is denied that the women are 'real prisoners', it is denied that the prisoners are 'real women'. This extreme denial of the existence of women's imprisonment in Scotland is constituted by, and partly mirrors, the similar contradictions which constitute the denied meanings of short-term imprisonment in general in Britain. In so far as these meanings are constantly affirmed in their very denial then that very same denial may at least partly account for the continuous increase in Britain's prison population.

9 The meanings of women's imprisonment in Scotland: Implications and questions for penal politics

'I've been through all this before — it's just a paper exercise. They won't *do* anything about it. You can't do anything about the drink unless you look at their other problems but it's still a terrible indictment on this society.' (Policeman No. 24, Edinburgh, 1981, his emphasis)

'I don't *want* to bring politics into this but you *have* to bring politics in. We are dealing with *political* questions. I don't think there is political motivation to change. The public is not interested and it doesn't matter which party is in power, none of them come up with anything new about prisons. There never has been a Great Debate about prisons, and it *should* be about argument and debate.' (General Secretary, Scottish Prison Officers' Association, 1981, his emphasis)

'Without counteracting policies, further increases in the prison population must be expected. The projection for 1986/87 is about 47,000. The numbers in Scottish penal establishments have also been increasing. Though the numbers are higher per head of total population than in England and Wales, the increase has been less marked, from 4,500 in 1968 to about 5,000 in later years. The increasing number of prisoners in the Scottish prison population who have been sentenced to long sentences make further increases likely. The projection for 1986/87 is 5,400.' (Home Office, 1980)

One does not need to read a sociological case-study to find out about the 'parlous state' of British prisons (though see Morris, 1978, for a good analytic description). A number of official reports have recently documented in startlingly sordid detail the overcrowded and insanitary conditions in the prisons. The same reports usually deplore the continued use of imprisonment for at least the following categories of offenders: fine defaulters, habitual drunken offenders, the homeless, prostitutes, the mentally ill, the mentally disordered, and all persistent petty offenders in general; (see, for examples, Banks and Fairhead, 1976; House of Commons Expenditure Committee, 1978; May Report, 1979; Home Office, 1980:2; Parliamentary All-Party Penal Affairs Group, 1980; Fairhead, 1981). This present study of the meanings of women's imprisonment in Scotland has attempted to unravel some of the complex processes which combine and make possible the continued imprisonment of these offenders. It has also shown that there has been absolutely no evidence of any political willingness to fund the alternatives to imprisonment which most of the reports recommend. Yet it is because Her Majesty's Institution, Cornton Vale, is in many ways different to other British prisons that this case-study of the meanings of women's imprisonment in Scotland challenges some of the assumptions inherent in contemporary penal politics. I will, therefore, by way of conclusion, address the specific policy issues which this particular study raises.

1 Short sentences

The Dutch experience suggests that sentence length has little effect on criminality and that the introduction of shorter sentences does not result in a massive crime wave, it simply reduces the prison population.' (NACRO, 1981b)

In recent years it has generally been considered that the imposition of shorter sentences will result in a decrease in the prison population. It has also been assumed that the imposition of shorter sentences will mainly affect those types of offenders who are at present receiving long sentences. This study of women's imprisonment in Scotland is a reminder that the implementation of this policy will only be seen as being rational and 'just' if most present categories of short-term prisoners are removed from the gaols.[1] If persistent petty offenders are not altogether removed from the prison system we could in future in Britain have the ludicrous situation presently obtaining for Scottish women offenders — the situation where it is mainly those who commit the least serious crimes who go repeatedly to prison. Secondly, this study of women's imprisonment in Scotland suggests that if shorter sentences do replace the present long term, prison regimes should be changed to ensure that the new short-term prisoners are not so grossly neglected as are the present short-termers. For short-term prisoners have recently been almost totally neglected both by prison officials and by prison researchers. *All* of the better facilities in prisons are only available to the long-term prisoners. The better education courses, the very small amount of interesting work available, the open units, the longer visiting times, and the many privileges relating both to association and to privacy are by and large denied the short-termer, such denial being most usually justified on the grounds either that 'you can't do much in a short time' or that 'she's not here long enough for it to make any difference.' Which brings me to my third word of caution regarding shorter sentences. Shorter sentences will most certainly benefit prison management by reducing overcrowding but they will not necessarily improve the lot of prisoners unless other radical changes are made. In sum, the move to shorter sentences will only have real significance if at the same time: imprisonment is reserved for the gravest offences; the criminal justice system is brought under greater control (see Hulsman, 1981; Carlen, 1982); and the penal authorities are made more accountable for their management of the prisons.

2 Small units

'We have always argued for a reduction in the prison population. But we have argued from the point of view that the prison buildings are inadequate, that one prison officer on a gallery of fifty prisoners cannot have much influence. Our argument has been all along for special units — not all like the Special Unit at Barlinnie — but special units in the sense that they would be special to the type of prisoner who needed a special custodial environment.' (General Secretary, Scottish Prison Officers' Association)

The argument that shorter sentences will reduce the prison population is often coupled with the implication that a diminution in prison overcrowding will in itself result in more humane and less repressive regimes for prisoners. I would argue that the Cornton Vale experience does not bear out that supposition. Throughout my investigations I found strong indications that prison officers themselves *want* the prison experience to be painful.[2] At Saughton Prison, Edinburgh, for instance, an Assistant Governor told me that, although he was indeed very concerned about the lack of facilities for short-term offenders, 'it could be argued that because nothing is done for them it has more of a deterrent value.' At Cornton Vale itself five of the ten senior prison officers formally interviewed said that in their opinion the regime should be harsher and, as we saw in Chapter Five, the view was generally expressed that one positive good associated with the imprisonment of the mentally disturbed is that their behaviour often serves to frighten the other prisoners. Furthermore, it is difficult to see how one could give 'special' status to small groups of prisoners unless it be to those very groups of prisoners who, it is argued on all sides, should be removed from the penal system altogether. Certainly it can be argued that many persistent petty offenders have special psychological needs but, once it is agreed that *their* problems cannot be dealt with in custodial discipline settings, it is difficult to see what types of 'special units' — other than replicas of the partly prisoner-run Barlinnie Special Unit — could be justifiably devised for other categories of prisoner.[3] The development of special units with a high prison officer/prisoner ratio would indeed protect the jobs of prison staff during any future contraction of the penal industry but the notion that there is a suitable type of specialised treatment for every prisoner is a highly dangerous one. As we saw in Chapter 5, the pains of imprisonment do not stem solely from overcrowding and brutal physical conditions, they can also emanate both from too-rigid structures of surveillance and from the more subtle disciplinary techniques which debilitate the mind rather than the body.

3   Criticism of contemporary penal policy should focus on the processes of imprisonment rather than on the prisons and the prison staff

> 'The problem of prisons is that we have so few links with the outside. Prison gets blamed for all the problems and we never have any successes. But people outside forget that we receive all society's failures and rejects — and they don't want them back either.' (Deputy Principal, Scottish Prison Service College, 1981)

The last ten years have seen an unprecedented growth in both prison overcrowding and in prisoner and prison officer unrest. It should, therefore, not be surprising that criticism has been primarily (though not entirely) focused upon the prisons themselves. Through the watchdog activities of groups such as PROP (Preservation of the Rights of Prisoners), RAP (Radical Alternatives to Prison) and the NCCL many of the penal system's abuses and injustices have been spotlighted, a few judicial victories have been won (for an example see Taylor, 1980). This surveillance of the penal system should not only be continued, it should be extended. Yet, at the same time, the prisons and the prison officers should not be criticised as if they are agencies and agents existing in and for themselves. The dangers of displacing the current ills of this society onto the visible agents of social control — whether those agents be either police officers or prison officers — are several. First, there is the obvious danger that criticism of individual prison abuses can be merely reformist insofar as it diverts criticism from the wider social conditions which make prisons what they are. Second, in the case of certain categories of prisoners it is difficult to see how prison personnel can avoid criticism *whatever* they do. Prisoners such as those at Cornton Vale who told me that outside prison they had been used to taking medically prescribed sleeping pills for their 'nerves' are a case in point. If the prison the prescription there is the suspicion that ing given *solely* for control purposes; es the prescription there is the accusa- is being denied the medication which ately prescribed outside.[4] To make this point is not to deny that in Britain in general the medical services provided in the prisons leave much to be desired, nor is it to condone the over-prescription of drugs; it *is* to argue that it may be counterproductive further to alienate prison personnel by scapegoating them for not being able to solve the problems which so far nobody else has been able to solve either. For (and this is my third and rather obvious point) while prisons exist, prison officers are in the front-line for implementing and changing penal policy. And, although such a claim may seem paradoxical, an increase in democratic control of the prisons must be dependent upon the opening up of formal channels of democratic communication with the prison officers. The prison service is presently as hierarchical as it ever was, working conditions are appalling, industrial relations are poor and public relations are non-existent. It is not surprising that in such a situation prison officers, like many others, are nowadays asking 'What are prisons *for*?' Instead of scapegoating prison officers for being the agents of a monstrous penal system which is not primarily of their own making we should, perhaps, search for answers to that question.

4 What are prisons for?

Analyses of the functions of penal incarceration at specific periods in history have been given by various writers (pre-eminently by Rusche and Kirchheimer, 1939 and by Michel Foucault, 1978) and I do not intend to repeat them here. Even official reports nowadays tacitly admit that prisons in Britain have traditionally been used as much for storing away those deemed to be socially useless as they have been used for the incarceration of those deemed to be either deserving of punishment or a danger to the public. Readers of the foregoing case study will know that this is certainly the situation presently obtaining in the Scottish women's prison. Again and again it was denied that the adult prisoners at Cornton Vale are either 'real criminals' or 'real prisoners'; again and again it was stressed that they are 'the women that nobody wants'. But (the views of some of the sheriffs and prison officers notwithstanding!) Cornton Vale *is* a real prison, and, moreover, many of the staff claimed that because it *is* a prison Cornton Vale must always be run as if it were full of 'real prisoners'. Others of the staff, being more pragmatic, claimed that as they are having to be 'more like mental nurses than prison officers' they should be given new, specialist training. This debate amongst the staff at Cornton Vale points up two of the dilemmas which might confront any executive which engages in penal decarceration. First, there might be the difficulty of justifying the continued existence of prisons once the 'real prisoners' have gone. Second, if the prisons remain to provide the 'secure discipline settings' for the 'disordered' and the alcoholic might it not be thought that their incarceration functions merely to keep the prisons in working order until such times as they are required to store away more and more people that 'nobody really wants'? Of course it might. Therefore, even if the prison population is drastically reduced in the near future, the question 'what are prisons *for*?' must be continually posed. I myself do not support the view that all prisons should be abolished but while prisons do exist we must never presume that we always already know what goes on behind the walls. For, as we can see from the way that Cornton Vale is adapting to cope with the alcoholic and the 'mentally disordered', while prisons exist the seeds of a new penology are always inherent in the old. And, finally, as we can also see from this study of Scotland's invisible women prisoners, while prisons *do* exist, it is unlikely that there will be any imprisonment so enduring as the imprisonment which is denied.

Appendix A

Table A Crimes and offences of convicted women prisoners over the age of 21 received into Cornton Vale in 1978
(Total prisoners over 21 657)

Class I Crimes against the person			
Murder		2	
Attempts to murder		1	
Culpable homicide		4	
Assaults		14	
Cruel and unnatural treatment of children		4	
Other		1	
	total	26	(4%)

Class II Crimes against property with violence			
Housebreaking		25	
Robbery, assault with intent, etc.		5	
	total	30	(5%)

Class III Crimes against property without violence			
Theft		183	
Reset		8	
Breach of trust and embezzlement		6	
Fraud		28	
Post Office offences		1	
	total	226	(34%)

Class IV Malicious injuries to property			
	total	1	

Class V Forgery and crimes against currency			
	total	7	(1%)

Class VI Other crimes not included above			
Mobbing and rioting		2	
Perjury and bribery		3	
Other crimes		4	
	total	9	(1%)

Class VII Miscellaneous offences			
Breach of peace		217	(33%)
Brothel keeping		2	
Education Acts, offences against		1	
Drunkenness		77	
Other offences against intoxicating liquor laws		1	
Prostitution		19	
Revenue and Excise laws		1	
Motor offences		1	
Vagrancy and Trespass Acts		3	
Other miscellaneous offences		36	
	total	358	(55%)

Adapted from Appendix No. 9 *Prisons in Scotland: Report for 1978, Cmnd 7749*, HMSO, Edinburgh, 1979

Table B Crimes and offences of convicted women prisoners over the age of 21 received into Cornton Vale in 1980
(Total prisoners over 21 569)

Class I Crimes against the person			
Murder		0	
Attempts to murder		0	
Culpable homicide		3	
Assaults		23	
Cruel and unnatural treatment of children		5	
	total	31	(6%)
Class II Crimes against property with violence			
Housebreaking		12	
Robbery, assault with intent, etc.		2	
	total	14	(3%)
Class III Crimes against property without violence			
Theft		148	
Reset		9	
Breach of trust and embezzlement		7	
Fraud		24	
	total	188	(33%)
Class IV Malicious injuries to property			
Fire raising			
	total	8	(1%)
Class V Forgery and crimes against currency			
	total	7	(1%)
Class VI Other crimes not included above			
Mobbing and rioting		1	
Perjury and bribery		4	
Other crimes		6	
	total	11	(2%)
Class VII Miscellaneous offences			
Breach of peace		177	(31%)
Brothel keeping		0	
Children and Young Persons (Scotland) Acts		2	
Education Acts, offences against		8	
Drunkenness		56	
Other offences against intoxicating liquor laws		0	
Offences against Police Acts, bye-laws and regulations		2	
Offences against Prevention of Crimes Act		1	
Prostitution		35	
Offences in relation to the railways		1	
Motor offences		1	
Vagrancy and Trespass Acts		4	
Other miscellaneous offences		21	
	total	308	(54%)

Adapted from Appendix No. 9 *Prisons in Scotland: Report for 1980*, Cmnd 8421, HMSO, Edinburgh, 1981

Table C Receptions under sentence: by age and offence, 1980
Adult females aged 21 and over

Offence		Number of females	
		Immediate imprisonment Total	In default of payment of a fine Total
All offences	Total	1,872	716
Violence against the person		171	22
Murder		2	—
Manslaughter		12	—
Other homicide and attempted homicide		3	—
Wounding		85	11
Assaults		51	11
Cruelty to children		3	—
Other offences of violence against the person		15	—
Sexual offences		2	1
Gross indecency with children		2	—
Other sexual offences		—	1
Burglary		95	18
Robbery		34	—
Theft, handling, fraud and forgery		1,172	315
Taking and driving away		18	2
Other thefts		856	173
Handling stolen goods		86	12
Frauds		191	122
Forgery		21	6
Other offences		398	360
Arson		12	1
Criminal damage		62	32
Drugs offences		83	12
Immigration Act 1971		4	5
In charge or driving under the influence of drink or drugs		—	1
Other motoring offences		4	27
Offences relating to prostitution		118	38
Drunkenness		—	97
Vagrancy		7	1
Other		108	146

Adapted from Table 5.1 *Prison Statistics England and Wales 1980*,
p. 80, Cmnd 8372, HMSO, London, 1982

Table D Prisons for women in England

Establishment	Accommodation for inmates	Number of Inmates	
		Average	Greatest
Holloway (closed prison)	253	355	451
Cookham Wood (closed prison)	56	63	76
Durham (closed prison)	39	37	38
Styal (closed prison)	204	227	260
total	552	682	
Askham Grange (open prison)	137	130	146
Drake Hall (open prison)	250	181	213
East Sutton Park	20	19	22
Moor Court	76	92	101
total	483	422	

Adapted from Appendix No. 7 *Report onthe Work of The Prison Department 1980*, p. 93 Cmnd 8228, HMSO, London, 1981

Appendix B

The purpose of this appendix is to indicate the range of topics discussed in the interviews.

Letter sent to prisoners

> Dear Ms
> I am a woman researcher from the University of Keele in England and I am trying to find out what difficulties (if any) women have had to cope with before they come to prison and what difficulties (if any) they have to face when they go out.
> The Governor has given me permission to request your help. If you agree to help I should like to have two fairly long talks with you. Naturally everything you tell me will be treated as strictly confidential.
> I hope you will agree to help because although much has been written about men who go to prison the situation of women has tended to be somewhat overlooked.
> Yours sincerely

Interviews with the prisoners

Prison Interview I   Interview number 000
First of all I want to ask you some factual questions and I'll fill in the answers on this sheet. Afterwards I'll be asking you to talk more generally, and then, if you agree, I'd like to tape-record your answers — so that you can make your answers as long as you like. [Answers recorded on separate sheet]

Factual information - name

1 Age 000   2 Age of leaving school (or full-time education)
3 Education qualifications
4 Single/Married/Divorced/Widowed/Cohabiting

5 Number of children
6 Who is looking after your children now?
7 Number of times in custody
8 Length of present term of imprisonment (if known)

List of previous sentences
Date (if remembered) 00 Offence 00 Length of sentence 00 (fine defaulter?)

Now I've got down some facts I'd like to tape-record the rest of the interview.
A First of all I'd like to ask you some questions about your life out-side prison:

1 *Health*
Do you think of yourself as usually being a healthy person?
How has your health been since you have been in here?
Have you been given any medicine since you have been here?
What was that for?

2 *Job*
Now could you tell me what kind of jobs you have had since you left school.
(Prompts – did you like that job? why did you leave that job?)

3 *Accommodation*
Now could you tell me a bit about your household?
(a) Where do you normally live?
(b) And who do you live with?
(c) Are you satisfied with your accommodation?

4 *Money Problems*
Before you came in here, did you have any money problems?
Prompt – Could you tell me what they were?
What do you think caused these problems?
Prompt – Unemployment; hire purchase debt; other debt? Gambling?
Man? (any reason) Low pay? Not good with money?

5 *Man and/or family*
And what about your man and/or family – how much help have they been when you've had difficulties/worries?

*6 (*Only for those who have been to prison before*)
Now I want to get your opinion about social workers and other people who are supposed to help you when you come out of prison.
(a) Each time you've been released from prison, what are the par-ticular problems (if any) that you have experienced?
(b) Have you asked anyone for help?
Prompt – Prison social worker, local authority social worker, other organisation.
(c) Can you think of any help which might have stopped you from coming back here?

Prison Interview 2   **Interview number**

Last time we talked mainly about your life in general. Today I'd like to ask you some questions about your experience of the court and the prison.

A *The court*
  1 When and how was it that you first came to the attention of the police?
  2 How much did you understand about your first court appearance?
  3 Were you represented by a lawyer (if not, why not?)
  4 Have you learned much about the law since that time?

B *The prison*
  Last time we talked about your life outside prison:
  1 Now that you're in here, do you think much about your life outside prison?
  2 What do you think about?
  3 Do you think that someone like yourself should be sent to prison? Why do you say that?
  4 How (if at all) has being in prison affected
    (a) you?
    (b) your relationships with people outside?
    (c) other aspects of your life outside?
  5 Is there anything else that you would like to add about women being sent to prison?

C *The future*
  1 How do you see your future when you leave prison this time? Prompt: job? accommodation? family? other (past) problems?
  2 (Only for those who have been in prison before)
    Can you describe to me how things went for you last time you were released from prison?

  Questions for women with children only
  1 Do your children normally live with you? How old are they?
  2 Who is looking after them now?
  3 How often do you get news of them?
  4 How well do you think they're being looked after?
  5 What advice did you get about, and who helped you to make arrangements about your children after you had been sentenced?

  Finally, to all women interviewed
  3 Is there anything you would like to ask me about this research?

Questions to be asked of prison officers

The purpose of this research is to find out about the lives and backgrounds of women who come to prison again and again. On the basis of your own personal experience I would be grateful if you would answer just four questions so that I have some idea of how the staff see the situation.

1 Could you first of all describe the women who return to prison again and again? Do they fall into any particular types or are they all very different?

2 What, in fact, do you think are the effects of imprisonment on these women?

3 A recent Report made two comments about women's imprisonment. Could you tell me if you agree or disagree with them — and give me your reasons:

   (a) 'In general, women in prison suffer more than men in prison?'
      Agree 000   Disagree 000   Do not know
Why?

   (b) 'Women in custody present special emotional problems'
      Agree 000   Disagree 000   Do not know
Why?

4 Would you like to see any changes in the ways women offenders are currently dealt with?

   (a) By the courts?
   (b) In the prison?

Open Question: Thanks for answering my questions. Is there anything else that you think should be known about the situation of women offenders — either in or out of prison?

Questions to ask Governor

A *Cornton Vale*

   1 Broadly speaking, on what kind of principles do you run Cornton Vale?

   2 What kind of values do you hope to impart to the women here?

   3 Do prisoners have any 'say' in the running of the prison?

   4 What kind of work/training/education is available to the women here?

   5 While they are here, what contacts do women have with the outside world?

   6 How would you describe the women who are recidivists — are they all different or do you think they have certain characteristics in common?

B *Women in prison*

   1 Do you think that imprisonment for women involves problems which are different to those attendant upon men's imprisonment?

   2 Do you think that women in prison need different types of regimes to those usually followed in men's prisons?

C *Prison policy in general*

   1 Has the female prison population changed very much over the last ten to fifteen years? i.e. is a different type of woman being sent here by the courts?

   2 To what extent do you have a say in penal policy?

Questions for social workers working within the prison

As you may know, the main purpose of the research is to find out how imprisonment affects women.

1 Could you, first of all, describe the job of the prison social worker?
2 I am particularly interested in what happens to the children of women in prison. When a woman with children receives a custodial sentence, what kind of arrangements are made for her children?
3 How often can they visit her in prison?
4 If a convicted woman is likely to have a baby born in prison what kind of advice is given to her?
5 If a baby is born while the mother is serving her sentence, how is the baby cared for:
   (a) within the prison?
   (b) outside the prison?
6 Is any kind of contraceptive advice given to women in prison?
7 What, in your experience, are the main worries of women while they are in prison?
8 How can these worries be reduced?
9 What kind of help is given to women concerning finding a job when they leave prison?
10 What kind of help is given to women for finding accommodation when they leave prison?

Questions for medical officer

1 Professor Gibbens found in a survey of prisoners entering Holloway Prison in 1967 that physical health was a major problem in one sixth of cases, mental health was a major problem in over 20 per cent. How would you assess the present population at Cornton Vale?
2 What are the main types of medication prescribed to the prisoners here?
3 What would you think of non-chemical means of alleviating stress, e.g. mixed prisons, conjugal visits, more contact with the outside world?

Questions for sheriffs and stipendiary magistrates

1 When you are considering sentencing a woman to imprisonment do you take into consideration any factors which are different from those which you consider when sending a man to prison?
2 When you ask for information prior to sentence do you either require, or receive, information of a different type from that which you require when sentencing a man?
3 When you sentence a woman to a *short-term* of imprisonment do you hope that it will have any beneficial effect or is the sentence imposed primarily as a punishment?

4　Why do you send alcoholic offenders to prison?
5　How is it decided whether an offender with a history of mental illness should be sent to a prison or a hospital?
6　Have you ever been to Cornton Vale?
7　Lastly, is there anything which you would like to add concerning women offenders in general?

Questions for policemen

1　Do you come across many drunken women when you're on the beat?
2　How do you usually deal with the situation?
3　What factors do you take into consideration when you decide to arrest?
4　Do you have many complaints from the public about drunken women?
5　Do drunken women cause much trouble for the public and/or the police?
6　Do you think that arresting and prosecuting these women is the best way to deal with them?

Appendix C
Social work training

Concern about the training of social workers was mentioned so frequently during my interviews with court liaison officers, sheriffs and prison officers that I decided to send out a questionnaire to the twelve CQSW courses available in Scotland. Strathclyde Regional Council had also investigated social work training as part of their intensive survey reported in *Who Cares?* A summary of the findings of both surveys is given below.

1 The survey by Strathclyde Regional Council's Services to the Offender Group

Method and Aims
The Services to the Offender Group sent out questionnaires to all colleges and universities running CQSW courses and gave a similar questionnaire to all staff who completed training in August 1977. The general aim was to establish current practices in training courses throughout Scotland; the three specific aims were to establish (a) what opportunities students had to supervise offenders in a variety of settings (b) whether visits were made to courts and penal establishments and (c) the availability of placements in penal settings. Five out of the twelve training courses replied to the questionnaire and sixty-nine recently qualified staff also participated.

Results
The main findings from analysis of the questionnaires sent to the training courses were: (a) that students in training would have few opportunities to supervise offenders; (b) that it was extremely difficult to obtain placements in penal institutions, and (c) that very few courses organise formal visits of observation either to courts or to penal institutions. The results from the staff questionnaire were as follows:

5.1 72 per cent of all staff completed a social background report for a court.

5.2 41 per cent were able to supervise a person on probation.

5.3 23 per cent were able to supervise a person on after-care.

5.4 32 per cent were able to supervise a person subject to fine-supervision order.

5.5 Only 9 per cent of students stated that formal visits of observation to a district court had been arranged by the college, and 10 per cent to a sheriff court, with 7 per cent to the high court. 12 per cent stated that formal visits had been arranged to a detention centre with 13 per cent to a young offenders institution and borstal, 46 per cent to prison and 8 per cent to the state mental hospital at Carstairs.

5.6 10 per cent of students had a placement in a prison, only 3 per cent in a young offenders institution, 4 per cent in a detention centre and 6 per cent in a borstal.

5.7 89 per cent of staff indicated that it was possible to complete a CQWS course without any practical work with the offender. (Strathclyde Regional Council, 1978)

Further, 46 per cent of the newly qualified staff had claimed that the amount of formal lecture time spent dealing specifically with legislation on the offender was unsatisfactory.

2 The survey for this book

Method and aims

I sent questionnaires to all the colleges and universities running CQSW courses. The general aim was to establish current practices in relationship to the teaching of subjects which might have relevance to the supervision of adult female offenders. Eight out of twelve courses replied but only seven questionnaires were completed as one course was experiencing severe staffing difficulties.

Results

Subject: Position of women in family, law, society (or other social institution)

None of the seven courses had a compulsory course specifically on women.

One of the seven courses offered an optional course on sexism and welfarism.

All of the seven courses ran compulsory courses where the position of women in society and/or law would be dealt with in specific lectures.

Subject: Criminology or deviance

Two of the seven courses had a compulsory course specifically on criminology.

Two ran optional courses and said that the number of students attending them varied considerably.

Two of the seven courses said that the topic would be dealt with on compulsory general courses.

One of the seven courses said that about 20 per cent of students might opt to specialise in the subject whilst participating in a more general compulsory course.

Subject: Criminal justice system
Five courses said that they ran compulsory courses on this topic.
Two courses said that the topic would be dealt with on other courses.

Subject: Alcohol and alcohol-related problems
Two courses said that they ran optional courses on the topic, with about 35 per cent (at one college) and 20 per cent students (at the other college) opting for the course.
The remaining five courses said that the topic would either be covered in either general courses, or by one day courses or by individual specialist seminars.

Subject: Penology
Two courses said that they ran compulsory courses on the subject.
One course said that they ran an optional course on the subject.
Four courses said that they had no courses solely on this topic but that the topic would be covered briefly in more general courses.

Other: The courses were asked to describe other courses which they thought might help their students to understand the problems of women offenders
(To maintain anonymity of respondents I have called the courses A-G)
Course A: Compulsory law course covers battered women, debt, homelessness and feminist issues.
Course B: No further information given.
Course C: Expert supervision available on topic of battered women.
Course D: Course on the relationship between mental illness and crime.
Course E: An optional course on 'Social Work, Offenders and the Courts'.
Course F: No further information.
Course G: Optional courses on 'Working with Offenders' and 'Normal Parenting'.

The second part of the questionnaire was directed at assessing how much practical training students were given *vis-à-vis* work with offenders.

1 *Are any students likely to be taken to visit a prison during the training period?*
Five of the courses said that visits to prisons would be arranged and that most students would be expected to visit a prison either in a group visit or individually. Two courses did not agree with arranging formal visits but both said that students would be encouraged either to visit a prison individually or to engage in some practical work at one.

2 *Are any students given any training in the preparation of reports for the courts?*
Four of the seven courses said that ALL students would be given some

training in preparing court reports. Three courses said that training in writing court reports would only be given to the 10-20 per cent of students who took the relevant optional course.

3 *Are any students given any training in preparation for the supervision of offenders on probation, parole or licence?*
Four of the seven courses said that ALL students would be given training in preparation for the supervision of offenders. Three of the seven courses said that training in the supervision of offenders would only be given to the 10-20 per cent of students who took the relevant optional courses.

Comment
My survey was directed mainly at assessing to what extent social work students were sensitized to penal issues and women's issues and the results suggest that, given the time available, most of the colleges cover these topics well. However, four of the courses spontaneously pointed out that there is a great difference between theory and practice and that their students would most likely have had few opportunities to practise (either on 'placement' or as part of in-service training) what they have been taught in lectures. This ties in with what Strathclyde Regional Council found, i.e. that students have few opportunities both to supervise offenders and to find placements in penal institutions. However, I did find that five of the seven courses replying to the questionnaire arranged prison visits for their students. (The discrepancy between this finding and Strathclyde Regional Council's finding that only a few courses arranged prison visits might have been because we had replies from entirely different courses!)

Notes

Chapter 1 The meanings of women's imprisonment in Scotland

1 The estimated population of Scotland in 1978 was 5,179,400; in 1980 it was 5,153,300.

2 Over a period of about ten weeks in the early part of 1979 industrial action was taken by the staff of the Scottish Sheriff and High Courts. As this industrial action affected prison receptions I have not used the Scottish prison statistics for 1979.

3 The formal and official distinction between long-term and short-term imprisonment can be inappropriate if used as a general starting point for categorically distinguishing between types of prisoner experience, e.g. some women I interviewed at Cornton Vale claimed that they were 'never out of the place' when in fact they meant that they were repeatedly serving very short terms of imprisonment. At the same time, it should be remembered throughout this study that when I refer in a general way to women's imprisonment in Scotland I am in fact mainly referring to the short-term imprisonment which is the experience of the majority of Scottish women prisoners.

4 'Outwith' is a commonly used Scottish word. Its meaning as given in *The Concise Oxford Dictionary* is 'outside', but its structure manages to convey the more subtle meaning of 'beyond (out) but not lacking (with)' which conveys the contradictory states of consciousness engendered by the competing definitions of the women.

5 The enforcement of law and order in Northern Ireland in recent years has been marked by so many features peculiar to the troubles there that maybe the meanings of imprisonment in Northern Ireland require separate analysis. For that reason I have limited my remarks here to England and Wales.

6 This 'invisibility' of female prisoners is mentioned in relation to the prison systems of several countries, e.g. Renée Short (1979:47) writing of Sweden, comments that even 'women's liberation in

Sweden has paid little attention to the manifold problems of women offenders.'

7   During the 1970s PROP (Preservation of the Rights of Prisoners) and RAP (Radical Alternatives to Prison) also campaigned against the building of a new, medically orientated Holloway in place of the old prison. The rapid rise in women prisoners, however, has resulted in the Home Office abandoning its previous medical model; women are being housed in increasingly overcrowded conditions and the new Holloway will not be completely finished until 1984 (Evans, 1980).

8   For a good discussion see Heidensohn, 1981.

9   I am not implying that prison is a suitable place for babies. I am merely noting that the incarceration of infants is a feature of English women's imprisonment.

10   The Fifteenth Report from the House of Commons Expenditure Committee (Education Arts and Home Office sub-committee) published in 1978 considered ways of reducing pressure on the prison system (House of Commons, 1977). During 1978 and 1979 they heard evidence for a separate study to be entitled *'Women and The Penal System'*. This study was not published because of the intervention of the 1979 general election.

11   Evans (1980:58) claims that 'between half and two-thirds [of the women in Holloway] have some sort of personality problem', though this claim begs many questions. See Chapter Eight of this book for a discussion of some of these questions.

12   'The increase in 1980 over 1979 in receptions of adult females under sentence of immediate imprisonment occurred among those with sentences of up to and including three months, and those with sentences of over six months and up to and including eighteen months' (Home Office, 1981b:76).

13   'In 1980 the population in Holloway at its peak was up to 78 per cent above the normal certified accommodation, in Styal up to 27 per cent ... and one open prison, Moor Court, was overcrowded by up to 32 per cent' (Matthews, 1981).

14   These prisoners were referring to the 'old' Holloway, though they expressed the view that prison life in the new buildings would be 'just as bad'.

Chapter 3   Women, family and the courts

1   At this point many readers will be wondering about the range of impositions which are neither custodial nor financial, the two obvious ones being community service orders and probation orders. These alternatives (or rather the lack of them) are so important that they will be discussed at length in Chapter Six. In the meantime, it can be stated that community service orders have only recently been introduced in Scotland and that many sheriffs will not make probation orders because they have little

faith in the Scottish social services' abilities to provide adequate or even minimal supervision.

Chapter 5 Papa's discipline: disciplinary modes in the Scottish women's prison

1 In fact there was evidence that some officers attempted to help the women maintain attractive appearances. Several prisoners told me that officers had cut or permed their hair and one officer told me that she had brought in some of her own cologne for one of the women about to be liberated. The women did not in the main complain about the prison officers; rather they complained about a system which appeared to be at best paternalistic and at worst deliberately obstructive of their own attempts to maintain individuality of expression.

Chapter 6 The dismissive society

1 The Scottish judicial system is different from that of England and Wales. The following extract from the Scottish Information Office's 'Factsheet No. 16' may be of use to readers unfamiliar with the structure of the Scottish courts.

Criminal Procedure
There are two types of criminal procedure — solemn and summary. In solemn procedure in both the High Court of Justiciary and the sheriff court trial is before a judge sitting with a jury of 15 laymen; and the alleged offence is set out in a document called an indictment. The judge decides questions of law and the jury decide questions of fact and may reach a decision by a simple majority. In summary procedure in sheriff and district courts the judge sits without a jury and decides questions of both fact and law. The offence charged is set out in a document called a summary complaint.

Proceedings in the criminal court are never initiated by the police, and only in a small number of special cases by individuals or officials of public bodies. Responsibility for prosecutions in all criminal causes in Scotland rests, except in the special cases just mentioned, with the Lord Advocate as senior Scottish law officer acting on behalf of the Crown. The department which handles criminal matters on behalf of the Lord Advocate is the Crown Office. In practice, most prosecutions are taken on behalf of the Crown by the Solicitor General (the second law officer) by ten advocates-depute and a staff of local prosecutors called procurators fiscal.

Procurators fiscal are civil servants. They must be either advocates or solicitors, but are usually solicitors. Police report details of an alleged crime to the local fiscal, who has discretion whether to prosecute subject to the discretion and control of the Lord Advocate and Crown Office. In Scotland, there are 46 full-time procurators fiscal. There are also depute procurators fiscal in busy areas.

Criminal courts

The supreme criminal court in Scotland is the High Court of Justiciary which sits in Edinburgh and also on circuit in several major towns and cities. It is a court which hears only cases taken on indictment, presided over by a judge sitting with a jury of 15, and has exclusive jurisdiction in certain serious crimes including murder, treason and rape. The High Court of Justiciary also sits (in a court of at least three judges) as the Court of Criminal Appeal, hearing appeals from the High Court as court of first instance and from the sheriff and district courts.

The sheriff court deals with offences committed within the area over which it has jurisdiction. Each sheriff court has jurisdiction within the sheriffdom in which it is located and at the head of the judiciary of each sheriffdom is the sheriff principal. There are six sheriffdoms: Grampian, Highland and Islands: Tayside, Central and Fife; Lothian and Borders; Glasgow and Strathkelvin; North Strathclyde; and South Strathclyde; Dumfries and Galloway. The six sheriffdoms are sub-divided into a total of 49 districts. There are 75 sheriffs; four are 'floating' sheriffs who, along with temporary sheriffs, undertake duties in any sheriffdom where an emergency occurs or where it is necessary to clear a backlog of cases so as to avoid delays.

The sheriff has jurisdiction in both summary and solemn criminal cases. In his summary court a sheriff may impose prison sentences of up to six months or a fine of £1000 for a common law offence. Under solemn procedure he may sentence offenders for up to two years, and has an additional power of remit to the High Court of Justiciary if he thinks a heavier sentence should be imposed.

District courts, set up under the District Courts (Scotland) Act 1975, are the administrative responsibility of the local authority. They preserve some of the traditional features of the former burgh and justice of the peace (JP) courts. The longest prison sentence which can be imposed is generally 60 days and the maximum fine £200.

The bench of a district court may be constituted by one or more lay judges or by a stipendiary magistrate, who is a professional lawyer of at least five years' standing and has the same summary criminal jurisdiction and powers as has a sheriff. Three stipendiary magistrates sit in the Glasgow district court.

Lay judges of the district court are justices of the peace drawn from three sources; justices appointed by the Secretary of State for Scotland on behalf of the Queen; magistrates and police judges who held office under the former structure of local government; and ex officio justices appointed by district and islands councils, up to a quarter of their number. An important provision of the Act requires justices to undergo training appropriate to their experience. (Scottish Information Office, 1981)

2 Until November 1973 the Scottish Home and Health Department was responsible for prison welfare work; since then it has been the responsibility of the social work departments in whose geographical areas penal establishments are situated.

3 Thirteen of the women interviewed had lived in Glasgow immediately prior to their present term of imprisonment, three in Edinburgh and one each in Aberdeen, Dundee, Hamilton and Whitburn.

4 Melissa's own story certainly illustrates just how difficult it is to 'rehabilitate' some of the women prisoners when they are released from prison. During the three weeks I was interviewing at Cornton Vale Melissa was both released from and returned to prison — this time for breach of the peace. The prison social worker had (after great difficulty) arranged for Melissa to take up a place in a hostel at Greenock. Upon liberation Melissa never made it to Greenock. She stopped off at Glasgow and for several days was reporting to the Salvation Army for breakfast 'each time with a good drink in her' (Salvation Army Captain). When she was returned to Cornton Vale she was very depressed, had a bandaged wrist and had asked for and been given valium and various other medications. When I talked with her she asked me if I thought a lot about my independence. When I replied in the affirmative she said sadly, 'Aye. You're like me', adding after a pause, 'But I haven't got mine.' A month after this conversation I went back to Cornton Vale to visit Melissa in a 'private' capacity. She was feeling very pleased and optimistic because the Governor had herself taken her to see some hostels and at one of them she had obtained a room for occupation upon her liberation from prison. This was in November. In December 1980 Melissa was released and we exchanged letters during the Christmas period. In the first week of January 1981 Melissa left the hostel and returned to Glasgow (at which point I lost contact with her).

5 For a survey of the training of Scottish social workers, please see Appendix C.

Chapter 7 Down, out, alcoholic and in prison

1 The terminology used to refer to people with alcohol-related problems is often disputed as to its 'appropriateness' or usefulness. The terms used in the list here do not imply any clinical diagnoses and are based on the women's assessment of their alcohol-related problem. *Homeless alcoholic* is used to refer to those women who claimed both that they had 'no fixed abode'

and that they had at some time previous been in hospital for 'alcoholism'. *Self-defined alcoholic* is used to refer to those women (homeless or not) who claimed that although no-one had so far defined them as 'alcoholic' they themselves felt that they were 'alcoholics'. *Women with drinking problems* refers to those women who were frequently in trouble either for drunkenness or at times when they had been drinking heavily but who were not considered either by themselves or by others to be alcoholics.

NB. These terms are only given the above meanings when used in the list on pp. 153-4. In the remainder of the chapter I use the terms 'women with drinking problems' to refer to the whole range of women offenders with alcohol-related problems.

2　The same thing is likely to happen with the new awareness and different conceptions of the public about homelessness. A report, *Single Homeless*, published in March 1982 by the Department of the Environment indicates that in England the homeless are no longer mainly alcoholic vagrants. Although one in four are women, 36 per cent are under thirty and many come from skilled or professional backgrounds. If the same holds for Scotland it is likely that the young, skilled, semi-skilled and professional people will in future be given priority over the alcoholic, unskilled and otherwise 'deviant' homeless.

Chapter 9　The meanings of women's imprisonment in Scotland

1　Both prisoners and prison officers commented again and again on what they saw as injustice — the fact that the prisoners at Cornton Vale in 1981 were, in the main, the women who had committed the least serious crimes. Likewise, prisoners also thought it unjust that the long-term prisoners who had been found guilty of serious crimes were the ones who received the best treatment in the prison.

2　Prison officers often remarked to me that they did not see why women should come into prison and expect to be better off than they had been outside.

3　Several prison officers at men's prisons told me that, although they agreed that most of the persistent petty offenders should not be in prison, they feared that once they had been removed the prison population would consist solely of the 'hard men'. Thus at present the persistent petty offenders *do* have a general function within the prisons, as the General Secretary of the Scottish Prison Officers' Association pointed out when he said 'Today there are more people in prison who are prepared to use violence. There is a harder element in the prison population and if the prison population is reduced the harder element will be more apparent. At the moment it is balanced by the others —

social inadequates, alcoholics and the large proportion of homeless people.'

4 It should be noted that Scotland does not have a prison medical service which is independent of the National Health Service. At Cornton Vale the medical services are provided by visiting general practitioners. Although it was generally asserted by both prison officers and prisoners that many of the prisoners housed in Sierra were on heavy doses of 'medication' the main complaint in regard to the medical prescriptions of the women whom I interviewed in Papa Block was that the doctor had told them that they should try to do without sleeping pills. Women like Kirsty King (who, according to an Edinburgh social worker who knew her, had been on various types of medically prescribed 'strong' drugs for years), Thelma Thompson (who described herself as 'a bag of nerves') and Melissa (when she returned distraught to the prison after cutting her wrists and failing to 'make it' to the hostel) were not, however, denied the relief which according to them they found in the medicine prescribed by the doctor.

Bibliography

Advisory Council on the Treatment of Offenders (1963) *The Organisation of After-Care*, London, HMSO.

American Psychiatric Association (1968) *Diagnostic and Statistical Manual of Mental Disorders*, New York, American Psychiatric Association.

Ardener, S. (1978) *Defining Females*, London, Croom Helm.

Banks, C., and Fairhead, S. (1976) *The Petty Short-term Prisoner*, Barry Rose, Chichester.

Bell, G.H. *et al.* (1968) *Textbook of Physiology and Biochemistry*, Baltimore, Williams and Wilkins, referred to in Camberwell Council on Alcoholism (1980).

Bettelheim, B. (1960) *The Informed Heart*, New York, Free Press.

Beveridge Report (1942) 'Report on the social insurance and allied services', Cmnd 6404, London, HMSO.

Bottoms, A. and McClean, J.D. (1976) *Defendants in the Criminal Process*, London, Routledge & Kegan Paul.

Boyle, J. (1977) *A Sense of Freedom*, Edinburgh, Canongate.

Brown, P. and Bloomfield, T. (eds) (1979) *Legality and Community: The Politics of Juvenile Justice in Scotland*, Aberdeen People's Press.

Burton, F. (1983) *Violence and Scottish Culture*, London, Routledge & Kegan Paul.

Butler Report (1974) 'Report of the committee on mentally abnormal offenders', Home Office and DHSS, Cmnd 6244, London, HMSO.

Buxton, J. and Turner, M. (1962) *Gate Fever*, London, Cresset Press.

Camberwell Council on Alcoholism and Campaign for the Homeless and Rootless (1976) *Out of Sight, Out of Mind*, London.

Camberwell Council on Alcoholism, (1980) *Women and Alcohol*, London, Tavistock.

Carlen, P. (1976) *Magistrates' Justice*, Oxford, Martin Robertson.

Carlen, P. (1982) 'On rights and powers in penal politics', in D. Garland and P. Young (eds) (1982).

Carlen, P. and Collison, M. (eds) (1980) *Radical Issues in Criminology*, Oxford, Martin Robertson.

Carpenter, M. (1970) *Juvenile Delinquents* (first published 1853) Montclair, New Jersey, Patterson Smith.

Chambers, G.A. (1979) *Social Work With Adult Offenders*, Edinburgh, Scottish Home and Health Department, Social Research Branch.

Chapman, J.R. (1981) *Economic Realities and the Female Offender*, Massachusetts, Lexington Books.

Chesler, P. (1974) *Women and Madness*, London, Allen Lane.

Christie, N. (1976) *Conflicts as Property*, Sheffield University Centre for Criminological Studies.

Clare, A. (1980) *Psychiatry in Dissent*, London, Tavistock.

Cohen, S. and Taylor, L. (1978) *Prison Secrets*, London, NCCL and RAP.

Crites, L. (1976) *The Female Offender*, Massachusetts, Lexington Books.

Curlee, J. (1968) 'Women Alcoholics', *Federal Probation*, vol. 32, pp. 16-20.

Dahl, T.S. and Snare, A. (1978) 'The coercion of privacy', in C. Smart and B. Smart (eds) (1978).

Davies, M. (1974) *Prisoners of Society*, London, Routledge & Kegan Paul.

Dell, S. (1970) *Silent in Court*, London, Bell.

Department of Health and Society Security (1978) *Report of the DHSS Advisory Committee on Alcoholism*, London, HMSO.

Department of the Environment (1982) *Single Homeless*, London, HMSO.

Dickson, T. (ed) (1980) *Scottish Capitalism: Class, State and Nation from before the Union to the Present*, London, Lawrence & Wishart.

Dobash, R.E. and R. (1980) *Violence Against Wives*, London, Open Books.

Donzelot, J. (1980) *The Policing of Families*, London, Hutchinson.

Edinburgh and District Council on Alcoholism (1980) pamphlet.

Edwards, G. and Grant, M. (eds) (1977) *Alcoholism: New Knowledge and Responses*, London, Croom Helm.

Ehrenreich, B. and English, D. (1979) *For Her Own Good*, London, Pluto Press.

Erikson, R. and Baranek, P. (1982) *The Ordering of Justice*, London, University of Toronto Press.

Evans, P. (ed.) (1980) *Prison Crisis*, London, Allen & Unwin.

Fairhead, S. (1981) *Persistent Petty Offenders*, Home Office Research Study No. 66, London, HMSO.

Foucault, M. (1976) *Mental Illness and Psychology*, London, Harper & Row.

Foucault, M. (1978) *Discipline and Punish*, London, Allen Lane.

Freeman, J. (ed.) (1978) *Prisons Past and Future*, London, Heinemann.

Garland, D. and Young, P. (eds) (1982) *The Power to Punish*, London, Heinemann.

Gavron, H. (1968) *The Captive Wife*, Harmondsworth, Penguin.

General Register Office (1968) *A Glossary of Mental Disorders*, Studies on Medical and Population Subjects No. 22, London, HMSO.

Ghodse, A.H. and Tregenza, G.S. (1980) 'The physical effects and metabolism of alcohol', in Camberwell Council on Alcoholism (1980).

Giallombardo, R. (1966) *Society of Women*, New York, Wiley.

Gibbens, T.C.N. (1971) 'Female offenders', *British Journal of Hospital Medicine*, September.

Gibson, Helen (1973) 'Women's prisons: Laboratories of penal reform', in Crites (1976).

Goffman, E. (1968) *Asylums*, Harmondsworth, Penguin.

Gunn, J. *et al.* (1978) *Psychiatric Aspects of Imprisonment*, London, Academic Press.

Hancock, D.N. (1977) 'Alcohol and crime', in Edwards and Grant (1977).

Heidensohn, F. (1981) 'Women and the penal system', in Morris (1981).

Henry, J. (1952) *Women in Prison*, New York, Doubleday.

Highett, J. (1960) *The Scottish Churches*, London, Skeffington.

Home Office (1970) *Treatment of Women and Girls in Custody*, London, Prison Department.

Home Office (1971) *Working Party on Habitual Drunken Offenders*, London, HMSO.

Home Office (1980) *The Reduction of Pressure on the Penal System: Observations on the Fifteenth Report of the Expenditure Committee*, Cmnd 7948, London, HMSO.

Home Office (1981a) *Report on the Work of The Prison Department 1980*, Cmnd 8228, London, HMSO.

Home Office (1981b) *Prison Statistics for England and Wales 1980*, Cmnd 8372, London, HMSO.

House of Commons (1978) *The Reduction of Pressure on the Prison System*, Fifteenth Report of the House of Commons Expenditure Committee, London, HMSO.

House of Commons (1978-9) *Women in the Penal System*, Expenditure Committee Minutes of Evidence, [Reports of] Sessions 1978-9, London, HMSO.

Howard League for Penal Reform (1977) *Probation in Scotland: A Programme for Reform*, Policy Review No. 2, Edinburgh, Howard League.

Howard League for Penal Reform (1978) *Women and the Penal System Memorandum to the House of Commons Expenditure Committee*, London, Howard League.

Hulsman, L. (1981) 'Penal reform in the Netherlands: Part 1 - Bringing the criminal justice system under control', *Howard Journal*, vol. XX pp. 150-9.

Hunter, E. (1979) *Scottish Woman's Place*, Edinburgh.

Hutter, B. and Williams, G. (eds) (1981) *Controlling Women*, London, Croom Helm.

Ignatieff, M. (1978) *A Just Measure of Pain*, London, Macmillan.

Kellas, J.G. and Fotheringham, P. (1976) 'The political behaviour of the working class', in A. MacLaren (1976).

Knox, J. (1558) *The First Blast of the Trumpet against the Monstrous Regiment of Women*, London, Southgate.

Lawton, [L.J.] (1973) *Weekly Law Reports*, pp. 857-83.

Litman, G.K. *et al.* (1976) 'Evaluation of the female alcoholic: a study in person perception', *Proceedings of the Annual Conference of the British Psychological Society, 1976*, referred to in B. Hutter and G. Williams (1981).

Logan, J. (1831) *The Scottish Gael*, London.

McBarnet, D. (1981) *Conviction*, London, Macmillan.

MacDonald, R. and Sim, J. (1978) *Scottish Prisons and the Special Unit*, Glasgow, Scottish Council for Civil Liberties.

MacLaren, A. (ed.) (1976) *Social Class in Scotland*, Edinburgh, John Donald.

McVicar, J. (1974) *McVicar by Himself*, London, Hutchinson.

Mathiesen, T. (1980) *Law, Society and Political Action*, London, Academic Press.

Matthews, J. (1981) *Women in the Penal System*, London, NACRO.

Mawby, C.I. (1977) 'Sexual discrimination and the law', *Probation Journal*, June, quoted in P. Evans (1980).

May Report (1979) 'Committee of Inquiry into the United Kingdom Prison Services', Chairman The Hon. Mr Justice May, Cmnd 7673, London, HMSO.

Mayo, M. (ed.) (1977) *Women in the Community*, London, Routledge & Kegan Paul.

Mechie, S. (1960) *The Church and Scottish Social Development, 1780-1870*, Oxford.

Mitchison, R. (1978) *Life in Scotland*, London, Batsford.

Moody, S. and Tombs, J. (1982) *Prosecution in the Public Interest*, Edinburgh, Scottish Academic Press.

Moore, G. (1979) 'New lamps for old?', *Scotsman*, Edinburgh, July.

Morris, A. (ed.) (1981) *Women and Crime*, Cropwood Conference Series, No. 13, University of Cambridge Institute of Criminology.

Morris, P. (1965) *Prisoners and Their Families*, London, Allen & Unwin.

Morris, T. (1978) 'The parlous state of prisons', in J. Freeman (1978).

Morrison Committee (1962) *Report of the Departmental Committee on the Probation Service*, Cmnd 1650, London, HMSO.

National Association for the Care and Rehabilitation of Offenders (1978) *Memorandum to the House of Commons Expenditure Committee (Education, Arts and Home Office Sub-Committee) Enquiry into Women in the Penal System*, London, NACRO.

National Association for the Care and Rehabilitation of Offenders (1981a) *Nacro News Digest*, March, London, NACRO.

National Association for the Care and Rehabilitation of Offenders (1981b) 'Dutch crime rates — are they affected by the shorter sentence in Holland?', *NACRO Briefing*, London, NACRO.

Neill, A. (1975) 'Socio-Cultural Aspects of Alcoholism in Scotland', paper presented at First Scottish School on Alcoholism, Edinburgh.

Okely, J. (1978) 'Privileged, schooled and finished', in Ardener (1978).

Otto, S. (1980) 'Single homeless women and alcohol' in Camberwell Council on Alcoholism (1980).

Parker, H. (ed.) (1979) *Social Work and the Courts*, London, Arnold.

Parliamentary All-Party Penal Affairs Group (1980) *Too Many Prisoners*, Chichester, Barry Rose.

Parsloe, P. (1979) 'After-custody: supervision in the community in England, Wales and Scotland', in H. Parker (1979).

Pitman, D. and Gordon, C. (1958) *Revolving Door*, Illinois, Free Press.

Pizzey, E. (1974) *Scream Quietly or the Neighbours will Hear*, Harmondsworth, Penguin.

Plant, M. (1952) *The Domestic Life of Scotland in the Eighteenth Century*, Edinburgh University Press.

Price, R.R. (1977) 'The forgotten female offender', *Crime and Delinquency*, vol. 23, pp. 101-8.

Prins, H. (1980) *Offenders, Deviants or Patients?*, London, Tavistock.

Probyn, W. (1977) *Angel-Face: The Making of a Criminal*, London, Allen & Unwin.

Richards, E. (1974) 'Patterns of Highland discontent', in J. Stevenson and R. Quinault (1974).

Rollin, H.R. (1969) *The Mentally Abnormal Offender and the Law*, London, Pergamon Press.

Rusche, G. and Kirchheimer, O. (1939) *Punishment and Social Structure*, New York, Columbia University Press.

Scottish Health Education Unit (1976) *Understanding Alcohol and Alcoholism in Scotland*, Edinburgh, HMSO.

Scottish Health Services Council (1965) *Alcoholics: Report of a Sub-Committee of the Standing Medical Advisory Committee*, Edinburgh, HMSO.

Scottish Home and Health Department (1958) *Report on Prisons in Scotland, 1957*, Cmnd 164, Edinburgh, HMSO.

Scottish Home and Health Department (1967) *Report on Prisons in Scotland 1966*, Cmnd 3319, Edinburgh, HMSO.

Scottish Home and Health Department (1969) *Report on Prisons in Scotland 1968*, Cmnd 4218, Edinburgh, HMSO.

Scottish Home and Health Department (1978) *Report on Prisons in Scotland 1977*, Cmnd 7391, Edinburgh, HMSO.

Scottish Home and Health Department (1980) *Report on Prisons in Scotland 1979*, Cmnd 8037, Edinburgh, HMSO.

Scottish Home and Health Department (1981) *Report on Prisons in Scotland 1980*, Cmnd 8421, Edinburgh, HMSO.

Scottish Information Office (1980) *Scottish Courts*, Factsheet No. 16, Edinburgh.

Scottish Information Office (1980) *Women in the Scottish Prison Service*, Edinburgh.

Scull, A. (1979) *Museums of Madness*, London, Allen Lane.

Sheridan, A. (1980) *Foucault: The Will to Truth*, London, Tavistock.

Short, R. (1979) *The Care of Long-Term Prisoners*, London, Macmillan.

Size, M. (1957) *Prisons I Have Known*, London, Allen & Unwin.

Smart, C. (1976) *Women, Crime and Criminology*, London, Routledge & Kegan Paul.

Smart, C. and Smart, B. (eds) (1978) *Women, Sexuality and Social Control*, London, Routledge & Kegan Paul.

Smith, A. (1962) *Women in Prison*, London, Stevens.

Smout, T.C. (1969) *A History of The Scottish People 1560-1830*, London, Collins.

Smout, T.C. (1976) 'Aspects of sexual behaviour in nineteenth-century Scotland' in A. MacLaren (1976).

Stair (1826) *Stair's Institutes of the Law of Scotland*.

Stevenson, J. and Quinault, R. (eds) (1974) *Popular Protest and Public Order: Six Studies in British History, 1790-1920*, London, Allen & Unwin.

Strathclyde Regional Council (1978) *Services To The Offender: Who Cares?* Strathclyde Regional Council.

Taylor, L. (1980) 'Bringing power to particular account: Peter Rajah and the Hull board of visitors', in P. Carlen and M. Collison (1980).

Thomas, J.E. (1972) *The English Prison Officer Since 1850*, London, Routledge & Kegan Paul.

Turner, M. (1964) *A Pretty Sort of Prison*, London, Pall Mall.

Weldon, F. (1978) *Praxis*, London, Hodder & Stoughton.

Widom, C.S. (1981) 'Perspectives of female criminality' in A. Morris (1981).

Williams, K. (1981) *From Pauperism to Poverty*, London, Routledge & Kegan Paul.

Wilson, E. (1977a) *Women and the Welfare State*, London, Pluto Press.

Wilson, E. (1977b) 'Women in the community', in M. Mayo (1977).

Woddis, R. (1972) 'The ballad of Holloway', London, *New Statesman*.

Woodside, M. (1974) 'Women offenders and psychiatric reports: Notes from a Scottish hospital', *Social Work Today*, vol. no. 11, pp. 341-2.

Woodside, M. (1976) 'Psychiatric referrals from Edinburgh courts', *British Journal of Criminology*, vol. 16, no. 1, January.

Young, J.D. (1979) *The Rousing of The Scottish Working Class*, London, Croom Helm.

Zaretsky, E. (1976) *Capitalism, the Family and Personal Life*, London, Pluto Press.

Statutes

Mental Health Act, 1959
Mental Health (Scotland) Act, 1960
First Offender (Scotland) Act, 1960
Social Work (Scotland) Act, 1968, 1972
District Courts (Scotland) Act, 1975
Criminal Justice (Scotland) Act, 1980

Index